Advance praise for

near black

"This book is the first of its kind: a study of racial passing focused on whites who pass as black. . . . It successfully collates a host of historical figures and fictional texts both canonical and marginal: the literature of the tragic mulatto, the memoirs of Euro-American jazz musicians living in African American communities, best-selling race-based journalism, contemporary mixed-race narratives, Hollywood films about racial performance, and the love and theft of African American culture."

—Joel Dinerstein, author of *Swinging the Machine: Modernity, Technology, and African American Culture between the World Wars*

D1570790

near black

near black

WHITE-TO-BLACK PASSING IN AMERICAN CULTURE

Baz Dreisinger

University of Massachusetts Press
Amherst

Copyright © 2008 by University of Massachusetts Press
All rights reserved
Printed in the United States of America

LC 2008028712
ISBN 978-1-55849-674-3 (cloth), ISBN 978-1-55849-675-0 (paper)
Designed by Karen Mazur
Set in Minion Pro, Meta, and Constructa by dix!
Printed and bound by The Maple-Vail Book Manufacturing Group

Library of Congress Cataloging-in-Publication Data
Dreisinger, Baz, 1976–
Near Black : White-to-Black passing in American culture / Baz Dreisinger.
      p.   cm.
Includes bibliographical references and index.
ISBN 978-1-55849-675-0 (paper : alk. paper)—ISBN 978-1-55849-674-3 (cloth : alk. paper)
    1. Whites—Race identity—United States.   2. Passing (Identity)—United States.
3. United States—Race relations.   4. Popular culture—United States.   5. Race in literature.
6. Race in motion pictures.   7. American literature—History and criticism.
8. Motion pictures—United States—History.   I. Title.
E184.A1D73   2008
305.809′073—dc22   2008028712

British Library Cataloguing in Publication data are available.

CONTENTS

ACKNOWLEDGMENTS

The ideas that color the pages of this book have been shaped by smart people from all walks of life and helpful institutions who have shown me support. It is my honor and pleasure to give them all a *big up*:

My undergraduate mentor at Queens College, Kathleen Kier, who gave me American literature. My advisers at Columbia University, who fostered the birth of this passing project: Ann Douglas, Robert O'Meally, and, especially, Rachel Adams—whose ceaseless encouragement deserves much of the credit for this book. The Ralph J. Bunche Center for African-American Studies at UCLA, where I held a Postdoctoral Fellowship in Ethnic Studies and had the pleasure of learning from and getting to know Richard Yarborough. My excellent colleagues at John Jay College of Criminal Justice, who have been supportive of my work and interested in hearing about it and me, particularly Chris Suggs, Valerie Allen, P. J. Gibson, John Matteson, Auli Ek, Jonathan Gray, and Pat Licklider. A Research Assistance Fund award from John Jay's Office for the Advancement of Research allowed me to complete the manuscript, and Celeste Moore did much of the legwork in this regard. Joel Dinerstein provided sage advice about final drafts of the book. My editors at the University of Massachusetts Press were enormously helpful: Clark Dougan delivered insightful critiques, and Amanda Heller vastly improved my copy.

Deepest thanks to my mentor, Louis Menand, and my mentorette/mothasista, Lynda Obst.

Thanks to my friends/family/intellectual sparring partners, with whom I've been blessed to debate everything from D'Angelo to deconstruction, race to reggae: Penny Vlagopoulos, Donna Augustin, Beth Skipp, Trish Perkins, Perry Salzhauer, Kirk Welcome, Anand Vaidya, Jessie Feinstein, Helene Sola, Tommy Smith, Carleene Samuels, Michael Ralph, Mike Wiltshire, Mom, Dad, Riv, Sar, Naomi. Thanks to Ian for the always spicy GT love.

And, especially, to Tam—for teaching me a world.

Acknowledgments

> I began wondering when white people started getting
> white—or rather, when they started losing it.
> —Chester Himes, *If He Hollers Let Him Go*

Introduction

When *do* white people lose their whiteness? Consider four scenarios:

In his *Picture of Slavery*, published in 1834, George Bourne describes the case of a seven-year-old white boy who is stolen from his parents and "tattooed, painted and tanned. Every other method was also adopted which wickedness could devise, to change the exterior appearance of the unfortunate creature, into one uniform dark tinge. In this wretched and forlorn condition, he grew up to maturity; driven, starved, and scourged, like the coloured people with whom he was forced to associate." Twelve years later, Bourne continues, the boy is stolen again, this time from his enslaved state by "some friends of freedom," who return him to his grieving parents.[1]

A Virginia legend from the same era tells of a wealthy planter's unruly mulatto son who is transported to New Orleans, where he is to be sold by a white half-brother who looks much like him. They embark on the steamer handcuffed together, but during a powerful storm the legally black son manages to steal his brother's handcuff keys and declare himself the master and his white brother the slave. The white gentleman's protests go unheeded and he is sold into slavery as a black man by his half-brother—who is said to have enjoyed himself with the profits.[2]

Almost one hundred years later, in 1946, Josephine Schuyler, white wife of the black writer George Schuyler, publishes an article in the *Negro Digest* titled "Seventeen Years of Mixed Marriage" in which she discusses her marriage to George and the relationships of her white friends who also have black partners.

In order to avoid conflict, she writes, most of these interracial couples "find it simple to explain that the paler member of the union has distant Negro ancestry, and under the American 'one-drop' theory, their marriage is accepted." [3]

Finally, in 1954 Memphis a young musician hurries into a local radio station for an impromptu on-air chat. His rendition of "That's All Right, Mama"— which would have been labeled a "race record" ten years before but had since been designated "rhythm and blues" (and would soon be called "rock 'n' roll")—has been heating up the airwaves, and the public is eager to hear from this rising star. Midway through the interview, the DJ asks a seemingly simple question: "Which high school did you attend?" The musician's response, "Humes High," is a revelatory moment. In an age of segregation, this answer did what the boy's singing and his manner of speech did not: it "outed" Elvis Presley as a white man.

These scenarios all involve what is sometimes termed the "reverse racial pass," which Philip Brian Harper has defined as "any instance in which a person legally recognized as white effectively functions as a non-white person in any quarter of the social arena." [4] In this book I explore such cases of "lost whiteness." I look at American narratives about white people who either envision themselves or are envisioned by others as being or becoming black. Historical anecdotes feature prominently in my project, but I am most interested in *narratives* about white passing: short stories, novels, films, autobiographies, and pop culture discourse. While I recognize that different genres use varying mediums, an interdisciplinary approach makes it possible to plot the patterns of a narrative that works its way through myriad facets of American culture. I tap into the ideologies—the conceptions of racial identity—that shore up narratives of white passing, and which are manifest in all aspects of culture from the high to the low, the aural and the verbal to the visual.

I am not concerned with whether whites "succeed" in passing—whether they fool anyone; in fact, I would argue that the enterprise of trickery, of "fooling our white folks," as Langston Hughes described black passing, is not a vital component of white passing. [5] Nor do I see white passing as necessarily motivated by what Carlyle Van Thompson describes as "strategy for survival and even socioeconomic investment." [6] Instead, I am interested in the moments of slippage in which whites perceive themselves, or are perceived by others, as losing their whiteness and "acquiring" blackness. Harryette Mullen asserts that "rather than 'passing for' white[,] . . . passing individuals actually become white or function as white"; the same might be said of white-to-black passers, who, in myriad ways, "function" as black. [7] Some do so via self-identification, as did jazz musician Mezz Mezzrow, who declared that playing jazz and living among blacks had literally darkened his skin. Others are, for a period of time, taken for black by a given community, as was Jewish critic Waldo Frank during his travels with Jean Toomer, or disc jockey Hoss Allen, master of R&B slang at Nashville's famed WLAC radio station. For some whites, including journalists John Howard Griffin and Grace Halsell, passing is a fleeting and deliberate experiment, while for others, such as Mark Twain's fictional white slave in *Pudd'nhead Wilson*, it is a near-permanent and accidental occurrence. Though some white passers actively claim a black identity, others merely disavow a white one—as does James McBride's mother, Ruth, in his 1997 memoir *The Color of Water*, or Belgian journalist Jean-Charles Houzeau, the editor of New Orleans's first black daily newspaper, who, during the 1860s, "never sought to deny the rumor that I had African blood in my veins." [8] Certain instances of white passing are anchored in essentialist notions of whiteness and blackness, but others destabilize racial identity altogether. In some scenarios race is defined primarily as a shade of skin, so passing whites must undergo physical alteration to "become" black; in others, race is defined in terms of cultural heritage, so that race changes occur by means of cultural and social transformations, not physical ones. [9] My protagonists span centuries and cross contexts, from slavery to civil rights, jazz to rock to hip-hop. They form an oft-forgotten, sometimes radically transgressive chapter of American culture, and they speak volumes about our conceptions of blackness and, especially, whiteness— which, as Chester Himes suggests, is most clearly discernible when it is taken off or lost. [10]

What conceptions of race and identity unite these disparate scenarios, allowing for a narrative of white-to-black passing? Central to the enterprise of white passing in American culture from the 1830s to the present day are ideas about proximity. Because "blackness," so to speak, is imagined as transmittable, proximity to blackness is invested with the power to turn whites black. Proximity, however, is an elastic term here, contingent on such factors as gender, historical period, and the context in which passing occurs. From one text to another, proximity has alternately sexual, homosocial, and geographical connotations. One thing, however, remains constant because it persistently undergirds rhetoric about proximity and racial transmission: space—cultural geography—plays a critical role in all of the narratives discussed in this book. Geography, after all, has long been crucial to racial formation; the very notion of the color line, writes Samira Kawash, "metaphorizes racial distinction as spatial division." [11] Far from being neutral, geography is invested with moral and cultural value. The difference between a vice district and a slum, for instance, is that the former is a literal space produced by social policies and economic factors, while the latter is "a representation, invented and popularized by social science, of the deteriorating neighborhoods, brothels, saloons."[12] The former, then, is a literal space and the latter a mythological one. Particular geographies and notions of proximity are vital to white passing because those who literally are "near black" become metaphorically "near black." While this concept arises during Reconstruction in the context of white anxieties about turning black, it is revised by later white passers for whom proximity to blackness becomes an authenticating badge and a celebrated mode of double consciousness.

My argument about passing, proximity, and the "spread" of blackness evokes Barbara Browning's theory about disease and contagion as metaphors for the spread of African diasporic culture, metaphors that are "invoked—often in the guise of a literal threat—at moments of anxiety over disaporic flows, whether migrational or cultural." Browning goes on to say that "the figure of infectious rhythm," as she calls this metaphor, "is not always negative: Artists and performers . . . recuperate the notion of African 'infection' by suggesting that diasporic culture *is* contagious, irresistible—vital, life-giving, and productive."[13] Similarly, white passing can be a product of either panic ("Surrounded by blacks and black culture, I'm becoming black") or pride ("I grew up among blacks, which makes me black").[14] This oscillation between anxiety and fantasy, pride and shame, remains a central feature of white passing narratives and is, interestingly enough, reflected in conflicting theories about the origin of the term "passing" itself: Is the word short for "trespassing," or does it refer to the "pass" slaves were given by their masters in order to obtain temporary free movement?[15] The former etymology connotes that passing is a dangerous, disreputable enterprise, while the latter emphasizes its role as a ticket to a better world.

My premise is that experiments in racial performance are intrinsic to American culture. As Ralph Ellison so flawlessly put it, "The melting pot did indeed melt, creating such deceptive metamorphoses and blending of identities, values, and lifestyles that most American whites are culturally part Negro American without even realizing it."[16] Recent years have given rise to numerous studies founded on this premise, but studies of passing particularly hinge on it. Cases of passing involve exaggerated and sometimes caricatured negotiations of racial boundaries. In many respects, traditional black-to-white passing narratives can be reread as white-to-black narratives because they often introduce "black" characters who pass into blackness as much as, if not more than, they pass into whiteness. When James Weldon Johnson's Ex–Coloured Man, for instance, speaks of having "pass[ed] into another world" as a child, he is learning, in a manner of speaking, how to "be" black: "From that time I looked out through other eyes, my thoughts were coloured, my words dictated, my actions limited by one dominating, all-pervading idea"—the "idea" of blackness, which his trip south helps him to comprehend.[17] Mimi Daquin, who in Walter White's *Flight* is reared in an idyllic, color-blind Creole world, actively "dated thereafter her consciousness of being colored from September, nineteen hundred and six"; she learns to perform this "colored" identity by visiting dancehalls with her boyfriend, Carl. Similarly, Douglas Sirk's film version of *Imitation of Life* includes a scene in which the light-skinned Sarah Jane, asked to help with kitchen work, charges into the living room with a basket of fruit on her head, feigns a southern accent, and quips that she learned such tricks from her mammy. Such moments of passing for black flourish in "traditional" passing narratives, and in cultural history, as well. Was Lena Horne passing when she darkened her skin in order to become a "blacker" entertainer? Was Arnold Johnson, the actor who played Putney Swope in the 1969 film of that name, passing when Robert Downey Sr. dubbed his own voice into the film, claiming Johnson's voice wasn't "black enough"? Are rappers passing for black when record executives encourage them to deliver exaggerated performances of "authentic" blackness—performances that have led critics such as Stanley Crouch to deem these rappers modern-day minstrels? These moments of *black* passing for black stand as a starting point for my work, which concerns those who, possessing not even "one drop" of black blood, cross the color line.

As race continues to be recognized as a social construct—"an unstable and 'decentered' complex of social meanings constantly being transformed by political struggle"[18]—most studies of passing are remiss in including little if any analysis of white passing.[19] Eric Lott's *Love and Theft* and David Roediger's study *The Wages of Whiteness* brilliantly link blackface to the construction of whiteness, but we cannot equate the entertainer T. D. Rice with John Howard Griffin or blackface with white passing. The former is an instance of performance and is recognized by its audience as such, while the latter is *not* mere performance and does *not* call attention to its own spuriousness.[20] Racial mimicry or masquerade is not the same as white-to-black passing, in the same respect that "white Negroes" must be distinguished from white passers, for the latter take their performance of "blackness" further than the racial masquerade of the former by, for a committed length of time, fully adopting, not simply idealizing and imitating, black culture.

The legacy of the white Negro, however, certainly rears its head here, because when the assorted figures in this book "eat" the Other, so to speak, the nutrients in their meal are not necessarily identical.[21] Some "consume" an African American culture that is bona fide, in the sense that it is fully conceived and in line with a time-honored African American aesthetic, manifested in vernacular traditions and musical styles, or a shared historical experience and consciousness with black Americans. Others fashion their passing identities not from a culture but from a *caricature*—a stereotype of blackness. The former obviously have a more three-dimensional conception of black identity and a more vexed relationship to their own crossover identities than did the white Negro posers on whom James Baldwin heaped his vitriol: those who "malign the sorely menaced sexuality of Negroes in order to justify the white man's own sexual panic."[22] Locating the moments at which passing becomes about cross-identifying with a caricature as opposed to a culture is part and parcel of my book.

What this distinction suggests, ultimately, is that there is no such thing as a uniform mode of white passing. Indeed, I look at sundry genres of passing, and I have labored against conflating them. There is cultural passing, which is the starting point for actual white passing; it involves cultural appropriation driven by heartfelt admiration for and identification with black culture. There are involuntary passers, such as white slaves, who did not choose their black identities. There is momentary passing and long-term passing. And yet despite these variations I find it tremendously helpful to discuss all of them, in a literary and cultural study, under the umbrella of "passing," for two reasons. One, it allows us to set the white passing tradition consistently in the context of its alter ego—black passing—which, because it has an established history that has been well theorized, forms a useful template for my work. It is worth noting, too, that although critics and readers are generally quite comfortable analyzing black-to-white passing as a homogeneous phenomenon, it is in fact anything but. Nella Larsen's *Passing*, for instance, presents two very different passers: Irene passes for an afternoon, almost as a sport, while her friend Clare passes for most of her life. There are intentional passers in so-called traditional passing narratives and accidental black-to-white passers, too; for instance, the protagonists of *Iola Leroy* by Francis Harper and *An Imperative Duty* by William Dean Howells pass without knowing that they are passing, since they were raised without knowledge of their "true" race.

Second, it is exciting to tease out vital similarities—especially shared conceptions about race and identity—that cut across the disparate texts and modes of passing discussed in this book. Together they form a narrative that is sometimes akin to traditional black passing scenarios and sometimes quite different from them. By collecting these various subgenres of white passing in a single study, I hope to fill a void in the scant existing studies of white passing. Brief readings and scattered references cannot stand in for a more systematic theory of white passing, one that begins with the genre's emergence during slavery and concludes with its contemporary incarnations. In *Crossing the Line*, for instance, Gayle Wald considers two white passers, Mezz Mezzrow and John Howard Griffin, in the context of black passing, drawing two distinctions between them. First, she writes, "in contrast to 'white' passing narratives, which embrace the efficacy of passing as a means of tearing down racial prejudice and establishing avenues of 'cross-racial' understanding, 'black' passing narratives cast doubt on passing as a form of racial 'liberation.'" I argue, however, that white passing is more complex than this, that it is at once a liberal and a conservative enterprise, one driven alternately by anxiety and fantasy, fear and hope. Second, Wald's assertion that black passers are often coded as feminine while white passing is "a masculinized (and often masculinist) enterprise" not only fails to take female white passers into account but also gives short shrift to the complexities of masculine identity in both white and black passing narratives.[23] While black passing narratives often locate masculinity in the realm of the private, the domestic, or the secret, white passers become enmeshed in very *public* identities, claiming their manhood by transforming a private passing enterprise into a public identity. In other words, they turn the "feminized" enterprise of passing into a masculine one by reallocating their identities from the private to the public sphere.

Black passing narratives are commonly, though not exclusively, fictional; white passing narratives, however, often merge the fictive with the factual and lean toward the autobiographical.[24] This may reflect fundamental attitudes at the heart of the two passing genres. Because black passing has most often been presented, especially during its Harlem Renaissance heyday, as a shameful enterprise, fiction may have been the most comfortable and effective venue for addressing the subject in sometimes subversive terms. White passing, however, emerges in fictional form but in its later incarnations becomes less fictionalized—because passing whites often relish the opportunity to boast of what they understand as not just a transgressive but a progressive deed. Boasting thus sits at the heart of white passing narratives, opportunities for whites to strut their self-declared authenticity and proudly transform their private history into something worthy of a public forum. Where white passing is motivated more by anxiety than by fantasy, however, the white boast is not operative—and the narrative more often takes the form of fiction, whether in literature or film. Fantasy and anxiety thus shape not only the theme of the white passing narrative but its form and style as well.

Part and parcel of this "white boast" is the didacticism that tends to pervade the narratives discussed in this book. Their tone of social urgency separates them from the jubilant, comic tenor of blackface; quite often it is also what makes these narratives aesthetically flawed. Intent on schooling the white folks, white passers sometimes devolve into droning moralizers. Their lessons overwhelm their stories. Or perhaps their lessons (about the nature of racial identity) become too complex for their stories, too messy to be contained in neat narratives. This is particularly true of Mark Twain's *Pudd'nhead Wilson*, which is a famously formalistic mess, but it applies to other white passing narratives as well. Quite frankly it is the very *badness* of many of these texts—their native flaws—that intrigues me. My reading of works such as *Black Like Me* and *Soul Sister* cannot escape a burning question, one that I find endlessly rich: What can we learn from texts that lack literary merit but abound in book sales? I am fascinated less by the formal qualities of individual stories than by the broad swath of white passing, by the cultural fabric of white-as-black.

Two additional generic features recur in white passing narratives. First, these narratives marry race and space, emphasizing particular regions in which passing occurs. Certain cities with marked racial divides—New York, Chicago, Detroit—are focal points for white passing, as are migrations between the spaces within these locales: uptown and downtown Manhattan, North and South Side Chicago, the segregated South and the integrated North. Proximity is crucial here, of course, because passing occurs within carefully constructed, clearly demarcated spaces; passing necessitates a line worth crossing. Second, white passing narratives often employ a literary convention that hinges on what Freud termed the "uncanny": doubling.[25] Skin-dyers, cultural appropriators, and white slaves (the very term destabilizes racial categories) turn familiar white identities into something radically unfamiliar, and narratives express this tension of the uncanny by way of doubles in the text. Such doubles (or split selves) may take the form of the formerly white self and its newly black incarnation, or perhaps the white passer and her more "authentically black" Other. Doppelgangers hint at the anxieties and fantasies of the white passing enterprise. By uncannily seeing themselves in another, white passers grapple, in panic or ecstasy, with their own identities.

Although my work eschews easy chronologies, I do suggest that three decades—the 1890s, 1920s, and 1990s—are intriguingly similar and thus play significant roles in the trajectory of white passing. In each decade, rhetoric about race mixing, cultural hybridity, and a potentially vanishing white population abounded, fueling passing narratives of both the black and white varieties. Though it has cut across American culture for centuries, the notion of a miscegenated America was—owing to a number of factors—particularly vibrant during these decades. Each of these three decades, too, produced demarcated racial spaces which I suggest are critical to white (and sometimes black) passing narratives. The 1890s saw Jim Crow laws become entrenched in the American South. The 1920s marked the moment at which, as Ann Douglas put it, "the Negroization of American culture became something like a recognized phenomenon,"[26] the time when, as James Weldon Johnson noted, America began to see the Negro "in a new light": "It is beginning to see in him the divine spark which may glow merely for the fanning."[27] During that era Franz Boas produced studies about the ways in which race was socially constructed and racial groups could change their characteristics over time. The 1920s also witnessed the rise of what Kevin Mumford has called "interzones," or "black/white sex districts" that were "areas of cultural, sexual, and social exchange."[28] In cities such as New York and Chicago, Prohibition and legal sanctions against crime did not eliminate vice but instead isolated it in marginalized African American neighborhoods (Harlem, the South Side of Chicago) which eventually became "slumming districts" for whites, places for them to enact, as Mel Watkins put it, "their rebellion against puritanical rural values."[29] Ironically, then, "Progressive repression of 'miscegenation' had resulted, ultimately, in the creation of a new urban margin in which black/white sexual relations thrived."[30] The "tough on crime" 1990s took a similar toll on urban geography. In Rudolph Giuliani's New York City, for instance, parts of Manhattan and Brooklyn, spaces where whites could partake of forbidden "vices," came to resemble 1920s interzones. Mumford equates the slumming tours of 1920s Harlem with travel narratives of the same era. "For the less affluent," he writes, "spending a night on the town in Harlem might represent the cultural equivalent of taking a Cunard cruise to Africa."[31] Contemporary trends of gentrification are often described in similar terms: a visit to Washington Heights offers a taste of Dominican "flava"; the D train to Flatbush leads to an "authentic" Caribbean "bashment." Such demarcated racial geographies sit at the heart of white passing stories, which often have all the texture and feel of travel narratives. The lines crossed in white passing narratives are as literal as they are metaphorical.

Chapter 1, "White Panic and White Passing: Slavery and Reconstruction," explores origins of white passing. I begin by considering accounts of white slavery in texts such as William Wells Brown's *Clotel* and William and Ellen Craft's *Running a Thousand Miles for Freedom* that were written during the slave era; I then contrast these accounts with two narratives involving white slaves that were written *after* slavery: Mark Twain's *Pudd'nhead Wilson* and George Washington Cable's "Salome Muller, The White Slave." I show that during slavery, the categories free/slave were as potent as those of black/white, which meant that whites could pass as slaves without necessarily passing as black. In slave-era narratives, then, white slaves are usually able to maintain their whiteness and ultimately to regain it; they are therefore passing as *slaves*, not as black. Yet during Reconstruction, when free/slave ceased being a social category, southern, mostly poor whites started to fear the breakdown of black/white lines and responded by institutionalizing Jim Crow. Some southerners began to fret that whites were indeed "turning black," and the narrative of white passing emerges from this prevalent anxiety.

In Twain and Cable, worries about "blackening" whites haunt both narratives. In these fictions, white characters pass as black not by altering their appearance but by "absorbing"—through literal and figurative proximity—black culture and black mannerisms. These stories bespeak the anxiety felt by southern (primarily poor) whites of Twain and Cable's own day, no longer separated from blacks by the free/slave divide and thus potentially capable of doing the same. White passing narratives, particularly in the context of late-nineteenth-century racial science, reveal the fear that perhaps whiteness is not an essence after all. I conclude the chapter by considering the legacy of *Pudd'nhead Wilson* as reflected in the work of William Pickens, a black activist (involved with the Niagara movement and the NAACP) whose short story "The Vengeance of the Gods," published almost thirty years after Twain's novel, is modeled after it. Pickens's work, which tinkers with Twain's paradigm in fascinating ways, speaks volumes about the lasting impact of the myth of white passing in the context of slavery and Reconstruction.

In the narratives at the heart of chapter 1, race is imagined as something other than skin color, something transmittable through physical, and therefore cultural, proximity. Such narratives stand in sharp contrast to those I consider in my second chapter, which are fixated on the physicality of race. In "Dy(e)ing to Be Black: "Mars Jeems's Nightmare," *Black Like Me*, and *Watermelon Man*," I turn to a second genre of white passing narrative in which whites physically alter their appearance to pass as black. Such narratives differ widely from those in chapter 1. First, these texts preserve the essential whiteness of their protagonists, who "become" black in skin tone only. Second, skin-dye narratives envision identity not as an interior-to-exterior process—in which, as in chapter 1, once individuals feel black, they are then perceived as such—but rather as an exterior-to-interior process, so that being perceived as black enables the men in these narratives to *feel* black. In these "skin-changing" (or "skin-dyeing") narratives, proximity is step two on the path toward acquiring blackness; what is really required in order to facilitate cultural exchange is a skin swap. Produced at crucial moments in the African American struggle for equality—the first just after Reconstruction, the second at the height of the civil rights movement, and the third during the era of Black Power—the three texts of this chapter are driven less by *anxieties* about whites turning black than by *fantasies* of this transformation, which is imagined as providing white men with a new sense of potency. These narratives are reminiscent of the Indian captivity narratives of Puritan America in which a white person would "become (for a while) Indian-like in her behavior" and gain "insight into the Indian heart," but then be "restored" to her old life "with newly opened eyes."[32] In the texts by Charles Chesnutt and John Howard Griffin, black and white are two essential entities, and therefore white men can become better whites through an excursion into blackness. Melvin Van Peebles's 1970 film, however, toys with the essentialism of such skin-changing experiments in intriguing (and amusing) ways. After close analysis of these three texts, I look briefly at latter-day incarnations of the skin-changing genre, considering why this genre of white passing possesses such lasting power in the public imagination.

Critics have emphasized that, particularly when it comes to passing, race and gender operate in tandem.[33] Chapter 3, "Black Like She: Grace Halsell and the Sexuality of Passing," looks closely at a text in which the two are particularly inseparable: Grace Halsell's *Soul Sister* (1969). The memoir is a remake of Griffin's *Black Like Me*, with three essential exceptions: it is staged after Jim Crow has been dismantled, it is written from a woman's perspective—thereby fusing, in interesting ways, discourses of civil rights and the women's liberation movement—and it locates itself in Harlem as well as in the South. Although Halsell dyes her skin, it is not by altering her physical appearance that she most vitally adopts blackness but rather through her contact with—her literal proximity to—black men. While chapter 2 is centered on *male* white passers who achieve "authenticity" through homosocial (and sometimes homoerotic) bonds with black men, chapter 3 considers the position of the *female* white passer who acquires "blackness" by way of sexual bonds with black men. This suggests, then, that proximity means one thing for white men and another for white women. Exploring the role of what might be called "sexual tourism" in passing narratives, I assert that for white women, sexual contact becomes the ultimate, and most literal, way of achieving proximity to blackness—and therefore of achieving blackness itself. Halsell's life story—her subsequent stints as a Native American and a Mexican are recounted in a 1996 memoir, *In Their Shoes*—is itself a kind of modern-day captivity narrative, in which a woman is allowed the thrill of immersion in the culture of the Other but from the position of ultimate safety: whiteness.

At the heart of this chapter is the question of why the popular imagination is more taken by interracial narratives about black men and white women than it is by stories of white men and black women. I argue that because whites envision "authentic" blackness as being located in black masculinity, black *men* possess the power to transfer their blackness, so to speak, onto white men and women, while black *women* cannot do the same. And because narratives about interracial affairs are frequently caught up in issues about white appropriation of black culture, the only interracial sex that truly matters must involve the black man, because only he is the bearer of the sought-after authenticity. In considering various narratives about interracial affairs during moments of particular anxiety about forms of white appropriation, I turn to Jack Kerouac's novel *The Subterraneans* (1958), which details the affair between a white hipster and his young black lover in the context of the white Negro movement, and to contemporary films that relate sexual tourism—the most literal form of proximity—to white passing, white posing, and white appropriations of black culture.

Can a white man play jazz? Are white rappers merely "wiggers"? Can music be an authenticating force? Chapter 4, "Contagious Beats: Passing, Autobiography, and Discourses of American Music," grapples with these questions in the context of autobiographical texts by two non-black musicians, Mezz Mezzrow and Johnny Otis, who envision themselves as black. Early white criticisms of jazz included the claim that jazz brought out the "uncivilized beast" in white men—that is, that jazz would essentially turn its listeners black; this sounds remarkably like the white fear, discussed in chapter 1, that proximity to black culture had transformative powers. But while such notions about proximity arise within the context of jazz as warnings and apprehensions, just as they did in Reconstruction narratives, they soon become appropriated by white musicians like Mezzrow and Otis, who claim that indeed they *have* become black by being close to blacks and playing "black music"—and they couldn't be happier about it. In both *Really the Blues* (1946) and *Upside Your Head* (1993), becoming black is a natural outgrowth of growing up among blacks and playing black music. And yet despite such assertions, Mezzrow's authenticity plagues him. His text is wrapped up in anxieties about being *really* (as his title puts it) black and *really* a jazzman, a racial quagmire he ultimately sidesteps by finally asserting that his race is altogether Other: music itself.

The next section of the chapter examines the ways in which these same ideologies—the belief that musicians become more authentically black by growing up among blacks, that culture is thus transmittable in certain neighborhoods but that ultimately the race of white musicians playing "black music" *is* the music itself—return in discourse about hip-hop culture. Hip-hop, like early jazz and rock 'n' roll, is often imagined by its opponents as awakening the "primitive" in whites, a racist critique that echoes fears about black music as an "infectious rhythm." And yet white rappers from Vanilla Ice to Eminem to Paul Wall wear their (alleged) upbringing in black neighborhoods as badges of authenticity, surrounding themselves with black people while onstage and ultimately invoking the claim that proximity gives one a special "pass" to black culture while simultaneously asserting that the culture they belong to is neither black nor white but "hip-hop culture."

Although critics claimed that black passing was "passé" by the 1960s,[34] the late 1990s witnessed an upsurge in memoirs by mixed-race individuals[35] as well as in black-to-white passing narratives: the book and film adaptation of Philip Roth's *The Human Stain*, for instance, Colson Whitehead's *The Intuitionist*, or the screen adaptation of Walter Mosley's *Devil in a Blue Dress*. It seems as if race is everywhere and nowhere in our culture: simultaneously recognized as a non-entity (or social construct) and yet hailed as the most crucial part of one's identity; the very same issue of *Newsweek* that denies the existence of whiteness continues throughout to refer to "whites" as if they do indeed exist.[36] In my concluding chapter, "Is Passing Passé in a 'Post-Race' World?" I consider how narratives of white passing operate at a time when, first, whites are hyperconscious of the ways in which they have historically appropriated black culture and, second, the notion of a "mixed nation" has become widespread. This discussion crosses generic lines, taking into consideration memoirs—such as *The Color of Water* by James McBride (1996), whose mother "refused to acknowledge her whiteness"[37]—novels such as Danzy Senna's *Caucasia*, contemporary hip-hop culture, and the "race traitor" movement, the last a group of contemporary scholars and activists (headed by Noel Ignatiev) whose goal is the abolition of whiteness.

One cannot write about white-to-black passing and the phenomenon of whites "assimilat[ing] and internaliz[ing] the degraded and devalorized signifiers of racial Otherness into the cultural construction of their own identity" without grappling with an über-question: Is it a progressive or regressive act?[38] During our contemporary era, increasingly defined in terms of its racial and cultural free-for-alls, are there judgments to be made about whites who claim blackness in some way, or have we relinquished any belief in cultural ownership and authenticity of identity? This question resonates loudly in pop culture since the triumph of Eminem, the surly faced, platinum-haired poster child for "wiggered"-out America, the man synonymous with contemporary discussions about cultural appropriation. At the height of his popularity, an influential hip-hop magazine, for instance, deemed Eminem "part of a dangerous, corruptive cycle that promotes the blatant theft of a culture from the community that created it" and urged readers not to "sit back while our culture is raped and pillaged."[39] Our discourse is engrossed by questions about race and appropriation but rarely untangles the quandaries at the heart of these issues: Can we draw a line between cultural theft and cultural influence or inspiration? Can we sift through the amalgam that is American culture? Take the case of "Hound Dog," a song penned by two Jews (Jerry Leiber and Mike Stoller), handed to a Greek man who passed as African American (Johnny Otis), sung first by a black woman (Big Mama Thornton) and then by a white man (Elvis Presley). Can we render judgment about who, in the end, stole from whom? Or consider the cakewalk, as LeRoi Jones sees it: "If the cakewalk is a Negro dance caricaturing certain white customs, what is that dance when, say, a white theater company attempts to satirize it as a Negro dance?"[40] Distinctions are too rarely made: Between literal (i.e., monetary) and metaphorical (i.e., historical) theft. Between a *trend* in the 1950s and a single *figurehead* in 2000. Between white Negroes like Elvis, George Gershwin, and Irving Berlin—who tapped black music for their art but grew culturally whiter with age and success—and those like Mezz Mezzrow, who grew darker over time. Between Elvis's early radio performances, which few guessed were the work of a white boy, and Eminem's lyrical flow, backed by his hyper-white persona. In an epilogue I confront such thorny questions in order to present an ethical breakdown of white passing and white-to-black identification. I assess the big picture, evaluating and comparing the various figures in this book in order to propose explicitly what I have implied all along: that there are indeed modes of passing and appropriating which are more progressive—more just, perhaps—than others.

White passing persists as a potent myth in American culture, one that has enabled blacks and whites alike to grapple with the color line in intriguing and inimitable ways. Recognizing the potency and the longevity of the white passing myth is thus crucial to our understanding of how whites and blacks look upon each other, whether with awe, fear, desire—or all three.

1

White Panic and White Passing
Slavery and Reconstruction

In his 1816 antislavery tract *The Book and Slavery Irreconcilable*, the Reverend George Bourne declared that "slave-holders would wade through seas of the blood of white men, as well as black men, to gratify their despotic propensities if they were not restrained."[1] Bourne may not have realized that slave owners were *not* restrained: cases of white slavery—the first recorded incidents of white people being taken for black—were a reality. White children were kidnapped and sometimes dyed black, immigrants placed on the market, and orphans shipped south. Most evidence of this is anecdotal.[2] In 1835 Edward S. Abdy reported the case of Nannie Pagee, a white woman from Virginia who was enslaved as an orphan. A Swedish writer and traveler similarly described her encounter with a "white" woman who was enslaved, as well as with a small "white" boy, with "cheeks as red as roses," who stood on the auction block. In 1835 a woman named Harriet, enslaved in Georgia, was declared white and free in a Tennessee court of law. And in 1681 a white servant named Irish Nell became enslaved by way of her marriage to a black slave known as Negro Charles.[3]

Yet despite such realities, the most significant narrative dealing with white passing and white slavery, Mark Twain's *Pudd'nhead Wilson*, was not published until 1894. The reason for this delay, as I will argue, is that the notion that white could pass for black did not truly enter the American cultural landscape until Reconstruction. What, then, of the cases just mentioned, all of which occurred during the slave era? In the first section of this chapter I answer this question by exploring slave-era narratives of white slavery. In these texts the black/white distinction is eclipsed by the free/slave one, making it possible to pass for *slave* without necessarily passing for *black*. After Emancipation, various historical shifts gave birth to the concept of white passing for black; these shifts provide the context for my reading of two texts at the heart of this chapter: Mark Twain's *Pudd'nhead Wilson* and George Washington Cable's "Salome Muller, The White Slave." These narratives reflect the ways in which myths of white passing—which become inextricably linked to ideas about proximity—first begin to take shape. Informed by nineteenth-century racial science, these texts reveal cultural anxieties about a potentially disappearing white essence.

Why should this anxiety find its most salient expression in fictional narrative? Frantz Fanon's discussion of "negrophobia" suggests one answer. "In the phobic," he writes, "affect has a priority that defies all rational thinking. As we can see, the phobic is a person who is governed by the laws of rational prelogic and affective prelogic."[4] Phobias, in other words, defy rational categories of thought. As products of "rational prelogic," they allow for the coexistence of opposites and the persistence of contradictions. In fictional narrative, creative "prelogic" reigns and contradictions thrive. Many literary texts are founded on ideologies that, when closely examined, stand in opposition to one another, reflecting profound ambivalences at the heart of the text. My close reading of Cable's and Twain's works suggests precisely such contradictions and ambivalences, for both texts, engaged in voicing certain cultural phobias while at the same time adhering to generic conventions, reflect what happens when the historical conflicts with the rhetorical. In expressing cultural anxieties about race while deploying particular literary genres, Twain and Cable end up writing deeply inconsistent texts, thereby demonstrating what happens when genre and ideology are at odds.

Whiteness, Slavery, and White Slavery

Antislavery writers in the 1850s faced a formidable challenge. How could they make slavery, which affected blacks in the South, relevant and real to whites in the North? Like good propagandists, they took a direct approach. It could happen to you, they asserted, because slavery is not necessarily about color. For this reason, two best-selling antislavery works, William Wells Brown's *Clotel* (1853) and William and Ellen Craft's *Running a Thousand Miles for Freedom* (1860), include narratives about a near-mythical figure in the history of white passing: Salome Muller. A German-born immigrant who arrived in New Orleans with her father and sister in 1818, Salome was sold into slavery soon after her arrival by John Miller, the planter in whose service Salome's father died. Too young to recall her origins, Salome remained enslaved until 1843, when she was discovered by Madame Karl, a German friend of the family. The 1845 Louisiana Supreme Court case that ultimately set her free became the stuff of legend: the Crafts, Brown, and Cable all wrote narratives about Salome—narratives that, as we will see, differ in crucial ways.

The Crafts make mention of Salome in the context of other cases of white slaves. Because the central goal of their narrative—a narrative of gender and racial passing—is to assert that "slavery in America is not at all confined to persons of any particular complexion," they begin part one by asserting that they have "conversed with several slaves who told [us] that their parents were white and free; but that they were stolen away from them and sold when quite young." [5] They cite George Bourne's description of the "tanned and stained" boy who was sold, and they mention, too, that Salome herself, during twenty-five years of servitude, had been "exposed to the sun's rays in the hot climate of Louisiana, with head and neck unsheltered, as is customary with the female slaves. . . . .Those parts of her person which had been shielded from the sun were comparatively white" (5). In opening their slave narrative with the story of Salome, the Crafts accomplish two things. First, they indict the slave system and the South, where, as they write, "there is a greater want of humanity and high principle amongst the whites, than among any other civilized people in the world" (6). Second, they establish the relative ease with which black and white can become interchangeable, something critical not only to the events of their narrative but also to their mission of making slavery applicable to a white readership.

Brown fictionalizes Salome's story in chapter 14 of *Clotel*, in which Althesa, Clotel's sister, encounters Salome at the home of the Mortons, her kindhearted owners. Salome does much of the talking in this chapter, titled "A Free Woman Reduced to Slavery." She tearfully recounts her story to Althesa and Mrs. Morton, who are horrified but powerless to help her. Salome is then moved to another home in the area, where she is finally discovered by a German woman (presumably Madame Karl) and emancipated. Like *Running a Thousand Miles for Freedom*, *Clotel* is invested in challenging racial categories; like Ellen Craft, Clotel—daughter of Thomas Jefferson, of all people!—stands on the auction block "with a complexion as white as most of those who were waiting with a wish to become her purchasers." [6] Both *Running a Thousand Miles* and *Clotel*, then, employ mulatto characters in order to enable white readers to personalize the horrors of slavery, and both introduce Salome in order to make slavery even more directly applicable to whites.

And yet what is so fascinating about both accounts of the Salome case is that in neither does Salome pass for *black*; instead she passes for *slave*. Even as she is "reduced to slavery," as Brown's chapter title puts it—thereby emphasizing the free/slave divide over the black/white one—Salome retains her whiteness. This fact is underscored in the Crafts' narrative by their addition of a crucial detail that is not present in any other Salome account, including the legal summary: the notion that Salome's skin was presumably darkened by the sun. In light of their claim that slavery is *not* about skin color, it seems odd that the Crafts add a detail implying that indeed it is—that in fact Salome's skin required altering in order to transform her from free woman to slave. This skin change implies that Salome's shift in status was not entirely cultural but also physical, and therefore her "acquired blackness," so to speak, can be easily undone: if exposure to the sun turned her slave, lack of it can turn her free. The important thing for the Crafts, however, is not that Salome turned from white to black— since, after all, this transformation is reversible—but that she turned from free woman to slave in a mere instant, which is the very thing that the Crafts decry in *Running a Thousand Miles*. "Above all, the fact that another man had the power to tear from our cradle the new-born babe and sell it in the shambles like a brute . . . haunted us for years" (3), they write—speaking of Salome herself, subject to this very reversal of fate. While narratives about mulatto slaves obscure racial lines but maintain the essential blackness of their protagonists, antebellum stories of white slavery question racial boundaries—but ultimately uphold the essential *whiteness* of their protagonists.[7]

The intractability of whiteness is evident in another novel of the antebellum era, *The Garies and Their Friends*, by Frank Webb. Like *Clotel*, the novel revolves around light-skinned protagonists, some of whom pass for white. Also like *Clotel*, the novel features a brief interlude in which a white character passes as black: the nefariously racist Mr. Stevens, who is attacked and tarred by a vengeful mob. For one harrowing evening he gets a taste of his own medicine, enduring racist harassment and going unrecognized by his own wife, who shrinks from him. But despite the fact that the novel, like *Clotel*, persistently undermines the physicality of race and blurs the line between white and black—only close examination of Mrs. Garie, for instance, exhibits her "true" identity as a black woman; Clarence Garie grapples throughout the novel with passing for white—during the one scene in which a white man passes for black, his physical appearance must be altered: "[Mr. Stevens] was, indeed, a pitiable object to look upon. . . . His lips were swelled to a size that would have been regarded as large even on the face of a Congo negro, and one eye was puffed out to an alarming extent; whilst the coating of tar he had received rendered him such an object as the reader can but faintly picture to himself."[8]

WHITE PANIC AND WHITE PASSING

Blacks pass as white in *The Garies* without changing their exteriors, but here a white man can pass as black only if he is assaulted and painted. Despite all of this, too, Mr. Stevens—like Salome in both the Crafts and Brown—remains essentially white, protesting throughout his traumatic ordeal that his is a case of mistaken identity. Clearly whiteness, unlike blackness, is an indelible essence in the novel, so durable that only tar can vitiate it, and even then only fleetingly, because that coating of tar, hard as it is to scrub off, cannot ultimately sully one's white identity.

Like *Running a Thousand Miles*, *Clotel* resolves Salome's story rather neatly by describing her restoration to freedom. What is fascinating about both texts, however, is that in neither one is Salome's identity as a white woman jeopardized in the least bit, despite the fact that she has spent nearly thirty years as a black slave. For Brown, this is because Salome never forgot who she was; although she was enslaved in her youth, Salome remains, in Brown's version of the story, fully aware that she is actually white. She carries it around with her as a badge of sorrow, lamenting to Althesa and Mrs. Morton, "I was once severely flogged for telling a stranger that I was not born a slave" (190). Like the Crafts, Brown seems invested in pointing out that Salome's transformation, her passing, is solely a matter of status. She never ceased being white or identifying as such; instead she ceased being free.

How different this is from Cable's version of the Salome story, published in 1889 as one of his *Strange True Stories of Louisiana*. In *Clotel*, Salome's voice is ever present. Fully secure in her identity as a white woman, she vocally commands her own narrative. Yet in "Salome Muller, The White Slave," that voice is scarcely to be found. Cable presents a Salome who is indeed secure in her identity—her identity as a black slave, not a white woman: "I am a yellow girl," Salome asserts to Madame Karl when she is first discovered. "I belong to Mr. Louis Belmonti, who keeps this 'coffee-house.' He has owned me for four or five years. Before that? Before that I belonged to Mr. John Fitz Miller, who has the saw-mill down here by the convent. I always belonged to him. Her accent was the one common to English-speaking slaves."[9] In Cable's narrative, Salome has no white identity because she has spent most of her life believing that she is a black slave. The central dilemma of Cable's story, to which I return later in this chapter, is then not simply how to restore someone's *freedom*, as it is in both *Running a Thousand Miles* and *Clotel*, but how to restore someone's *whiteness*. Brown and the Crafts present narratives in which a free white person passes for slave, but Cable writes a story in which a white person passes for black.

Ultimately, the slave-era narratives of white slavery are, as I propose with regard to *Running a Thousand Miles* and *Clotel*, more concerned with the free/

slave distinction than with the black/white one. After all, Salome remains essentially white in both Brown and the Crafts; only her status changes. This is in line with David Roediger's argument in *The Wages of Whiteness* that between 1860 and 1865 white workers were developing a firm identity as whites, so that discussions of white slavery, which began in the 1830s, never implied that whites were becoming black but rather that "they were threatened with slavery." Whites were rarely imagined, during the slave era, as having the potential to turn black; instead they were imagined as having the potential to turn slave (though these workers often hesitated to employ terms such as "white slave," Roediger notes, for fear that it too closely allied them with blacks).[10] An 1835 cartoon, in which white slaves work beside black ones and are called "whities," underscores the fact that slave-era visions of white slavery did not jeopardize white identities: the "slaves" in this cartoon remain, despite their socioeconomic status, white. The crucial divide in antebellum America was that between free and slave, leading one Louisiana judge in 1856 to declare, "There is . . . all the difference between a free man of color and a slave, that there is between a white man and a slave."[11] Informed by such ideologies, slave-era texts present whiteness as an unalterable essence, one that slavery can do little to vitiate.

And yet in Cable's narrative, whiteness is anything but an essence. In his tale white identity is jeopardized precisely because it can be put on and taken off. Whence this questioning of a racial science that separated white and black? What happened to the southern cultural landscape between Emancipation and Reconstruction, between Brown and Cable, so as to make white-to-black passing an imaginative possibility?[12]

Racial Difference and Reconstruction

What happened, in short, was that many whites became literally and figuratively closer to blacks than ever before. In her study of segregation in the South, Grace Elizabeth Hale makes this crucial observation: "In their culture of segregation, white Southerners, despite their best and most violent efforts to segregate and to contain Southern blacks, recognized at some unconscious level and deeply feared an interdependence, a grayness, an area of 'racial' sameness."[13] According to C. Vann Woodward, this interdependence was particularly evident during the period between Emancipation and Jim Crow, during which northern visitors often noted an "intimacy of contact between the races in the south, an intimacy sometimes admitted to be distasteful to the visitor."[14] With the breakdown of the free/slave divide and the increase in day-to-day contact between black and white, many whites began to get nervous about the status

WHITE PANIC AND WHITE PASSING

of whiteness, anxiously questioning nineteenth-century "scientific" claims that black and white were two distinct essences. If, after all, a mere drop of black blood could turn white black, then just how vulnerable was white blood? Tom Watson, a racial theorist in the postbellum South, deemed it quite vulnerable, asserting that unless whites devised a way to control blacks, then emancipation—which represented what he called a "sudden injection into the body politic of a horde of black savages to . . . overshadow the social world with the ever-present terror of the 'black peril'"—would result in a loss of white "civilization." In response to such fears, the myth of the diseased Negro took hold during the 1880s, as racist doctors such as Hinton Rowan Helper claimed that blacks must be kept separate from whites in order to prevent "pollution" due to contact.[15] One member of the Freedmen's Bureau tried to dispel such fears, asserting that no "causes have existed to transform one type of man into another—as the white man into a Negro, or *vice versa*," but his words seem to have fallen on deaf ears.[16]

Fears about blackness being contagious, transmittable via proximity, were particularly invoked in panicky rhetoric about miscegenation—which results, after all, from literal (i.e., sexual) proximity. As one racial theorist, Watson Quinby, put it, "It is a rule and law that when the white man mixes his blood with the darker races, that the dark races will eventually gain the ascendancy." Miscegenation was so great a threat to whiteness during Reconstruction that even Cable, an antiracist activist, issued a disclaimer of sorts with regard to his "Freedman's Case in Equity," stating that it "does not hint the faintest approval of any sort of admixture of the two bloods." Miscegenation thus always lurks as a kind of subtext in the narratives I discuss—even if it never forms the central thread of the story—because it is capable of "darkening" one's offspring, and is thus the most literal path from white to black. As Eric Lott notes with regard to minstrelsy: "It should hardly seem strange that miscegenation is suggested . . . in accounts of white men's fascination with and attraction to black men and their culture, for these are accounts in which the cultures merge. The logic of such accounts is that fascination may be permitted so long as actual contact is avoided."[17]

With the end of slavery and the advent of Reconstruction, then, the notion that white could become black—the fear that whiteness was not an essence—became a terrible reality in the minds of many whites. Whites were eager for the establishment of a physical space between black and white that would replace the now lost social space between free man and slave; they began to think that only segregation could prevent the "contagion" of blackness, which was transmittable via proximity and, of course, miscegenation. And as blackness became something that could be transmitted, there was created in the white mind "a new and curious kind of mulatto—a mulatto who was in fact genetically white but morally black. In sum, 'Negro' became an *idea*."[18] By the turn of the century, whites could "become" black by way of association with blacks, or by acting in a manner that was identified with blacks, as when Robert Hancock, a white Republican senator from North Carolina who was accused of sexual assault, was described in "Negro-like" terms by numerous reporters.[19] The Radical era gave birth to this figure of the so-called "white nigger," but this was really the logical extension of Reconstruction ideas about blackness being contagious in the wake of a disappearing free/slave divide. It is interesting to note that even Reconstruction anxieties over the contagion of blackness have their roots in an earlier age; in the eighteenth century, Dr. Benjamin Rush spoke of blackness as a potentially contagious disease and encouraged whites to avoid "connections" with blacks that could "infect posterity with any portion of their disorder."[20]

The danger of becoming black was most tangible to poor whites, for whom Reconstruction constituted a social and economic nadir. White farmers were often subject to the same exploitative labor system (including crop liens, verbal contracts between sharecroppers and landlords, and the convict lease system) as blacks. The Farmers' Alliance of the 1880s was formed in response to the deepening recession faced by white farmers, and the "plantation paternalism" rhetoric of the era applied to blacks and whites alike. Further obscuring the line between poor whites and blacks was the fact that whites began to fill what had previously been considered black jobs. In a Mississippi cotton mill in 1876, for instance, most of the five hundred employees were white, as were the majority of cotton mill workers in and around Petersburg, Virginia, in 1874; this state of affairs led to objections regarding what one reporter called "a mingling of the races in Southern cotton mills."[21] Whites were employed in household and field jobs as well, causing one Florida farmer and physician to note that "white women are taking the place of the Negroes in our village."[22] As Noel Ignatiev points out, the whitening process is inextricably linked to labor roles. The Irish were "blackened," for instance, by performing the same jobs as African Americans but became white, he argues, once a separate sphere of labor—"white man's work"—established them as "white" working class.[23] White identity thus becomes vulnerable when whites perform the same labor as blacks—as was occurring in the wake of Emancipation.

In terms of their socioeconomic status, then, poor whites could be perceived as becoming black, a fact underscored by what Woodward has called their "excessive squeamishness or fussiness about contact with Negroes."[24] Perhaps in response to a deep-seated anxiety that they were being "blackened," poor whites (by this time called "crackers" or "tarheels") were desperate to be physically separated from blacks, and were therefore the most outspoken segregationists in the South. Among poor whites, writes W. J. Cash, "race obsession and passion for getting the Negro safely bound again in his old place were most fully developed."[25] Because of the increasingly tenuous boundary, physical and economic, between black and white, poor whites were more susceptible to the "contagion" of blackness.[26]

Poor whites, however, were not the only ones taking over formerly black jobs. In 1869 Father Abram Ryan's *Banner of the South* called for the replacement of black labor with immigrant labor, and by 1870 the arrival in Mississippi of Danes, Swedes, Norwegians, Swiss, and Irish was being hailed by a local paper as "the dawn of a new era in Southern labor." Between 1881 and 1884 Italians replaced blacks in South Carolina phosphate mines, and in 1880 Louisiana sugar planters contracted with seven hundred Portuguese to replace black laborers. The labor landscape of the South was transformed during the 1880s and 1890s as whites and immigrants filled African Americans' shoes and then struggled to maintain their white identities. Immigrants were often unsuccessful in this regard, as the general population, especially in the South, refused to acknowledge the "whiteness" of these newcomers. " 'You don't call . . . an Italian a white man?' a West Coast construction worker was asked. 'No, sir,' he answered, 'an Italian is a Dago.' "[27] Like blacks, immigrants—Chinese, Italians, Jews—often faced lynch mobs and tragic deaths. As more and more workers who looked white were suddenly performing black jobs, it became increasingly difficult for whites to feel secure in their own whiteness. They began to wonder whether whiteness was indeed an essence after all.

Amplifying such claims were developments in racial science in the late nineteenth century. Two theories of racial origin were circulated at the time: monogenism, which claimed that the races evolved from a single source and had degenerated, and polygenism, which argued that the races were endowed with distinctly unequal attributes from the start. By the 1860s and 1870s Darwinian evolution had begun to replace both theories and emerge as the dominant paradigm. Many scientists promoted a "Lamarckian process" of evolution (named for the French biologist Jean Lamarck), by which traits acquired during one's lifespan could potentially be passed on to future generations. The effects of such scientific theories on popular conceptions of "black" and "white" were quite significant. Because, as Louis Menand writes, "a general type is fixed, determinate, and uniform" while "the world Darwin described is characterized by chance, change, and difference," thinkers began to "drop the language of [racial] types and essences, which is prescriptive (telling us what all finches should be), and adopt the language of statistics and probability, which is predictive (telling us what the average finch, under specified conditions, is likely to do)." Darwinian science asserted that species were constantly in flux, which meant that one could no longer speak with certainty about racial essences—including white essences. Neo-Lamarckian ideologies reinforced the notion that identity (notably racial identity), altered by one's cultural environment, was a profoundly ephemeral thing. Just as the line between the white and black worlds was becoming blurred, scientific paradigms were shifting in such a way as almost to reinforce such blurring. If humans were a changeable species, molded by their surroundings, then what was to stop white from turning black?[28]

It is in this cultural climate—in which, as racial science began to abandon its emphasis on racial essences, black proximity was imagined to mean black contagion, whites could "become" black by behaving in certain ways, and white workers were in socioeconomic terms filling black shoes—that notions about white passing for black first assume their narrative possibility. In her work on rituals of purity and contagion, the anthropologist Mary Douglas argues that such rituals reflect cultural ideas about boundaries. Citing the abominations of Leviticus, she claims that holiness "is exemplified by completeness" and ultimately "means keeping distinct the categories of creation." According to Douglas, uncleanness—"that which must not be included if a pattern is to be maintained"—results from a dangerous crossing of social barriers, an inappropriate tampering with critical social patterns. Therefore, "wherever the lines are precarious, we find pollution ideas come to their support. Physical crossing of the social barrier is treated as a dangerous pollution."[29] Douglas's analysis helps explain why white passing is envisioned in the nineteenth century as a form of contagion: it reflects exactly this sort of boundary crossing, of rigid social patterns being unraveled. Blackness becomes envisioned in terms of pollution and contagion only when the lines that separate it from whiteness become indistinct.[30]

One response to such boundary blurring is reflected in the nineteenth century's most popular form of cross-cultural play: minstrelsy. Though it flourished during the period in which white passing was born, minstrelsy is, with regard to cultural exchange, not anxious but jubilant. This is so because minstrelsy did just the opposite of suggesting a hazy line between the two races. Whites who blacked up were not *becoming* black but *performing blackness*—a crucial difference. Instead of *passing*, minstrels were *posing*, an enterprise for which they "often emphasized the spurious or ersatz caricature they created."[31]

WHITE PANIC AND WHITE PASSING

Even in blackface, minstrels were clearly and essentially white; passers were not. If minstrelsy allowed whites to play with a black mask that could easily be taken on and off—implying its retention of basic distinctions between the two races—white passing reflected anxiety about the haziness of distinctions between black and white. It is here that we can turn to two narratives that are so profoundly wrapped up in this anxiety. Both are set in the slave era, yet both reflect the racial ideologies of a post-slavery moment.

"Salome Muller, The White Slave"

I have already begun discussing the ways in which Cable's story places Salome's white identity in jeopardy. As an object of interpretation throughout the narrative, Salome barely speaks, and when she does, it is usually to deny that she is Salome Muller, German woman, at all. Her lawyers and Madame Karl take center stage in making her case, indicating that Salome herself has little sense of her identity as a white person. By living and marrying among blacks, by passing as black, and by imagining that she *is* black, Salome embodies the post-Emancipation fear that physical and cultural proximity to African Americans could cause whites to lose their whiteness. While the Crafts and Brown neatly resolve Salome's story with a description of her emancipation, Cable's tale offers no simple resolution. Salome is freed, Cable recounts, but she has difficulty finding her place in society:

> Salome being free, her sons were, by law, free also. But they could only be free mulattoes, went to Tennessee and Kentucky, were heard of once or twice as stable-boys to famous horses, and disappeared. A Mississippi River Pilot, John Given by name, met Salome among her relatives, and courted and married her. As might readily be supposed, this alliance was only another misfortune to Salome, and the pair separated. Salome went to California. Her cousin, Henry Schuber, tells me he saw her in 1855 in Sacramento City, living at last a respected and comfortable life. (191)

How, after all, could a white woman who spent most of her life as a black woman live happily ever after? A sense of unease lingers with the reader who finishes Cable's tale—perhaps the same unease faced by many southerners after the war: What if, because of radical social upheaval, whites were turning black? Many poor whites were, after all, confronting just the sort of racial identity crisis that Salome faces: confusion about what, in the context of the South's new racial economy, separates white from black. Salome's 1845 court decision notes that the plaintiff, Louis Belmonti, "always thought she has something resembling the colored race in her features, but this opinion may have been induced by the fact, that he had always seen her associating with persons of color."[32] Salome—"for twenty-five years dragged in the mire of African slavery, the mother of quadroon children and ignorant of her own identity" (166), as Cable describes her—passes for black by way of proximity to the black world, a proximity that allows her to absorb black culture. Her environment, then, alters her essence. That very notion cuts to the heart of the panic felt by poor whites of Cable's era, who lived in similar cultural proximity.

In a related point, Cable brings issues of his own day to bear on his story by emphasizing the Mullers' position as part of an immigrant group that was, as we have seen, increasingly envisioned in the nineteenth century as nonwhite. He begins his story with a description of Salome's homeland, the German-speaking town of Langensoultz in Alsace, France, where "there was a widespread longing among [the residents] to seek another land where men and women and children were not doomed to feed the ambition of European princes" (146). By opening his tale with a description of a displaced people seeking liberty, Cable foreshadows the very *lack* of liberty that they ultimately face—but he also sets up a parallel between the journey of these poor immigrants and that of the black slaves, both sailing into southern harbors during the same era. As the German-French community awaited departure from Holland, Cable writes, "provisions began to diminish, grew scanty, and at length were gone. . . . [M]any of them, without goods, money, or even shelter, and strangers to the place and to the language, were reduced to begging for bread" (149). When the ships finally depart—their decks "*black* with people" (150; emphasis added)—passengers endure storm, famine, and illness; of one ship's 700 passengers, Cable says, only 430 survived. They arrive in America only to be scattered about, much as black slaves were: "The people were bound out before notaries and justices of the peace, singly and in groups, some to one, some to two years' service, according to age" (157). Cable's implicit parallel between immigrant and black again calls attention to the increasingly indistinct line between white and black, which made white passing an imaginative possibility.

"Salome Muller, The White Slave" is an unstructured tale; Cable seems more concerned with documenting his story than with crafting its narrative. And yet two aspects of the narrative are intriguing in light of their relationship to *Pudd'nhead Wilson*, to which I turn next. First, Cable makes subtle use of doppelgangers in his story. Adding an unusual detail that is not found in Salome's legal account, Cable tells us that his heroine bore a strange resemblance to her cousin, "whose face was strikingly like Salome's" (149). This cousin is revealed to be Madame Karl, whose life takes a dramatically different turn from Salome's: "The little girl cousin of Salome Muller, who as a child of the same age had been her playmate on shipboard at the Helder and in crossing the Atlantic, and who looked so much like Salome, was a woman of thirty, the wife of Karl Rouff" (164). It is Madame Karl, the respectable gentlewoman, who discovers Salome, a fact that sets up a strange doubling between the two women, one slave and one free, one white and one "black"—and yet ultimately of the same family. Such doubling is crucial to the story because it literalizes the two potential paths open to poor whites and/or immigrants in Cable's day: whiteness or blackness. For Cable, writes Ronald Takaki, "whites had a special responsibility to preserve their racial purity: they were the custodians of mind and civilization."[33] Cable implies that if they abdicate this responsibility, their fate is to become not Madame Karl but Salome Muller.

The second way in which Cable takes creative license with his tale is by peppering it with physical evidence. As if to make Salome Muller (or Sally Miller, as she becomes known) bona fide to his readers, Cable incorporates her signature into his story twice. He also includes a photo of her court papers as well as reprints of the court's declarations.[34] The most important piece of physical evidence in the tale, however, concerns an aspect of the Salome story that is mentioned neither by the Crafts nor by Brown, and is only cursorily noted by the legal brief. As Salome's case stands before the Louisiana Supreme Court, the burden of proof is deemed to be not on Salome but on those claiming that she is in fact black. And yet Salome's lawyers set forth dramatic evidence that "Sally Miller" is "Salome Muller": two birthmarks that Salome's relatives had previously attested to, documented as genuine by a physician whose letter is reprinted by Cable. These birthmarks, initially ignored by the district court but finally acknowledged by the Supreme Court, serve as physical markings that Salome is white. They become tangible proof of her identity, even as the rest of the tale is invested in deeply questioning that identity. It is as though Cable's story, which interrogates Salome's ability to retain whiteness, simultaneously asserts that her whiteness is in fact physically provable, something that can be determined by appearance, while also declaring that "neither this man's 'instinct' nor that of any one else, either during the whole trial or during twenty years' previous knowledge of the plaintiff, was of the least value to determine whether this poor slave was entirely white or of mixed blood" (177–78). On some level, then, the tale—even as it centers on a white "black" person who undermines the connection between race and skin color—nevertheless hinges on the idea that physical appearance is indeed a reliable indicator of identity. At its core, "Salome Muller, The White Slave" speaks from both sides of its mouth on the issue of whether identity is a physical matter or not, a point to which I will return.

The tale is also, finally, ambiguous about whether "lost" whiteness can ever be regained. After all, by *passing* as black, Salome essentially *becomes* black: She forgets her past and is but tenuously reintegrated into the white world. In this respect, the first narrative of white passing is both similar to and different from classic black-to-white passing narratives. On the one hand, the story radically questions white and black identity, implying, as Samira Kawash puts it in her analysis of *The Autobiography of an Ex-Coloured Man*, that "identity is not what we are but what we are passing for."[35] Yet at the same time, in no story of black passing does the black passer lose all memory of a black identity as Salome loses sight of her white identity. That is because in black passing narratives—from *The Autobiography of an Ex-Coloured Man* to Jessie Redmon Fauset's 1929 novel *Plum Bun* and *Imitation of Life*—blackness is ultimately an essence that passers are, as critics have noted, punished for denying. By contrast, in the postbellum white passing narratives discussed in this chapter, whiteness is *not* essentialized but is a deeply vulnerable entity, one that can be obliterated by mere contact with a drop of black blood. Blackness is an essence that can never be wiped out, but whiteness can be taken off, sometimes permanently. This changes, we will see, as white passing becomes a fantasy and not a nightmare. Latter-day white passers are actually persistently aware that their own whiteness can never be fully eradicated—that, in other words, whiteness is more stubborn than they might like it to be. But in its early incarnation, white passing, born in the context of contagion and amnesia, suggests that whiteness can be swiftly swallowed by blackness. Salome does not consciously decide to be a passer, as many African American passers do; rather she has passing foisted upon her. Furthermore, through proximity to the black world Salome "absorbs" blackness and loses whiteness. Nowhere in black passing narratives does proximity take on this sort of transformative power—a power that reflects the very cultural panic I have been discussing, and that is captured more cogently in Twain's 1894 novel.

Pudd'nhead Wilson

Like "Salome Muller, The White Slave," Mark Twain's novel *Pudd'nhead Wilson* was published at the end of the nineteenth century but set in an earlier moment. Why, asks Shelley Fisher Fishkin, did Twain choose to set both *The Adventures of Huckleberry Finn* and *Pudd'nhead Wilson* in the antebellum era? Because, she suggests, he was seizing upon "the freedom this remote setting gave him to explore contemporary issues that may have been too threatening to explore directly."[36] I propose that one of these issues is the "blackening" of poor white America. By the 1880s Twain had become less a humorist with regard to race and more a moralist; perhaps this was a result of political and cultural changes that led many toward "a sense of reconstruction having failed, of immigration getting out of hand, of assimilation no longer a boon but a possible threat to the development of a national character."[37] If this is indeed the case, we might read *Pudd'nhead Wilson* as a product of disillusionment and anxiety with regard to racial and economic dividing lines in postbellum America.

Anyone who writes about *Pudd'nhead Wilson* must grapple with Hershel Parker's definitive work on the history of the manuscript, in which he asserts that we cannot ultimately make any real claims about the fragment of the novel that we are privy to. "How," he asks, "can we talk sensibly about characterization 'throughout' a novel when chapters survive from stages when a character [Tom] was white and a stage when he was part black?"[38] Parker emphasizes the impossibility of offering an analysis of Tom (as many critics do), since Tom is an inconsistent character, half the time conceived as black and half the time as white. Yet this reading ignores the fact that two characters in the novel *are* consistent and seem to have been with Twain from page one: Pudd'nhead Wilson and Chambers, the white slave. Much has been said about Wilson's role in the novel but nearly nothing about Chambers's, an odd fact considering that he remains an invariable figure in Twain's work.[39]

Chambers, however, plays a crucial role in the narrative, because it is through Chambers—the white passer—that Twain explores the ominous possibility of a "blackening" white population. *Pudd'nhead Wilson* is, like "Salome Muller, The White Slave," a narrative that revolves around doubles, one slave and one free, one "black" and one "white"—each reflecting, perhaps, potential identities for the poor whites of Twain's era. Although Chambers does not appear in the narrative nearly as often as Tom does, his role as Tom's doppelganger, his other half, reverberates throughout the novel. This role emerges during their childhood interactions. "Tom got all the petting, Chambers got none. Tom got all the delicacies, Chambers got mush and milk, and clabber without sugar," Twain writes. "In consequence, Tom was a sickly child and Chambers wasn't. Tom was 'fractious,' as Roxy called it, and overbearing, Chambers was meek and docile."[40] Critics ceaselessly debate the prickly question posed by the novel—Is Tom's petulant behavior a product of nature or nurture?—but one thing seems certain: whiteness is easily malleable. Chambers adapts readily to his role as servant, a fact that perhaps underscores the vulnerability of whiteness, which can be overpowered by a mere drop of "black blood"—or of black contact. White identity is hardly essentialized in Twain's novel, for not only does Chambers easily "become" black but also, as we will see, he never quite becomes white again.

As Tom "cuffed and banged and scratched" his ur-twin brother, the latter "learned that between meekly bearing it and resenting it the advantage all lay with the former policy" (19). And yet the two boys, with their mutual dislike for each other, seem bound together most powerfully. Tom's childhood games depend on the presence of Chambers:

> In the winter season Chambers was on hand, in Tom's worn-out clothes, with "holy" red mittens, and "holy" shoes, and pants "holy" at the knees and seat, to drag a sled up the hill for Tom, warmly clad, to ride down on; but he never got a ride himself. He built snow men and snow fortifications under Tom's direction. He was Tom's patient target when Tom wanted to do some snow-balling, but the target couldn't fire back. Chambers carried Tom's skates to the river and strapped them on him, then trotted around after him on the ice, so as to be on hand when wanted; but he wasn't ever asked to try the skates himself. (20)

This passage speaks not only to the profound and sometimes subconscious dependence of owner on slave—consider Melville's Babo and Benito Cereno in this light, particularly the scene in which "master and man stood before him, the black upholding the white"[41]—but also to the way in which Chambers is such an indispensable fixture in Tom's childhood that he is taken for granted, much as Chambers's role in the narrative may seem to be secondary but is in fact vital to our understanding of the novel. Chambers's omnipresence is noted, after all, by Tom's enemies, who begin referring to Chambers as "Tom Driscoll's Nigger-pappy" (21), a phrase we might read as symbolic for Chambers's position as the unheralded father of the narrative itself. From the opening of the novel, Twain arranges it so that we cannot think of Tom without thinking of Chambers, a fact he later highlights by having Roxy begin calling "Tom" by his given name of "Chambers," and by putting both names in quotation marks for the duration of the novel. Chambers seems to appear magically at critical moments in the text, as when he enters Tom's room after Tom has first discovered his past: " 'Tom' blushed scarlet to see this aristocratic white youth cringe to him, a nigger, and call him 'Young Marster' " (19). Even when Chambers is not physically on the scene, then, he is present—whether in name or in spirit.

Tom, after all, cannot seem to survive without Chambers. When they were children, Twain tells us, "Chambers was [Tom's] constant body-guard, to and from school; he was present on the play-ground at recess to protect his charge" (19). This is because while Tom grew up weak and inept, "Chambers was strong beyond his years, and a good fighter; strong because he was coarsely fed and hard worked about the house, and a good fighter because Tom furnished him plenty of practice on white boys whom he hated and was afraid of" (19). Chambers is also "good at games of skill" and a masterly diver (19); Tom, by contrast, needs to be rescued time and again. As a result, Tom envies Chambers's masculine prowess, which motivates his immense desire to overpower Chambers: "Tom did his humble comrade these various ill turns partly out of native viciousness, and partly because he hated him for his superiorities of physique and pluck, and for his manifold clevernesses" (20).[42] Implied here is that Tom degenerates by passing as white, but Chambers advances by passing as black.

If Chambers is made a better man by passing, then two approaches to white passing sit side by side in *Pudd'nhead Wilson*. On the one hand is an exultant fantasy of white passing—the "love" in Eric Lott's "love and theft" paradigm—in which whites are able to "play black" and to take on the idealized traits of blackness, as Chambers does. On the other hand, however, is a pervasive feeling of panic, a fear that poor whites were, like Chambers, becoming black. Chambers, after all, is characterized by many of the same traits exhibited by poor whites of Twain's day. His passing consists of three cultural exchanges, all of which are made possible by proximity. First, he takes on a typically black job. Second, he changes his clothes, a point noted by a number of critics who have discussed the crucial relationship between clothing and identity in the novel. Indeed through clothing, Chambers comes to look like what Roxy calls an "imitation nigger" (35).[43] And the third way in which Chambers passes is by his adoption of black speech patterns, a crucial factor since it is the only thing the written page can make visual. Chambers's passing takes the form of altered dialect, and even Roxy, too, is initially identified as a sort of passer by virtue of her speech patterns: from her "manner of speech, a stranger would have expected her to be black, but she was not. Only one-sixteenth of her was black, and that sixteenth did not show" (8). By living in close proximity to blacks, both Roxy and Chambers absorb black speech; the same was true of poor southern whites of Twain's day, who, in the words of the English actress Frances Kemble, complained that white southern speech was being "corrupted" by black speech. "The Negro jargon has commended itself as euphonious to her infantile ears," she wrote of her confidante, "and she is now treating me to the most ludicrous and accurate imitations of it every time she opens her mouth."[44] Speech would become a fundamental feature of white passing scenarios in the decades that followed, one that I will return to in later chapters, but for now I simply highlight Twain's use of dialect as a way of making visual what cannot be seen: white passing for black.

As I noted earlier, Twain's approach to white passing might be compared to the one represented by an early genre of American literature: Indian captivity narratives. "The Indian's way of life was not totally alien to the Puritan," Richard Slotkin writes. "In it he recognized just enough of his own behavior and feelings to be deeply troubled with self-doubt."[45] If we substitute "black" for "Indian" and "white" for "Puritan," then Slotkin's statement becomes perfectly applicable to Twain's and Cable's era, in which whites struggled to separate white from black. Puritan fears of being debased by the Indian wilderness parallel later white anxieties about turning black, and captivity narratives—like white passing narratives—became a method of both exploring and shunning the fantasy of "going primitive." In a similar vein, narratives of white passing—suffused with fear and desire, love and theft—allowed whites to vent their concerns about absorptions of black culture while enabling them to toy with the guilty pleasures of this same scenario.

This fantasy/anxiety, however, is not necessarily an easy one for whites to address openly; it is for this reason, perhaps, that both Twain and Cable defuse the contemporaneity in their stories by setting them in earlier eras. It may also explain why Twain, perhaps hesitant to grapple with the full implications of his own character, did not fully flesh out Chambers's character (a point to which I will return). And yet in certain respects, Chambers is not the only white passer in the novel; Tom, as a number of critics have pointed out, is also passing for black. Or, as Warren Hedges says, explaining that Tom embodies racial rhetoric which described dissolute white men in terms of their "black behavior," Tom is "a legally black person passing for a white person who acts like the racist idea of a black person."[46] To make things even more bewildering, we might say that Tom is a visibly white person passing for a legally black person who passes as white—and then discovers that he "is" black. Tom's moment of discovery, the discovery that "changed his moral landscape," is described by Twain in a masterly passage:

> His arm hung limp instead of extending the hand for a shake. It was the "nigger" in him asserting its humility, and he blushed and was abashed. And the "nigger" in him was surprised when the white friend put out his hand for a shake with him. He found the "nigger" in him involuntarily giving the road, on the sidewalk, to the white rowdy and loafer. When Rowena . . . invited him in, the "nigger" in

him made an embarrassed excuse and was afraid to enter and sit with the dread white folks on equal terms. (44–45)

Tom's discovery that he "is" black makes him—prior to this discovery—one of several accidental black-to-white passers in literature.[47] But in many ways this passage presents Tom as passing for *black*, since he must actively alter his consciousness in order to act the part of a black man. In order to pass for white, it seems, Tom must first learn to be black. This phenomenon is a central feature of traditional passing narratives. In *The Autobiography of an Ex-Coloured Man*, for instance, the protagonist first discovers that he "is" black one day in class, when a school official "outs" him; it is only once he has "learned" to be black that he chooses to pass as white. In Walter White's *Flight*, only after Mimi learns about her blackness (from her boyfriend Carl, who takes her to black cultural events) can she elect to pass out of it. Tom Driscoll, like the Ex-Coloured Man and Mimi—and William Dean Howells's Rhoda—must pass as black in order then to pass as white. In this vein, Twain (like Johnson, White, and Howells) radically questions the nature of racial identity—and presents us with the second white passer in the novel.[48]

Minor characters further blur the racial lines of *Pudd'nhead Wilson*. Just as Cable employs German immigrants as a "not-quite-white" group in his story, Twain includes the Italian twins in his. Critics have often noted that the story revolves around two sets of doubles, Tom and Chambers and the Italian twins—who, in Twain's famous "literary caesarean section"—had to be separated from each other as well as from the novel.[49] But Eric Sundquist points out the relevance of the twins as indicators of a "blackening" white population: "It is inconceivable that Twain was not impressed by the Italo-American crisis and the light it cast on the blurring of the color line caused by non-Anglo immigrant races."[50] The twins, after all, are associated with an Irishman named John Buckstone, another member of a "not-quite-white" immigrant group. And like Cable, Twain draws subtle links between Italian and black by having the twins repeatedly describe their struggle with debt and exploitation as a "slavery" from which they escaped, only to end up traveling "about Germany, receiving no wages, and not even our keep. We had to exhibit for nothing, and beg our bread" (28). That the twins ultimately return to Europe indicates the difficulty of their being integrated into either side of the racial divide in Dawson's Landing. Twain's parallel between immigrant and black implies that he was, in his work, grappling with the ways in which racial lines are created and destroyed. If immigrants who look white could be defined as nonwhite, then what was to stop American "whites" from losing their whiteness?

As the ending of *Pudd'nhead Wilson* makes clear, Twain does not ultimately resolve such issues. Like "Salome Muller, The White Slave," *Pudd'nhead* remains ambivalent about the relationship between the internal and the external. Twain's portraits of Roxy, Tom, and Chambers blatantly defy "literal" readings—that is, they make us question our reliance on visual clues—but at the same time, visual readings of the body do not conclusively fail in the novel. Just as Cable's story ends up employing physical evidence (birthmarks) as an irrefutable identity marker, Twain's novel hinges on a tangible deus ex machina: fingerprints. In the novel's firmest assertion about the immutability of identity, Wilson declares, "Every human being carries with him from his cradle to his grave certain physical marks which do not change their character, and by which he can always be identified—and that without shade of doubt or question" (108). Like Salome's birthmarks, Tom's and Chambers's fingerprints serve, almost in lieu of race, as physical proofs of identity, evidence that even in a tale about a white slave, identity remains a physical matter. Or does it? *Pudd'nhead Wilson*, like "Salome," cannot seem to make up its mind about this.

Why this ambivalence in both narratives? Here we return to my discussion, at the beginning of this chapter, of those moments in which content and genre clash. *Pudd'nhead Wilson* is a detective story, and Cable's story, too, follows the generic conventions of a courtroom drama or mystery. "All the detectives on earth couldn't trace me now; there's not a vestige of a clew left in the world," Tom says to himself after murdering his adoptive father, Judge Driscoll (95). He is, of course, mistaken: Pudd'nhead, the consummate detective, does uncover a clue.[51] Francis Galton, who discovered the art of fingerprinting, was ultimately *not* able to locate racial characteristics in fingerprints, but the climax of Twain's novel turns on the fantasy that indeed all truths reside in Tom's print.[52] Fingerprints serve here as the ultimate clue, solving the mystery and serving up truth beyond a shadow of a doubt. If, as Franco Moretti suggests, in detective fiction "innocence is conformity; individuality, guilt," then Tom's fingerprint—a guilty mark that is utterly individual to him—is his undoing, leading to "the victory and the purge of a society no longer conceived of as a 'contract' between *independent entities*, but rather as an organism or social *body*."[53]

The most salient feature of detective fiction is its structure, which is always propelled toward a clear-cut solution. In order to satisfy the demands of detective fiction, then, Pudd'nhead must solve the crime; in order to conclude a courtroom mystery successfully, Cable must have Salome's case solved beyond a shadow of a doubt. Such generic conventions are at odds with the conceptions of race that are at the heart of both narratives. Race—whiteness, in particular—is an elusive entity in both texts, an entity bound up in the very enigmas that detective fiction is meant to decipher and thus resolve. In their attempts to grapple with race-related ideological tensions while remaining within the confines of generic conventions, both *Pudd'nhead Wilson* and "Salome" end up pitted against themselves. Their genres stipulate an answer, while their central theme, so to speak, demands a question. Whiteness defies physical "clues," and yet these are precisely what successful mysteries demand. By expressing social ideologies and phobias in the form of literature and not, say, historical tracts, both Twain and Cable end up producing texts that speak from two sides of the same issue. The tension between the physical and the antiphysical is a product of genre versus ideology.[54]

It thus makes sense that another genre—one more in tune with the racial ambiguities at the heart of Twain's text—comes into play in *Pudd'nhead Wilson*: the supernatural. Pudd'nhead is identified as a "witch" by Roxy and a "prophet" by Tom; his palmistry is labeled "rank sorcery," and his revelation in the courtroom is declared "miraculous" (16, 110). Early detective fiction often bonded the mysterious to the supernatural, but in *Pudd'nhead Wilson*, key scenes involving racial revelation are rife with supernatural undertones. Wilson's "miraculous" presentation in the courtroom reveals Tom's "true" race to all; the first race-related revelation in the novel—Roxy's confession to Tom—occurs in a "two-story log house which had acquired the reputation a few years before of being haunted" (40). By invoking the supernatural throughout his novel, particularly at moments of racial revelation, Twain nods to a genre that is less about decisive fact than speculative hearsay—a genre that is thus more of a piece with the racial ambiguity on which his text hinges.

Despite such generic play, Twain's novel, like "Salome," does not finally resolve the fate of its white passer, and this underscores the fact that whiteness is not an essentialized entity in the text. After the trial, Chambers, like Salome, is left free but displaced, his whiteness elusive. Wilson declares, in his speech to the court, that "'A was put into B's cradle in the nursery; B was transferred to the kitchen, and became a Negro and a slave'—[Sensation—confusion of angry ejaculations]—'but within a quarter of an hour he will stand before you white and free!'" (112). It is significant that Wilson separates "Negro" from "slave" and "white" from "free," since, as we have seen in the case of Brown and the Crafts, it is indeed possible for one to be both white and slave; Chambers, however, has turned *black* and slave, leaving Wilson with the task of making Chambers not just free but white as well. He can achieve the former in a court of law but not the latter, and here I quote at length from Twain:

> The real heir suddenly found himself rich and free, but in a most embarrassing situation. He could neither read nor write, and his speech was the basest dialect of the Negro quarter. His gait, his attitude, his

gestures, his bearing, his laugh—all were vulgar and uncouth; his manners were the manners of a slave. Money or fine clothes could not mend these defects or cover them up, they only made them the more glaring and the more pathetic. The poor fellow could not endure the terrors of the white man's parlor, and felt at home and at peace nowhere but in the kitchen. The family pew was a misery to him, yet he could never more enter into the solacing refuge of the "nigger gallery"—that was closed to him for good and all. But we cannot follow his curious fate further—that would be a long story. (114)

A long story indeed, and one that Twain seems reluctant to tell. It is as if the implications of white passing are too threatening, or too downright perplexing, for white authors such as Twain and Cable to come to grips with. Both authors present narratives of white passing in which the white passer is returned to freedom, but not to whiteness. Both Salome and Chambers are permanently "blackened" by the experience of passing; they become what they passed for. Proximity is thus a potent and dangerous force in Twain and Cable, since it possesses the power to turn white black. In this light it is significant that Twain refers, in the quoted passage, to the *spaces* in which Chambers feels he belongs (the "black" spaces) and to those in which he does not feel at home ("white" spaces), since it is in his change in location, his move from the front of the house to the back of the house, so to speak, that Chambers's passing consists.

As I have mentioned, nowhere in narratives of black passing do we find black figures permanently whitened by their passing enterprise; we never hear of, say, the Ex–Coloured Man's altered dialect, or Clare Kendry's distorted gait. Even as they pose as white, black passers remain essentially black—but white passers do not remain essentially white. A novel such as *Iola Leroy*, which is contemporaneous with *Pudd'nhead Wilson*, is further evidence of the intractability of black identity. The novel revolves around a series of characters who, though they wear white skin and were raised to conceive of themselves as white, ultimately come to embrace their essential black identities. Harry does so first—"Now that I have linked my fortunes to the race, I intend to do all I can for its elevation," he declares—and Dr. Latimer is the last to accept his "true" identity. Iola progresses toward eventual celebration of the fact that she is "truly" black. Her climactic scenes of dialogue with Dr. Gresham, during which he pleads for her hand in marriage, intimate that Iola can choose her own race. She concedes that, yes, "public opinion" is what designates her black—it "assigns me a place with the colored people"—but public opinion "is stronger than we are," which means her choice is made for her. "I feel that our paths must diverge," she tells the good doctor. "My life-work is planned. I intend spending my future among the colored people of the South."[55] Choice is an illusion in the novel; Iola—like Harry and Dr. Latimer—is always and ever black. She is the inverse of the pre-Emancipation Salome: years of passing for a particular race cannot make her belong to that race. As early Salome is essentially white, Iola is essentially black.

Thus black identity cannot be tainted by drops of white blood, but white identity can be "soiled" with ease. If the white passing narrative is motivated by anxiety that whiteness, surrounded by blackness, is being lost, then that narrative presents whiteness as a besieged identity and white identity as anything but stable. It is this conception of whiteness as fragile that makes proximity so potent in the white passing narrative. Echoing a racial science that focused on the mutability of blackness and whiteness, *Pudd'nhead Wilson* and "Salome Muller, The White Slave" dare to propose that whiteness is not an essence after all. They give voice to a powerful fear, one that is later transformed into fantasy: What if whiteness is weak?

Pudd'nhead Revisited

The story of nineteenth-century white passing would end here if not for William Pickens and a story titled "The Vengeance of the Gods," published in 1922.[56] Pickens, a Yale graduate who was a leader in both the Niagara movement and the NAACP, was the son of a tenant farmer, and he, like Twain and Cable, chose to set his narrative in an earlier era: the turbulent 1890s.[57] But as a story about debt slavery, "The Vengeance of the Gods" could just as easily be set in the slave era. Plainly modeled after *Pudd'nhead Wilson*, Pickens's narrative concerns two boys—one white and one legally black, one slave and one free—who are switched at birth. The story takes place on the plantation of John Elliot, who holds a number of blacks in debt slavery. One of these is Aunt Katy, a "matronly looking black woman" with "clear and beautiful black skin," whose daughter Essie, fathered by Elliot's brother, is "of a rich cream color decorated with vanishing rose tints" (15). During the same year John Elliot fathers two children: one, borne by his wife, is named William, and the other, borne by Essie, is named Jimmie. The latter boy, third in a generation of lightening blacks, has "dark hair, dark eyes, and skin—*white*" (15). Distraught over the dismal future her son faces and eager for revenge on the man who raped her daughter, Aunt Katy switches the two infant boys, who are—more explicitly than Twain's duo—brothers; the specter of miscegenation in Twain becomes a stated reality in Pickens. As they grow older, the two boys "enter the two most important schools of their divergent careers: William was to enter the State

University, Jim was to enter the State Penitentiary" (44). When Jim is falsely accused of theft and murder, he manages to escape by tying his own father up, but in the story's climax, Jim is lynched at the very moment when Mrs. Elliot learns that she has just lost her son. After this, Pickens writes, "Mrs. Elliot never regained her reason. 'Vengeance of the Gods!' is her only coherent utterance" (85).

Like "Salome," "The Vengeance of the Gods" reduces identity to physical markings on the skin: young Jim's burn scar and a tattooed "W" secretly given to William. And like Twain's novel, Pickens's tale makes ample use of doppelgangers, presenting not one but two sets of doubles: William and Jim, and Aunt Katy and Mrs. Elliot. While Mrs. Elliot is vilified as cold and heartless, Katy's maternal instincts, like Roxy's, drive the narrative: "There is no other mother heart on earth like that which beats with African blood," Pickens asserts. "The Negro mother is . . . *the greatest mother in the world*" (50). Also like Twain, Pickens makes clothing central to his use of contrast; in one scene, for instance, the two boys switch hats, causing their mothers to gasp in astonishment. William's aunt openly declares that "only their clothes make it possible to tell one from the other," to which Mrs. Elliot, "the proud white mother," retorts, "Why, if they were lost till they were grown, you could tell the white man and the nigger when you found them" (48). Mrs. Elliot, of course, ends up eating her words. The tale is filled with moments of dramatic irony. In one poignant scene Mrs. Elliot remarks that if black boys "had any ambition to learn and work and do what they *can* do, they might make *their* mothers happy instead of causing them so much trouble" (53); she then refuses to accept Katy's point that such troublemaking is the result of training, not genetics.

This tension—between nature and nurture—is the explicit theme of "The Vengeance of the Gods," which is subtitled "Blood or Opportunity?" The story opens by declaring: "There is an old unsettled war 'twixt blood and chance. Heredity or environment? Which has the major influence on the destinies of men?" (11). But while Twain, to the dismay of many critics, ends up muddying the issue by simultaneously attributing Tom's ill will to nature *and* to nurture, Pickens, by contrast, makes his position crystal clear: "No; Environment is not omnipotent, but it is so almost all-powerful that it deserves the major consideration in the making of a man on earth" (35). As an activist, Pickens is invested—much as Richard Wright was in *Native Son*—in demonstrating that environment is everything, that African American life would be radically improved by social changes. "Who can refrain from speculating," writes Pickens, perhaps slipping into fund-raising mode, "as to how much more good even the one hundredth part of that money and time and attention might have accomplished, had they been bestowed on the education and training of this human being thru his childhood and youth?" (75). Whereas William grows up to become "an autocrat," Jim evolves into "a revolutionist, a radical" (38). Yet although Jim's lack of schooling and privilege sends him down the wrong path and into prison, Jim, like Chambers, ends up radically improved by being raised as a black man. He is powerful, chivalrous (in defending his sister Mary), and proud—in part, we are told, because his mother taught him that he was as good as any white boy. Proximity is everything in Pickens's story, in which environment conquers all.

In some sense, however, Pickens attempts to have it both ways, insisting that blacks have the best of both nature and nurture. This is evident in the fact that while Twain makes his black passer a villain, Pickens's William is presented as sympathetic and caring. While Tom and Chambers are at odds from birth, William and Jim remain "two little playmates in perfect accord and brotherhood, with not a thought of difference or caste" (31). In essence, William and Jim are both innately good; it is their milieus that cause them grief: Jim is denied the opportunity to thrive, and William is raised by two people, the Elliots, who remain the villains of "The Vengeance of the Gods." The story's trajectory, after all, moves toward giving the evil plantation owners their just deserts. In a moment of supreme irony, Aunt Katy hysterically tells the lynch mob, with "William" in mind, that they have killed Elliot's own son, but they flippantly reply, with "Jim" in mind, "we know that"; it is only John Elliot who refuses to acknowledge his illegitimate son—until he has lost his legitimate one.

It is in his willingness to center his story not on the black passer, as Twain does, but on the white passer that Pickens most emphatically rewrites *Pudd'nhead Wilson*. For Pickens's white passer emerges not out of some general sense of panic that white is turning black but rather from the felt need to assert that a white man in a black man's shoes could not defeat the forces aligned against him. Pickens is invested in declaring not that whites are losing their whiteness but that, if only given the opportunity, blacks could achieve all they set out to do. This fact is underscored by the ending of the story, which focuses on the black man's victory instead of the white man's losses. Indeed, by killing Jim off, Pickens sidesteps the dilemma of finding an appropriate ending for a white passer, which neither Twain nor Cable successfully resolves. He ends with justice: Elliot becomes an anti-lynching activist who saves Essie and Mary when they run off to France to live with "William," now an officer in the French army, who "has been given a liberal portion of the Elliot money" (85). Aunt Katy is killed by the mob, but her spirit lives on. In the story's final lines, Pickens tells us that her gravesite became known as "'Witch's Hole' where a great 'conjure woman' or sorceress is said to have disappeared" (86).

Pickens's reference to the supernatural lends the story a myth-like quality.

And indeed Pickens seems to be working with—and in a sense rewriting—the myth of the white passer that had been established in the nineteenth century. While pre-Emancipation writers had not grappled with the concept of white passing, Twain and Cable, in the context of a potentially "blackening" white population, did. They established a kind of paradigm for the early white passing narrative, one that involved three central features. First, the narrative of white passing is a hash of contradictions, radically questioning whether identity is a visible entity but in the end resorting to very visible traits—birthmarks, tattoos, fingerprints—as markers of identity. Second, it relies on the use of dark and light doubles, just as many narratives of black passing do: Angela and Virginia in *Plum Bun*; Irene and Clare in *Passing*; and Shiny and the Ex–Coloured Man in Johnson's novel. Third, and most important, the early narrative of white passing is premised on the notion that proximity is powerful. It is through physical and cultural intimacy with blacks that white passers become black, a fact that bears tremendous historical relevance in the context of late-nineteenth-century racial politics. Once moved from the free cradle to the slave one, from the front of the house to the back, white passers are enduringly blackened. Because they have been near black, they can never again be white. And it is this conception of proximity's power that lends these early narratives their sense of alarm—and tragedy.

2

Dy(e)ing to Be Black
"Mars Jeems's Nightmare,"
Black Like Me, and *Watermelon Man*

Socially speaking, white passing involves a move from the center to the margin. Why might such a move be made? In the texts discussed in chapter 1, it was made by slaves, who had this shift foisted upon them; they were products of what Jane Gaines has called "coerced passing."[1] In this chapter I consider the move from center to margin as made by those who do possess varying degrees of power over their fate. These passers also possess another fundamental characteristic that differentiates them from the white passers of chapter 1: an altered skin tone.

The narratives I discussed in the preceding chapter were invested in detaching race from physical traits, instead linking it to cultural traits and proximity to blackness. Yet at the same time these narratives did, in some respects, remain committed to the physicality of race by pointing to things physical— birthmarks, fingerprints—as markers of identity. The texts discussed in this chapter are founded on the essential physicality of race. Each involves what Michael Awkward has called "transraciality," which he defines as "the adoption of physical traits of difference for the purpose of impersonating a racial other."[2] As the pun in my title would have it, the narratives to which I now turn present men who are not merely dying, in the sense of aspiring, to become black, but who are literally *dyeing* (or otherwise altering) their skin in order to do so. There are traces of transraciality in the texts discussed earlier: the swapping of "black" (i.e., tattered) and "white" (i.e., lavish) clothing in *Pudd'nhead Wilson* and "The Vengeance of the Gods" implies that indeed some form of visible alteration is necessary in order to transform white to black. But for the most part the characters enact their transformation by absorbing slave culture, a transference facilitated by physical and social proximity. In the texts discussed in this chapter, cultural proximity hinges on alteration of one's skin as the necessary first step in any passing enterprise—a fact that reflects altogether different conceptions about the relationship between race and proximity, as well as the nature of racial identity more generally.

Awkward differentiates texts of transraciality from traditional passing narratives, arguing that the latter are less subversive than the former, which involve "an individually determined, surgically and/or cosmetically assisted traversal of boundaries that putatively separate radically distinct social groups." He draws another critical distinction: "Unlike narratives of passing, which are concerned fundamentally with exposing the ease with which racial barriers can be transgressed, texts of transraciality generally insist on the impenetrability, the mysteriousness, of the racial other's cultural rituals and social practices."[3] While the narratives of chapter 1 are founded on the blurring of racial lines, skin-dyeing narratives maintain a sharp distinction between black and white. They insist that race, purely a matter of skin tone, creates an unequivocal, visible distinction between two groups—separate, hostile, unequal. This may be because the texts I discuss here—Charles Chesnutt's short story "Mars Jeems's Nightmare," John Howard Griffin's memoir *Black Like Me*, and Mario Van Peebles's film *Watermelon Man*—actively seek to change the racial landscape, which often means working from the starting point that there *are* two distinct groups to reconcile. The works by Chesnutt and Griffin are indeed generically different and born of disparate contexts, but what they do have in common is that they are both, at their core, activist texts, didactic productions that either imagine or enact a racial experiment. Though the real-life Griffin and the fictional Jeems each undergo skin swaps, the real parallel here is between Griffin and Julius, Chesnutt's storyteller, because they are the ones with agency in the stories; by telling a tale about a white man turned black, Julius describes the "what if" scenario that Griffin enacts: What happens when the white man turns (temporarily) black? It should thus not be surprising that the two distinctly different narratives hinge on shared conceptions of racial identity: the notion that black and white are two essential entities, and that white men can become better whites through an excursion into blackness.

Before turning to twentieth-century texts, I want to look back briefly. The narratives of this chapter are racially anachronistic, echoing the pre-Emancipation white passing stories of the preceding chapter. One slave-era text illustrates this parallel poignantly. In 1836 Robert Montgomery Bird published the novel *Sheppard Lee*, about a man who spends his life inhabiting various bodies. One such body is that of a black slave, making this one of the earliest texts about skin swapping. Several features of this narrative are worth noting. First, before Sheppard Lee is transformed into a slave, he wears the identity of an abolitionist who, captured by anti-abolitionists, is sold to body snatchers. About to be subjected to the anatomist's knife, he makes a mad dash toward a group of Africans and utters a desperate cry: "It is better to be a slave than a dead man."[4] His words become a wish, and as wishes are agents of transformation in the novel, Sheppard Lee becomes Tom, a slave from Virginia. This transformation is intriguing on several levels. For one, Lee's "descent" into blackness occurs in stages. As a white person about to be sold, he first occupies the socioeconomic sphere of blackness. Next he is physically transformed. This shift in skin tone serves the purpose of maintaining, in the way other slave-era narratives of white slavery do, sharp lines between black and white. Instead of his becoming a liminal figure (like Cable's Salome and Twain's Chambers), Lee's status changes and he becomes (like the Salome of *Clotel* and *Running a Thousand Miles*) unequivocally black, unable to recall his previous identity. "I forgot that I once had been a freeman, or, to speak more strictly, I did not remember it, the act of remembering involving an effort of mind which it did not comport with my new habits of laziness and indifference to make," Lee declares. "I could not have been an African had I troubled myself with thoughts of any thing but the present" (171). Lee is never a white man turned black; he is, quite distinctly, a free white man and then an enslaved black one. This division between free and slave eclipses, as in other pre-Emancipation narratives, the line between black and white; Lee gives little thought to his identity as a black man but a great deal of attention to his new social status as a slave.

In addition to its sharp division between black and white, *Sheppard Lee* is predictive, in a second way, of later skin-altering narratives. As a slave, Lee deems himself supremely content. As such, he laments the circulation of an abolitionist pamphlet among his fellow slaves which "had the effect to make a hundred men, who were previously contented with their lot in life, and perhaps as happy as any other men ordained to a life of labour, the victims of dissatisfaction and rage, the enemies of those they had once loved, and, in fine, the contrivers and authors of their own destruction" (200). Montgomery's novel is highly conservative, not only maintaining clear-cut distinctions between white and black but also insisting that these critical divisions remain unscathed.

Both facets of *Sheppard Lee*—the novel's radical division between the races and a racial conservatism that stems from it—resonate in the narratives to which I now turn. Though they span a century, these works dramatize fascinating and at times dissimilar experiments with skin dye. By the same token, the progression from Chesnutt to Griffin reflects a crucial shift: the move from white passing as *anxiety* to white passing as *fantasy*. As we will see, fantasy and anxiety take their turns in white passing narratives throughout the twentieth century, but a significant shift from one to the other distinguishes early white passing narratives from later ones. Part and parcel of this vacillation is, first, a conservative approach to race that follows the same lines as does Montgomery's novel (though in terms hardly as extreme). Second, as texts produced by and about men, these narratives make the homosocial bond crucial to their fantasy of passing as black, and to their conception of race more generally.

"Mars Jeems's Nightmare"

Charles Chesnutt published "Mars Jeems's Nightmare" as part of *The Conjure Woman* in 1899, less than a decade after the publication of both "Salome Muller, The White Slave" and *Pudd'nhead Wilson*. Like those two texts, Chesnutt's work harks back to the slave era, employing conventions of the plantation genre. Yet while Twain and Cable, peering through post-slavery lenses, depict a world in which white and black bleed into each other, Chesnutt's world sets the two races quite distinctly in their places. Though a contemporary of Twain and Cable, Chesnutt writes a piece that conforms to a very different model of white passing, indicating that dissimilar notions about the white/black divide evolved side by side. His is a story that, in its clear partition between black and white, more closely resembles slave-era accounts of white passing. Like Mr. Stevens in *The Garies*, or the skin dye scenario described in my introduction—in which a young boy is tanned and stained, sold into slavery, then returned to his parents—Chesnutt's story presents a white person who against his will acquires a taste of blackness but then safely returns to the white world with lessons in tow. He lacks agency, yes, but he is not left ambiguously raced, as both Salome and Chambers are. And because white and black are, in Chesnutt, two visibly separate entities, he must undergo a literal skin change in order to pass.

Written in the dialect style of plantation fiction, "Mars Jeems's Nightmare," like all the tales in *The Conjure Woman*, employs a complex framing device: John, a white plantation owner, narrates tales told to him and his wife, Annie, by his slave Julius. Critics have written at length about Chesnutt's subversive use of the plantation genre. By presenting Julius's sly stories by way of John, to whom they are intended to teach a lesson, Chesnutt manages to mitigate the offensiveness of Julius's occasionally militant voice—a voice that persistently chastises the white man and indicts slavery. Chesnutt's use of John also serves to give his readers a lesson in what constitutes the correct response to his tales, as John is presented as a model reader.[5] Chesnutt had no illusions about whom he was writing for. "The object of my writings would not be so much the elevation of the colored people as the elevation of the whites," he once wrote.[6] This point underscores a key feature of the skin-dyeing narrative: its didacticism. The genre is caught up in teaching white folks a lesson about how to "read" race, and it does so via stories of skin swaps.

In "Mars Jeems's Nightmare" it takes a conjure woman to perform such swaps. The tale begins as John hires Julius's grandson on the plantation, then fires him because he finds him "absolutely untrustworthy."[7] When Julius protests, John, claiming to have "hardened my heart" (26), pays him little mind, leaving Julius to find another mode of influence: tale-telling. Using the sight of an ill-spirited neighbor beating his horse as a starting point, Julius presents John and Annie with a story about a cruel master, Mars Jeems McClean—grandson of this same neighbor—and his slave Solomon. Jeems, who "said he wuz n'raisin niggers, but wuz raisin' cotton" (28), is despised by his slaves and becomes the victim of Aun' Peggy, the conjure woman's, scheme. Handing Solomon a root to slip into Jeems's soup, Peggy tells him, "I has ter be kinder careful 'bout cunj'in w'ite folks; so be sho' en lemme know, w'ateber you do, des w'at is gwine on roun' de plantation" (33). When Jeems leaves the plantation for several days, he has his cruel white overseer, Nick, mind the slaves. Nick buys, abuses, then sells a new, unruly black slave who was "puttin' on airs, des lack he wuz a w'ite man" (36), as Nick puts it. Peggy, as part of her scheme, sends Solomon off with a potato for the exiled slave. The next morning Solomon discovers Jeems sleeping under the same tree that shaded the slave, "dress' lack a po' w'ite man, en wuz barefooted, en look' monst'us pale en peaked, ez ef he'd come th'oo a ha'd spell" (35). Jeems explains that he has had a terrible nightmare: he dreamed that he was a slave on his own plantation. Upon returning to the plantation, Jeems is a new man. He fires Nick, begins treating his slaves with kindness, gets married, and prospers. "Solomon useter say," Julius concludes, "dat Aun' Peggy's gopher had turnt Mars Jeems ter a nigger" (38). The story has its desired effect on Annie, who soon rehires Julius's grandson.

Chesnutt's narrative echoes that of his contemporaries Twain and Cable in several ways. His use of "white trash" in the story reflects the post-Emancipation blurring of the line between poor whites and blacks which, I have argued, is the impetus for Twain's and Cable's works. Julius's description of Nick, for instance—"all de niggers 'spised 'im ez much ez dey hated 'im, fer he did n' own nobody, en wa'n't no bettah 'n a nigger, fer in dem days any 'spectable pusson would ruther be a nigger dan a po' w'ite man" (29)—seems poignantly applicable to post-slavery poor whites. It is also significant that when Solomon discovers Jeems in the woods, Jeems is dressed as a poor white. It is as if Jeems, after spending time as a black man, is fully rehabilitated to his former white status only after passing through gradations of whiteness: from slave, to poor white, to white.

Jeems's "white trash" masquerade highlights another similarity between Chesnutt's story and the narratives of chapter 1: its use of doubling as a narrative device. "Mars Jeems's Nightmare" is constructed around various sets of doubles, foremost of which are Jeems and Nick. In his excessive cruelty Nick is a caricature—and an offensive caricature, since Nick is poor white trash—of Jeems himself. That Jeems awakens wearing Nick's style of dress signifies that Jeems has finally caught a glimpse of this caricature; in banishing Nick from the plantation, then, Jeems perhaps banishes the part of himself that exhibits such "low-class" behavior. Other doubles in the story include Jeems and John, our narrator, who is being warned *not* to behave like Jeems, and even Solomon and Jeems, who, though at opposite ends of the power spectrum, are reunited with their women at the story's close (a point to which I will return).

But the most obvious double in Chesnutt's work exists within one person, Jeems himself, in the form of the new slave and the white master—Jeems's white and black selves. Forced to wear blackness for a short time, Jeems alternates between white and black identities. Perhaps the free man who is suddenly enslaved represents the ways in which the newly freed black men of Chesnutt's own era grappled with dual identities as slaves and freemen.[8] "Mars Jeems," after all, is one of the only conjure tales in which a white man is conjured, implying that perhaps Jeems is symbolically black, not white. Such a reading is also suggested by the original title of "Mars Jeems's Nightmare": "De Noo Nigger." Eric Sundquist suggests that the "new Negro" in the tale is Jeems's grandson, who is lazy and unruly.[9] But perhaps the "new Negro" is really Jeems himself, who represents a post-Emancipation black population at odds with itself, caught between two identities: one slave, one free.

Yet Jeems also represents the fantasy of a white man turned black, and it is in this respect that Chesnutt's story begins to diverge from those of Cable and Twain. First, only in Chesnutt does the most significant doubling occur within a *single* figure who is white one moment, black the next, then white again—a pattern that follows the pre-Emancipation model. More important, this doubling is marked solely by skin change. When Nick complains that the new slave acted like a white man, we are left to imagine that the only difference between Jeems's white and black selves is skin tone. How different this is from the examples of Chambers and Salome, whose moves from white to black entail a completely new identity, and who are never quite rehabilitated to whiteness.

Jeems's return to whiteness is a simple process, merely requiring a change of skin color. In Cable and Twain, white passes for black and then passes for slave; in Chesnutt, white must physically *become* black in order to pass for slave, implying that far more than proximity is required to make white become black. And this is so because, as I will show later, proximity can only be truly experienced if preceded by a change of skin. The very fact that in Chesnutt's tale it takes supernatural forces to turn white to black implies that the two races are separate and distinct entities.

And these two distinct races must, in Chesnutt's story, learn lessons from each other. "Mars Jeems's Nightmare" is dripping with didacticism in a way that the texts discussed in chapter 1 are not. Peggy teaches Jeems a lesson, and Julius uses Jeems to teach Annie and John a lesson. Jeems must become black in order to learn something crucial—which, as Susan Gubar points out, underscores the notion that wearing black skin is a form of chastisement.[10] Jeems is penalized for excessive cruelty by having to serve time in black skin, after which he is restored to whiteness. In order for Chesnutt to make his tale a palatable lesson for his white readership, he must maintain the sharp divide between black and white; he must leave white readers with no doubt that their white identities are essential and inherent. As white authors without didactic aims, Twain and Cable could give voice to cultural anxieties without fear of upsetting their white readers. Chesnutt's return to an earlier mode of white passing is a product of his aim to educate a white readership in the most effective way possible, leaving them secure in their whiteness while causing them to question the injustice of racial lines. His nod to white readers is in line with what Sundquist has called Chesnutt's "literary cakewalk": Chesnutt adopted various voices and points of identification in his tales, Sundquist argues, which enabled white readers to identify with his tales and—unwittingly—to learn lessons from them, just as Jeems learns his lesson.[11]

Jeems, after all, becomes white again, but this whiteness is never what it once was, because he who undergoes a skin change is, like a victim of Indian captivity as described by Richard Slotkin, "restored to his life with newly opened eyes."[12] When Jeems regains his white skin, one small side of him remains, in some way, black. Having been, however briefly, a black man, he retains some level of identification with blackness. At his wedding feast, for instance, Jeems and his black slaves "wuz fiddlin' en dancin' en funnin' en frolic'in fum sundown 'tel mawnin'" (38). Whereas Cable's and Twain's narratives are pervaded by a certain *anxiety*, skin-dyeing narratives reflect, at bottom, a *fantasy*: that a white man, after a taste of blackness, can safely return to whiteness—carrying a little bit of blackness within. The skin dyer remains essentially white, however, and this little bit is, of course, the idealized part of blackness, the double consciousness that allows for heightened sensitivity and keener insight.

In addition to new insight, black skin often provides white men with something else: their manhood. When the story begins, Jeems has a "junesey," Miss Libbie, who soon leaves him because, she reasons, "he mought git so useter 'busin his niggers dat he'd 'mence ter 'buse his wife" (28). It is Libbie's rejection that sets off the tale's chain of events. Bitter over his loss, Jeems forbids Solomon to see *his* girlfriend, which in turn leads Solomon to go to the conjure woman for help. Once Jeems returns from his adventures in black skin, his newly acquired kindness causes Libbie to forgive him, which results in both their marriage and Solomon's reunion with his girlfriend. We might say, then, that Jeems's stint as a black man ultimately makes him a man: it paves the way for a happy marriage and firm footing as head of the plantation. If black men are often presented as possessing the penis without the phallus—"an excessively physical masculinity stripped of traditional patriarchal privilege"[13]—the white men who pass as black get the best of both worlds: the penis *and* the phallus. Jeems's experience of wearing black skin provides him with the former, and when he returns to a privileged position of whiteness, he reacquires the latter.

Chesnutt wrote one of the earliest white passing narratives, but he is best remembered for his *black* passing narratives, particularly *The House Behind the Cedars* (1900), which makes for an interesting comparison with "Mars Jeems's Nightmare." *House* tells the story of John and Rena Walden, two light-skinned siblings from North Carolina who move to South Carolina, where they have no difficulty passing as white. John, a lawyer, arranges for Rena to marry Tryon, a white man, but upon discovering Rena's racial secret, he spurns her. Distraught, Rena flees and is pursued by two men, one a mulatto named Jeff Wain and the other a dark-skinned childhood friend, Frank Fowler. In a melodramatic conclusion, Rena dies before Tryon has an opportunity to reconcile with her, and before she can marry any of her suitors.

The House Behind the Cedars, a richly layered work, shares its essential mission with "Mars Jeems": both aim to make white readers identify with blacks, "Mars Jeems" by presenting a white passer and *House* by having as its protagonist a black man who not only looks white but also insists he *is* white. In certain respects, *House* radically questions racial lines and the one-drop rule: John's move from one state to another literally turns him white. (Of the one-drop rule, John declares: "It don't apply to me. It says 'the negro.' A negro is black; I am white, and not black.")[14] Unlike Jeems, John remains white—even as his sister cannot do the same. Chesnutt's allowance for male but not female passing speaks to his reliance on conservative categories of race; once the womb is involved, it seems, racial lines become more binding. Furthermore, *House* does ultimately rest on the same essentialized racial categories as does "Mars Jeems." Rena's three suitors—one white, one black, one mulatto—exist as three separate races in the novel, just as black and white are two distinct entities in the short story. The question that Chesnutt sidesteps by having Rena die is: Which of the three "races" shall triumph?

Marriage and domesticity thus remain at the crux of both *House* and "Mars Jeems"—just as they do in all passing narratives, in which the color of the passer's betrothed becomes the heart of the matter. Philip Brian Harper points out that with respect to gender roles, passing narratives adhere to a pattern: by the end of the narrative, the passer is returned to a private or domestic sphere. This formula holds true for both *House* and "Mars Jeems"; the former substitutes death for marriage, and the latter closes with Jeems's wedding.[15] The interesting thing about Harper's theory in light of both of Chesnutt's passing narratives (one black, one white) is that while both conclude by returning passers to the domestic sphere, in white passing narratives this return is not emasculating but empowering. For white male skin dyers such as Jeems (however unintentionally) and Griffin, the return to the domestic is a return to patriarchal privilege; in the context of their private spheres they become vested with a newfound potency, one that—as we will see in Griffin—enables them to turn these private spheres public.

Although Chesnutt's story reflects a black fantasy about the white man walking a mile in the black man's shoes, this fantasy eventually becomes adopted by white men, like John Howard Griffin, who seek the best of both worlds: the supremacy of whiteness merged with the masculinity and the double consciousness of blackness. Perhaps it was during the 1920s that the narrative of white passing began to be motivated by fantasy as well as anxiety. A number of the major passing novels, written (or, in the case of *The Autobiography of an Ex-Coloured Man*, republished) during this era, make reference to white passing. "It's easy for a Negro to 'pass' for white. But I don't think it would be so simple for a white person to 'pass' for coloured," says Irene Redfield in *Passing*.[16] The Ex-Coloured Man, too, speaks of "several cases" involving "a white man [being] taken for coloured."[17] George Schuyler's *Black No More* is peppered with references to whites passing for black. The preface presents us with a Mr. Bela Cati who, "very tanned by the sun," passes.[18] In a wonderful moment of irony, Bunny takes a white girl in a Harlem nightclub for black, muttering, "You never can tell!" until Max declares he can "tell a cracker a block away" (20); whites are scrutinized and "read" in this scene exactly the way light-skinned blacks typically are. Later in the novel Schuyler describes the streets of Harlem as flooded with whites who seem "on the most intimate terms with the Negroes, laughing, talking, dining and dancing in a most un-Caucasian way" (59). Schuyler's description cleverly captures a time when whites rushed up-town to Harlem to taste black culture for themselves.

In the context of such romanticized journeys, it makes perfect sense that what once sparked anxiety—the notion of white passing for black—suddenly became tinged with fantasy. Painter Miguel Covarrubias's caricature of Carl Van Vechten, famous white patron of the black arts, presented him as a black man and bore the caption "a prediction"; was this wishful or fearful thinking? Jean Toomer spoke of his white grandfather's passing for black in terms of its benefits, not detriments: it helped him win political office in Reconstruction Louisiana. We witness, then, a gradual reconfiguration of white passing from an anxious endeavor to a fantasy-driven one. That said, the scenario is rarely so straightforward. As we will see, twentieth-century narratives of white pass-ing are often suffused with *both* fantasy and apprehension, often at one and the same moment.

"Mars Jeems's Nightmare" sets the stage for a reading of a latter-day influen-tial experiment in skin dye: Griffin's *Black Like Me*. In Chesnutt's story I have noted the deep divide between black and white, grounded in the notion that skin color is the only essential difference between the two. I have also pointed out the didacticism of skin-dyeing narratives, as well as the fantasy on which they rest, that black skin can provide the white man with prized possessions: insight, masculinity, and the white woman. Though written over a half-century later, *Black Like Me*—by virtue of its use of the skin dye trope—hinges on many of these same beliefs.

Black Like Me

Time magazine's 1960 review of *Black Like Me* presents the reader with not one but two photos of the book's author. The first is titled "John Griffin (colored)" and the second "John Griffin (white)."[19] Perhaps unwittingly, the photos hit on a central theme of *Black Like Me*: the fact that the book, like "Mars Jeems's Nightmare," is structured around a man and his double, both of whom are re-ally the same man—John Howard Griffin, white and black. Three critics who have written extensively about *Black Like Me* make much of this doubling, pointing out that, as Eric Lott sees it, Griffin's stint in black skin ends up being a journey into his own whiteness, and that, as Gayle Wald puts it, "though the 'black' Griffin attempts to 'lose' himself in passing, the observing Griffin never suspends his disbelief, never completely loses himself in the illusion of having 'become' the other." Wald astutely notes that as both the subject and the object of his experiment, Griffin seeks to "appropriate black 'experience' without compromising a presumed white entitlement to speak for that experience" and to "lose [himself] in the 'other' without losing control." [20] Indeed, there are two John Howard Griffins in *Black Like Me*. "I became two men," Griffin writes, "the observing one and the one who panicked, who felt Negroid even into the depths of his entrails. I felt the beginnings of great loneliness, not because I was a Negro but because the man I had been, the self I knew, was hidden in the flesh of another." [21] Griffin writes repeatedly about feeling estranged from himself. He struggles to reconcile his two selves, an onerous task considering the fact that in *Black Like Me*, as in Chesnutt, black and white are essentially discrete entities. At times, readers can forget which of the "two" Griffins is talking, as when he laments the fact that "my own people" could be so hateful. Who, exactly, are "my people" (69)?

I want to unpack further the theme of doubling in *Black Like Me* by exploring the ways in which this doubling changes over the course of the text, as well as how it plays into a vital aspect of Griffin's work that has not been adequately analyzed: space. *Black Like Me* is, at heart, a travel narrative, a characteristically American story of the open road. There is something kinetic about the narrative, which never remains in one place for very long. In this sense *Black Like Me* is a text about the relationship between race and space.

On the first page of his book Griffin lays out, in simple terms, the reason for his experiment: "How else except by becoming a Negro could a white man hope to learn the truth?" he asks (7). The rhetorical question is an odd one. Cannot the white man simply ask a black man about "the truth"? Cannot proximity to blackness and/or discussions with black folk teach this truth? Griffin offers an answer: "Though we lived side by side throughout the South, communication between the two races had simply ceased to exist. Neither really knew what went on with those of the other race. The Southern Negro will not tell the white man the truth" (7). Proximity, in other words, is neither transformative nor threatening in Griffin, as it seems to be in Cable and Twain. In *Black Like Me*, living close to black people hardly turns white to black; instead it boldly intimates the wide gulf between the two. The reason why Griffin must dye his skin black is that proximity to blackness is contingent on skin color. Closeness to black people is possible only for one who wears black skin, and any experience of particular geographies is limited and defined by external appearances. Skin dye is thus the necessary first step in achieving the proximity to blackness that comes easily to the figures discussed in chapter 1. The central point, according to Griffin, is that space is experienced differently by blacks and whites, and for this reason *Black Like Me* is ultimately a book about how one man experiences the very same spaces—in two different skins.

Griffin begins his journey in New Orleans, a resonant starting point in light of the fact that New Orleans, with its rich Creole heritage, often plays a cameo role in classic passing narratives.[22] Immediately after checking in at the hotel, Griffin goes for a walk and begins meditating on his sense of place. He recalls having been blind when he lived before in New Orleans—Griffin lost his sight because of diabetes but regained it ten years later—and becomes excited as he "walked miles, trying to locate everything by sight that I once knew only by smell and sound. . . . Every view was magical, whether it was a deserted, lamp-lit street corner or the neon hubbub of Royal Street" (10–11). Already the author, reconciling the blind Griffin with the Griffin who has sight, feels his own dualism by experiencing physical space in a new, exhilarating way. He eats a lavish dinner—"the same meal I had there in past years" (11)—and anticipates how it will feel to live in this very same space as a black man, just as he had earlier invoked the blind Griffin in the context of space: "Surrounded by elegant waiters, elegant people and elegant food, I thought of the other parts of town where I would live in the days to come. Was there a place in New Orleans where a Negro could buy *huitres variees*?" (11). The next morning Griffin, still wearing whiteness, takes a walk through the black section of town near South Rampart Street. Though he stands close by black people there, he cannot be *close to* any of them: "I searched for an opening, a way to enter the world of the Negro, some contact perhaps. As yet, it was a blank to me" (12). Griffin cannot experience this "black" space yet because his skin is white.

But he returns there when, after he undergoes dyeing procedures, his skin has become black. Deciding he can at last "pass over," Griffin takes a street-car to Canal Street and walks through the center of town. He passes "the same taverns and amusement places where the hawkers had solicited me on previous evenings" but experiences these places anew: "Tonight they did not solicit me. Tonight they looked at me but did not see me" (17–18). The clerk at the drugstore he has patronized each day since his arrival shares no banter with him now. Griffin begins experiencing familiar spaces in an unfamiliar way. This process of reexperience continues as he returns to the black section of town, which had previously been closed off to him. With his new skin, Griffin is able to book a room, chat with the locals, and share in the "talk, laughter, and juke-box jazz from the bar downstairs" (18). As he makes his way through the neighborhood the next morning, Griffin again remarks on his unfamiliar view of familiar places: "I had seen them before from the high altitude of one who could look down and pity. Now I belonged here and the view was different" (22–23). He makes his way back to the French Quarter, where he encounters Sterling Williams, the shoeshine man whom he had befriended as a white man. Griffin discovers, however, that his new black skin—even when recognized as artificial—has the power to transform not only physical space but also social space. Williams, who had previously been cordial, becomes downright friendly, all because of skin color: "Within a short time he lapsed into familiarity, forgetting I was once white. He began to use the 'we' form and to discuss 'our situation.' The illusion of my 'Negro-ness' took over so completely that I fell into the same pattern of talking and thinking. It was my first intimate glimpse" (29).

Griffin spends the remainder of his time in New Orleans engaged in "incessant walking" (42), traversing the same streets repeatedly but experiencing them anew on account of his skin tone. Griffin's New Orleans becomes divided into three spaces, a fact that underscores the doubling at the heart of his text. White space is that which Griffin experiences in his white skin. Black space is the world he enters wearing black skin, the space that is unfamiliar and sometimes ominous to him: "The whites seemed far away, out there in their parts of the city. The distance between them and me was far more than the miles that physically separated us. It was an area of unknowing. I wondered if it could really be bridged" (41). The third space in *Black Like Me*, in which the bulk of the narrative transpires, lies between these two extremes; it is the space that is simultaneously black and white, experienced in black skin but suffused with Griffin's memories of having been there in white skin. When Griffin ogles the menu at Brennan's, a famous New Orleans restaurant, for example, he is momentarily enraptured by memories of having experienced the spot as a white man, "realizing that a few days earlier I could have gone in and ordered anything on the menu. But now, though I was the same person with the same appetite, the same appreciation and even the same wallet, no power on earth could get me inside this place for a meal" (46). The reality of his black skin jolts Griffin out of this reverie; loitering in front of the restaurant, he looks up to face "frowns of disapproval" (46). The white Griffin and the black Griffin are not simply two different people; they also inhabit two different spaces—even when these spaces are in the very same location.

It is no accident that space is so central to the theme of doubling in *Black Like Me* and, more generally, to the book as a whole. The text was, after all, written to counter segregation, which sought to contain race by way of physical space. Griffin is fixated on reexperiencing physical space because to him as a civil rights activist during the era of Jim Crow, the color line is a very literal thing. Samira Kawash notes that "throughout the modern era . . . the delimitations of racial difference have been understood to correspond to a global map."[23] Griffin's text revolves around just this sort of racial map. His conception of race is intimately bonded to physical spaces, just as it cannot be detached from physical skin tone. *Black Like Me* presents race as an entity that rears its head in particular locales, so that Griffin's attempt to "discover" life as a black man must entail journeys through particular geographies. Attempts to rewrite *Black Like Me* after Jim Crow had been dismantled lose their potency precisely because they cannot be suffused with the sense of place in which Griffin's text is grounded. These later texts cannot invite their readers to visit the "other world" in their own backyards, as *Black Like Me* can. Proximity and space form the crux of the racial struggle in 1950s America.

They also continue to shape Griffin's narrative. His travels take him to familiar spaces, while his black skin defamiliarizes these spaces. He moves from New Orleans to Hattiesburg, then back to New Orleans with his friend P. D. East. He takes a bus to Biloxi and then hitchhikes to Mobile, where he offers an extended meditation on his newly acquired sense of racial space. "I walked through the streets of Mobile throughout the afternoons," he writes.

> I had known the city before, in my youth, when I sailed from there once to France. I knew it then as a privileged white. It had impressed me as a beautiful Southern port town, gracious and calm. . . . Now, walking the same streets as a Negro, I found no trace of the Mobile I formerly knew, nothing familiar. The laborers still dragged out their oxlike lives, but the gracious Southerner, the wise Southerner, the kind Southerner was nowhere visible. I knew that if I were white, I would find him easily, for his other face is there for whites to see. (101)

Finally, Griffin makes a definitive statement about racial space: "I concluded that, as in everything else, the atmosphere of a place is entirely different for Negro and white" (101).

Hitchhiking through swamp country between Mobile and Montgomery, Griffin is allowed a proximity to black folk that his white skin would have denied him. He shares dinner, even a bed, with a black man and his family. But overcome by loneliness—and perhaps by fear as well—Griffin begins to contemplate "passing as white." The more time he spends isolated in his Montgomery hotel room, the more he longs to have his white skin back. So he scrubs his skin "almost raw" and steps into the black space wearing white skin (120). At once he becomes a stranger to the black men he encounters, because without his black skin, "there was no longer communication between us, no longer the glance that said everything" (122). His stint in New Orleans is turned on its head: Griffin experiences Montgomery, a space he had previously encountered in his black self, as a white man. Haunted by memories of his black self in the very same space, Griffin discovers a magical thing happening: "Montgomery, the city I had detested, was beautiful that day" (123). Until, that is, he wanders into a black section of town, where he "was a lone white man in a Negro neighborhood," and has therefore crossed the line into a space in which he no longer belongs (122). When Griffin reapplies his black skin color in order to visit Tuskegee, he has an interesting encounter with a white man who, carping about the color line, tactlessly offers to share a drink with him. At once Griffin sees his former self in this well-meaning white man who cannot understand that when it comes to being close to a black person, skin color makes all the difference.

Griffin's duality is underscored by the division of space that I have been discussing, but this doubling changes over the course of the narrative, becoming literalized as Griffin proceeds in his travels. He starts taking his black skin on and off, "zigzagging back and forth" in order to "traverse an area both as Negro and white" (124). He writes, "I would go through an area as a Negro and then, usually at night, remove the dyes with cleansing cream and tissues and pass through the same area as a white man" (124). The two Griffins, who had previously existed in one black-skinned body and only in the realm of Griffin's mind, become quite literally, as for Mars Jeems, two separate selves—one with skin dye and one without. Marked by altered skin, they are always situated in a particular space. Movement—walking, hitchhiking, traveling—is central to Griffin's experiment. *Black Like Me* is said to be a text about a white man who alters his skin and passes as black, but it is really a work about a man who passes as both black *and* white, since Griffin spends the bulk of the narrative alternating between the two. He travels to Atlanta as a black man, but upon his arrival he rushes into the bathroom and turns himself white. He later returns, with a photographer, to New Orleans, where he must blacken his skin again in order to be photographed and thus passes, in a sense, for his former self: he becomes the white Griffin passing for the white Griffin who had put on black skin and stood in these same spots weeks before. Throughout *Black Like Me*, which is in fact structured as a travel narrative, spatial experience and proximity to blackness are contingent on one thing: skin color.

And yet once his skin dye is removed, Griffin, like Mars Jeems, is never the same again. While wearing black skin, Griffin begins to imagine the possibility of its permanence. Watching a group of poor black children, he contemplates their position of inferiority and writes, "It became fully terrifying when I realized that if my skin were permanently black, [society] would unhesitatingly consign my own children to this bean future" (113). After returning to his white skin, Griffin finds things "always confusing. I had to guard against the easy, semiobscene language that Negroes use among themselves, for coming from a white man it is insulting" (131). Growing attached to his black self, Griffin feels "strangely sad to leave the world of the Negro after having shared it so long— almost as though I were fleeing my share of his pain and heartache" (143). And in fact Griffin never fully sheds his blackness. In the final pages of *Black Like Me* he writes of his relationship with a black youth who works in his home: "The youth knew me and had no reticence in talking since he was sure I was 'one of them' so to speak. Both Negroes and whites have gained this certainty from the experiment—because I was Negro for six weeks, I remained partly Negro or perhaps essentially Negro" (158–59). Like Jeems, Griffin returns to whiteness, but he retains more than a bit of blackness within; indeed he re-mains "essentially Negro." Reviewers of the book took note of this retention: "It was a joy to see a white man become black for a while and then re-enter his own world screaming in the tones of Richard Wright and James Baldwin," wrote Hugh Smythe in the *Saturday Review*.[24] The film version of *Black Like Me*, released about a decade after the book (to scathing reviews), includes a number of scenes in which Griffin moans about forgetting what his true race is, and even visits a church in an effort to find solace.[25] Yet the film closes with a shot of Griffin literally crossing a line in the road to return to his wife, signify-ing his unambiguous rehabilitation to whiteness. Skin dyers, unlike those who do not alter their appearance, are permitted this clear-cut return to the white world, since their return entails something as straightforward as altering their skin tone.

Yet as I discussed in the context of Chesnutt, there is a powerful fantasy at work here, one in which the white passer's newly insightful white identity in-cludes a bit of blackness. In "Mars Jeems's Nightmare" this new identity paves the way for a reinvigorated masculinity, and according to Eric Lott, *Black Like Me* is no different in this regard. Lott argues, in "White Like Me," that Griffin's experiment in black skin is bound up with his desire to form homosocial bonds with black men. In a sense Jeems's passing involves similar homosocial bonding: his skin change is the product of an exchange between Jeems and Solomon, with whom Jeems reconciles in the end. Even *The House Behind the Cedars*, in which John and Tryon form a potent bond, makes the homosocial central to its plot. Clearly the homosocial male bond plays a crucial role in white passing narratives about men, a fact that proves true with regard to the works discussed in chapter 1 as well: Salome forms few bonds at all, while Tom and Chambers are intricately bound up in each others' lives.

Just as women figure prominently in the background of Chesnutt's tale, Griffin thinks often of his own wife, who becomes representative of his formerly white self, and to whom he has trouble writing while wearing his black self. In skin dye narratives, white women serve as that which anchors the white passer in his whiteness; because a white wife waits in the wings, Griffin, like Jeems, will surely reclaim his former status. *Black Like Me*, a text centered on the relationship between race and space and narrated by a man who is throughout the text really *two* men, reflects the white fantasy that skin dye does retain a measure of permanency—just enough to make a white man a wiser, more worldly, more masculine white man. Like Jeems—and unlike black passers—Griffin makes a triumphant return to whiteness. He assumes a public role as a speaker and activist; and by becoming a spokesman on the basis of his private experiences, he transforms his return to the private sphere into a very public, empowering act.

As a text that is fixated on skin color, *Black Like Me* differs from the texts I considered in the preceding chapter. In white passing narratives that do not involve skin change, identity is an internal-to-external process: the behavior (i.e., speech) of Salome and Chambers and their proximity to blackness affect people's perceptions of their physical appearance and social role, enabling them to pass as black. In skin-dyeing narratives such as *Black Like Me*, identity operates in the reverse fashion, from external to internal: people's perception of Griffin's physical appearance (i.e., skin color) affects his behavior and his proximity to blackness. Once he puts on black skin, Griffin begins to *feel* black. This occurs not only during his discussion with Sterling Williams, in which he claims to begin thinking like the black man Williams imagines him to be, but also when he stays with a black family in the Alabama swamps. Walking back from the well with his host, Griffin "felt more profoundly than ever before the totality of my Negro-ness, the immensity of its isolating effects" (109). Griffin's conception of identity as something that works from external to internal is what makes skin so central to his narrative. The premise behind most skin-dyeing narratives is that if one *looks* black, one can *feel* and *act* black. The premise behind white passing narratives that do not involve skin altering is, in contrast, that if one *feels* and *acts* black, one can *look* black, or at least be perceived as such. In the 1947 film *A Double Life*, in which Ronald Colman stars as a British actor, Tony, who has been cast to play Othello, Tony suddenly finds himself *becoming* Othello, feeling his rage and jealousy—as if the mere fact of performing blackness, or wearing black skin, is enough to make one black inside.[26] This notion of identity as an external-to-internal process stands at the heart of the skin dye genre. In these narratives skin becomes, as Judith Halberstam has noted in a different context, "a kind of metonym of the human," the essence of identity, the marker of a racial self.[27] It is also a passport, providing passers with proximity to the "nonwhite" spaces that allow them truly to experience that racial self.

Interestingly, only black skin is invested with this sort of transformative power. Such is suggested by *Black No More*, which—since its plot is essentially their inverse—makes for an interesting companion piece to Chesnutt's and, especially, Griffin's texts. Like them, Schuyler's novel essentializes the differences between black and white. When protagonist Max Disher first whitens his skin, he is elated: "The world was his oyster and he had the opensesame of a pork-colored skin!" (35). Soon, however, his enthusiasm is dampened; he cannot find much fun in the "ofay places of amusement" because "it was all so strained and quite unlike anything to which he had been accustomed. The Negroes, it seemed to him, were much gayer, enjoyed themselves more deeply and yet they were more restrained, actually more refined. Even [the whites'] dancing was different. . . . [A]t best they were gymnastic where the Negroes were sensuous" (40). Max grows nostalgic for "the almost European atmosphere of every Negro ghetto: the music, laughter, gaiety, jesting and abandon" (40). Like Griffin, Max finds that his skin swap allows him access to another world—albeit a lackluster one—but unlike Griffin, Max understands that the change is only skin deep. Despite wearing white skin, Max never feels white, and in fact remains essentially black throughout the novel. In a fit of nostalgia, for instance, he goes up to Harlem to find "peace" by viewing "the old familiar sights: the all-night speakeasies, the frankfurter stands, the loiterers, the late pedestrians, the chop suey joints, the careening taxicabs, the bawdy laughter" (41). It's small comfort to Max, and he ultimately ends up "outing" himself to his wife, who is indifferent to the fact that their baby, as she acknowledges, will be black. Wearing white skin has done little to whiten Max's essential self, or that of his offspring: the one-drop rule holds firm here. Black skin is a potent transformative agent in the narratives discussed in this chapter; white skin, by contrast, is merely cosmetic: skin deep.

To demonstrate the pervasiveness of this thinking, I want to digress for a moment in order to take a look at a film about a different sort of passing: *Gentleman's Agreement* (1948), Hollywood's second-ever film about anti-Semitism.[28] The story of a white journalist, Philip Schuyler Green, who passes as a Jew for six weeks in order to write a first-person exposé on anti-Semitism, the film bears an uncanny resemblance to *Black Like Me*, particularly since both narratives make the fate of the nation hinge on our ability to be tolerant (a product, perhaps, of cold war anxieties), both narratives are extremely didactic, and both suggest that passing drives a wedge between man and wife.[29] The more time he spends as a Jew, the more Phil Green doubts that his fiancée, Kathy, is as open-minded as she seems. As in *Black Like Me*, Green's estrangement from his lover is not long-lived; after Kathy learns a lesson in tolerance from Dave, Phil's Jewish friend, she and Phil reunite during the film's final moments. Phil is restored to "whiteness," but only after his stint as a Jew has affected his psyche. "If I were Jewish, that's how I would have felt," he says to himself after Kathy's polite bigotry offends him. Like Griffin, Green begins struggling with an emerging double consciousness. Being *perceived* as Jewish causes Green to *feel* Jewish—just as being seen as black causes Griffin to experience his "Negro-ness."

Yet the critical difference between passing as black and passing as Jewish is that Jews presumably lack physical identity markers, which makes it far more difficult for Green to be perceived as a Jew than for Griffin to be perceived as black.[30] *Gentleman's Agreement* repeatedly pays lip service to the idea that Jews are physically no different from whites. Upon deciding to pass, Green looks in the mirror and declares, "Phil Green—I could be anybody . . . dark hair, dark eyes." When he "outs" himself to his secretary, Green calls attention to his physical traits. "I'm the same man I was yesterday," he exclaims. "Same face, same eyes, same nose, same suit, same everything. Here—take my hand—feel it. Same flesh as yours, isn't it?" The film even introduces a professor named Lieberman, who points out that the only reason Jews, who are *not* a race, continue to call themselves "Jews" is solely out of stubborn pride in a world that "makes it an advantage for us not to do so."

But if *Gentleman's Agreement* is, like Griffin's book, founded on the premise that how one is seen by the world profoundly affects one's psyche, then it must indeed find a way to make Jewishness a physical, visible thing so that Green can be quickly identified as Jewish in the same way that Griffin is identified as black. The film accomplishes this by two means. First, it employs surnames in lieu of skin color. Instead of altering his skin, Green alters his name, which stands in for skin color. The moment Phil identifies himself as "Greenberg" instead of "Green," his "race" is revealed (just as his secretary, Miss Wales, "outs" herself by admitting that her real name is Walofsky). Second, the film goes out of its way to make its Jewish characters—Miss Wales and Dave Goldman—look quite different from its white ones. Dave, played by John Garfield (who was himself Jewish), is shorter than the other actors and has curly hair; Miss Wales has a prominently larger nose than the other women in the film. Clearly the film is signaling that Jews *do* indeed look different—a point that a review in *Commentary* was quick to underscore. Criticizing the film's message that tolerance is "conditional on uniformity," the reviewer noted that the Jewish characters do not look like everybody else: "Dave is visibly different from Phil, as you can see from the picture; his son, too, will be noticeably different from Phil's."[31] Because *Gentleman's Agreement* is invested in the notion that identity is an external-to-internal process, it must make Jewishness something as physical, as clearly visible, as skin color. The paradoxical way in which Jewishness is simultaneously an essence and a non-essence in the film is, according to Daniel Itzkovitz, part and parcel of the way in which Jewishness has been imagined over the years. Itzkovitz suggests that "chameleonism" was considered the essential trait of the Jewish "race": the Jew's "skill at blending into his surroundings is attributed to both 'tradition' and 'instinct.' His chameleonism is thus culturally and naturally determined; the 'natural place' of the Jew is in passing."[32] Jews, in other words, have been envisioned as most essentially Jewish when they are passing as essentially *non*-Jewish. Phil Green, in an act of "chameleonism," takes on a Jewish last name and immediately begins to feel like a Jew—just as Griffin puts on black skin and comes to feel like a black man.

Ultimately, this external-to-internal conception of how identity operates allows white experimenters a kind of comfort zone: if black identity is acquired by a mere change of skin, then whiteness is easily reacquired by the same process. Skin dye separates the passer's white self from his black self, and it heightens the transitory nature of his black identity. When Mr. Stevens in *The Garies* struggles to eradicate the "obnoxious tar," that "infernal stuff," from his face—and in the end goes to bed when it was "almost day . . . with the skin half scraped off from his swollen face"—the reader never doubts that his nightmarish stint in blackface will be short-lived, and thus the scene is more comic than dramatic.[33] The doubling process I have been describing is a kind of safety net for white passers, allowing them to maintain distinctions between their black and white selves. Anything the white passer experiences as a black man is obliterated the moment he removes his skin dye, precisely because these events were experienced by a different man: the man with black skin. Wearing skin dye, passers can cling to essential distinctions between two very distinct races. One who does *not* alter his skin could not retain such distinctions and, additionally, would feel the trauma of racism in a more personal sense since he encountered this racism while in his very own skin. The passer who has not dyed his skin is denied the luxury of imagining that the man who faced bigotry yesterday looked any different from—and thus *was* any different from—the man he is today.

Illustrating this difference is the case of author and critic Waldo Frank, who, in the spring of 1920, was invited by Jean Toomer on a tour of the South, "which meant of course to live with him among Negroes as if I were a Negro." Frank's memoirs detail this journey, which resembles Griffin's in obvious ways:

Frank, too, was a white man who passed as black and was given "a chance to see and feel the Negro from within the inside angle of the Negro." Unlike Griffin, however, Frank never alters his skin: "No questions would be asked about my race; it would be quietly assumed that if I came with Toomer I must be a Negro. I had seen Negroes in the South more 'white' than I: pale-skin men and women with blond hair (mine was black) whom a drop of Negro blood categorized as 'colored' forever. Toomer himself, tall, lemon-colored, could easily have passed as white."[34] Ironically, Frank passes as black by way of association with a "black" man who appears white himself, and thus Frank is compelled to confront the irrationality of racial distinctions in a way that Griffin is not.

In many respects Frank never acquires the "inside view" he had so desired; his depiction of the southern blacks he encounters is a romanticized portrait drawn by an outside observer: "They were intelligent, sensitive, neurotic. To be born a colored was a trauma they all suffered together." And yet Frank does write of the panic that pervaded his passing experience: "Lying in the dark sleep I would dream I was a Negro, would spring from sleep reaching for my clothes on the chair beside the bed, to finger them, to smell them . . . in proof I was white and myself."[35] Though Frank retains his white perspective throughout his journey as a black man, his moment of anxiety is fueled by the fact that unlike Griffin, he "becomes" black without changing his skin; this leads to moments of terror in which he realizes that his white and "black" selves are not separated by skin tone. While Griffin can take comfort in knowing that his black identity looks altogether different from his white one, Frank must grapple with the notion that although he is being taken for a black man, he is in all respects the same man he was before; he cannot imagine his passing experience as having occurred, in some sense, to another man.

Frank, after all, was Jewish—a fact that perhaps amplified his sense of terror at being taken for black.[36] During an age of rampant xenophobia, for Frank to envision himself as suddenly black was to exaggerate his already powerful sense of outsidership; it was, in some sense, to wear this outsider status on his sleeve. This Jewish-black "tour of the South" was, interestingly enough, repeated about a decade later by George Gershwin and Todd Duncan, a singer and voice teacher at Howard University who would originate the role of Porgy in Gershwin's Porgy and Bess. The two visited Charleston together in order to soak up black music and speech, and although Gershwin did not, as Frank did, pass for black, he did entertain Duncan's teasing for being "blacker" than Duncan, retorting only that Duncan was more Jewish than he was himself. I will have more to say about black-Jewish passing in chapter 4, when I turn to Mezz Mezzrow—the ultimate Jewish Negro—but for now I simply note that during trips down South, Jews who passed for black, as Frank did, suddenly confronted a very new reading of their very same skin. Without doing a thing to their pigmentation, such Jews became more than not quite white; they became black—in a way that Griffin never does.

The Essential Question

A critical question remains: If the skin-dyed Griffin (or the un-dyed Frank) looks black and even feels black, *is* he then black? For one reviewer of *Black Like Me* the answer was absolutely not. "Orwell was not *really* poor in his 'down and out' period just as Griffin was not *really* a Negro when he made his journey through the South," Bruce Cook wrote in *Commonweal*. "In each case, the simple fact somehow dulls the point of the book, reducing the effort essentially to a kind of well-intentioned voyeurism."[37] Griffin might even, to some extent, agree with Cook. "I would merely change my pigmentation and allow people to draw their own conclusions," Griffin writes of his plan, indicating that his essential white self would remain intact; only his outer shell would change. This essentialist approach to identity pervades the book, enabling Griffin to speak as a white man—his "true" self—even as he is identified by the world as a black man. And yet during those moments when Griffin begins to *feel* his black skin and to allow his exterior to shape his interior, he comes around to adopting a more constructionist view of identity, later referring (in an interview with Bradford Daniel) to his stint in black skin as a time "when I *was* a Negro," not when he "looked like" one.[38]

The tension at work here is plainly laid out in Walter Benn Michaels's essay "Autobiography of an Ex–White Man," which asserts that "passing becomes impossible because, in the logic of social constructionism, it is impossible not to *be* what you are passing for." In a culture invested in what Gayatri Spivak consistently refers to as "chromatism"—the reduction of race to visible differences in skin color—the only way to pass, Michaels argues, is by the alteration of color. But, he continues, "if you do somehow manage to alter the color of your skin, are you really passing? Are you pretending to belong to one race when you really belong to another, or have you in fact stopped belonging to one race and begun instead to belong to the other?" *Black Like Me* never quite answers this question. On the one hand, Griffin (and Jeems as well) was indeed a black man when he wore black skin, both because the world treated him as such and, more simply, because his skin was in fact black. But on the other hand, Griffin persistently points out that his essential white self lived on even while shrouded in black skin. To a great extent, this maintenance of an essential white identity in skin dye narratives is in line with their function as experiments and/or lessons learned: white people can venture into black skin, or happily learn lessons from it, but only when they are guaranteed safe return to a secure and solid whiteness. The problem of essentialism stands unresolved in all passing narratives, particularly, as Michaels points out, in skin-alteration passing narratives. *In Black No More*, for instance, protagonists dye their skin white yet retain essential black identities—even as Schuyler famously claimed that "the Aframerican is merely a lamp-blacked Anglo-Saxon." In his analysis of Michael Jackson's transraciality, Michael Awkward ends up concluding that Jackson's experiment, while invested in anti-essentialism—in the notion that one can literally turn oneself into someone else—is also suffused with those essentialist moments in which Jackson insisted on profound racial pride. "Even the most enlightened constructionist gesture," Awkward finally concludes, "is susceptible to strategic essentialist reading." [39]

Once we have noted its persistence, the problem of essentialism offers little resolution, except perhaps to declare the skin-dyed Griffin neither black nor white but something in between. Race is rarely so nice and neat. If we propose that racial identity consists of (at least) two ingredients—how the world sees a given individual, as well as how that same individual sees himself or herself—then it is possible to be simultaneously black and white. The skin-dyed Griffin becomes black, on the one hand, but white on the other; his identity is epitomized by the half-white, half-black effigy of Griffin that is hanged in his hometown. And yet our next skin-altering narrative, released in 1970, leaves little room for racial ambiguity. In Melvin Van Peebles's *Watermelon Man*, one *is* one's skin.

Watermelon Man

When Jeff Gerber wakes up one morning to discover that he has turned black, he is beside himself. "It's a nightmare!" he repeats, a phrase that echoes (unintentionally, I'm sure) Mars Jeems's identical nightmare. [40] But unlike Jeems, Gerber never wakes up to white skin. *Watermelon Man*, one of Van Peebles's first films (and one that has been essentially ignored by critics), explores a possibility that neither Chesnutt nor Griffin was prepared to grapple with: What happens when the white passer's black skin will not rub off?

Gerber, a racist of the Archie Bunker variety, has a wife, two children, and a particularly powerful sunlamp, under which he spends more time than even Griffin did. He shares racist banter with a black waiter at his local diner, and his favorite pastimes include sexually harassing the female secretaries in his insurance office and racing his bus to work each morning. Upon turning black, Gerber discovers that race is more than skin deep. His bus race acquires new meaning when performed in black skin: a black man running through the neighborhood inevitably causes a stir, and Gerber is promptly arrested. Althea, Gerber's wife, asks him a poignant question when she discovers him: "How do you know you're you?"

Indeed, who *is* Jeff Gerber? Is he white or black? Jeff is actually played by Godfrey Cambridge, a black comedian who initially wears whiteface (and, quite intentionally, looks as absurd in it as James Whitmore looked in black-face in the film *Black Like Me*); this fact suggests that *Watermelon Man* is in fact about a black man's refusal to be what he "really" is. Gerber's hilarious experiments with skin creams and milk baths, in the context of the civil rights and Black Power movements, lampoon the un-progressive black man's desperate attempts to erase his racial identity. As Gerber comes to accept his blackness, even telling his blonde lover that he will be neither worshipped nor reviled for his skin, the film's tone progresses from over-the-top comedy to one of didactic intensity. Like Chesnutt's story, Van Peebles's film is concerned with teaching the white racist and the self-hating black man a lesson. And yet unlike Jeems or Griffin, this white "passer" really is black, a fact that speaks not only to the interconnectedness of white and black in American culture, reflected in the "white" Gerber's constant references to black culture and the fact that Gerber and Althea—Jefferson Washington Gerber and Althea Jemima—bear stereo-typically black names, but also to the notion that race can indeed be reduced to skin color. Once Jeff looks black, he *is* black. The fact that he may possess a "white self" within is irrelevant; his physical appearance is the sole determinant of racial identity. The concept, present in *Black Like Me*, that identity is an exterior-to-interior process is taken to absurd extremes in *Watermelon Man*. Black skin does not merely affect one's psyche or enable proximity; it literally transforms white to black, plain and simple. The film turns the essentialism of other skin dye narratives on its head. The skin dyer indeed has an essential identity—but it's a black, not a white, one.

Accordingly, the underlying fantasy of skin change narratives—that a white man can obtain a "taste" of blackness and then return to whiteness bearing a bit of black insight within him—is modified by *Watermelon Man*. Gerber does not simply take on a smidgen of blackness; he remains a new and improved *black* man. At the start of the film, Gerber is, quite simply, a failure of a man: despised by his community, derided at his job, mocked by his children. Most important, he cannot fulfill his "husbandly" duties. "If you spent as much time in bed as you did under that sunlamp, we'd have more children," Althea laments. The film opens with Jeff launching his elaborate morning exercise routine as Althea sits, frustrated and unsatisfied, in bed. His hours under the sunlamp may represent his—and, by extension, white America's—subconscious desire to be black, but at the very least it attests to his pathetic narcissism. He remains a sorry figure—until he acquires black skin. By the end of the film Jeff has slept with a beautiful blonde, made sums of money, stood up to his boss, and opened his own business; he has, in other words, reclaimed his masculine status. This fact is underscored by the film's final shots, in which Jeff relaxes with a drink in a *Shaft*-like bar as a half-naked black woman undulates behind him.

The film's closing scene affirms this equation of black power and black consciousness with black masculinity. Jeff, surrounded by other black men, engages in martial arts as part of what appears to be training in the mode of the Black Power movement. The ultimate product, black skin, then, signifies an acquisition of the black phallus, here represented by martial arts.[41] Though in one respect *Watermelon Man* ends where it began—with Jeff engaging in a choreographed exercise routine—the film has also seen Jeff come a long way. In wearing black skin, he, like Jeems and Griffin, at last becomes a man. Despite the fact that it initially seems to be a narrative about anxieties and nightmares, Van Peebles's film is ultimately driven by the same hypermasculine fantasy as "Mars Jeems's Nightmare" and *Black Like Me*. Jeff's new exterior dictates his new interior—and for him, the results are priceless.

Latter-Day Skin Dyers

To this day the fantasy that changing one's skin can change one's essential identity remains a potent one in American culture. Although *Black Like Me* and *Watermelon Man* are very much products of their eras, the themes of these texts reverberate in more contemporary skin dye narratives. In the 1976 comedy *Silver Streak*, Richard Pryor disguises Gene Wilder by covering him in shoe polish, which he obtains from a shoeshine man not unlike Griffin's Sterling Williams. As he is blacked up by Pryor, Wilder grows anxious. "What're you—afraid it won't come off?" Pryor prods him, perhaps echoing *Watermelon Man*.[42] Wearing his natural "Jewish afro" as well as a Michael Jackson "Thriller"-style jacket, a Rastafarian's tam cap, sunglasses, and a mini–boom box, Wilder starts talking jive and learns a thing or two about rhythm from both the shoeshine man (who spies his sad attempts at dancing in the men's room) and Pryor ("How come you whiteys got such a tight ass, man?"). During an unusually somber moment in the film, Wilder, removing his blackface, looks in the mirror and imagines his white lover's voice; there is always, as we have seen, a white woman in the background during moments of white passing. (And during classic moments of blackface as well: whenever Al Jolson so famously applies blackface in *The Jazz Singer*, his beloved Mary is always present, whether in spirit or in person.) When Wilder does finally embrace his white woman, she spies the bit of blackness that he has unwittingly retained: a dab of shoe polish behind his ear.

Two years later Armistead Maupin invoked John Howard Griffin in D'orethea, the character in *Tales of the City* who dyes her skin black in order to get modeling jobs and to escape a father who works, aptly enough, in a Twinkies factory.[43] And in 1994 a college student named Joshua Solomon dyed his skin black and followed in Griffin's footsteps, traveling through the South in order to "know what it's like." Unlike Griffin, Solomon survived only a few days in black skin. "The anger was making me sick and the only antidote I knew was a dose of white skin," he wrote in the *Washington Post*.[44] Like Griffin's, Solomon's metaphorical journey also involves a literal one. Instead of confronting the racism in his home town of Washington, D.C. Solomon was attempting to re-create the setting of Griffin's experiment, to come as close to the Jim Crow days as possible, by visiting one of the most racist towns in the South. Such an extreme choice of setting guaranteed results—Solomon was sure to experience racism of the most virulent sort—and also veiled the oddness of reenacting Griffin's experiment in the 1990s, a time when whites should presumably be able to accept black accounts of "blackness" instead of calling for white accounts of it, an era when it should not have taken skin dye to prove that whiteness equals privilege.

In 2006 documentarian R. J. Cutler and rapper/actor Ice Cube brought skin swapping into the twenty-first century with their cable television series *Black. White.*, in which two families—the Sparkses, a black family from Atlanta, and the Wurgel-Marcotullis, a white family from Santa Monica, California—lived together and, aided by an astoundingly adroit makeup team, took turns in each other's skin. The show echoed Griffin's experiment in obvious respects. Bruno Marcotulli, the white male protagonist, actually proved to be the precise flip side of Griffin: whereas the latter was motivated by certainty that racism is omnipresent, the former seemed determined to prove just the opposite, that racism is overrated. "They really wanted me in this show to really come off at the end as, 'Gosh, I see' and 'Oh, my heart is open,'" Marcotulli told the *New York Times*. "But you know what? Life is tough for millions and millions of people. And I can't just say, you know, 'Yes, the African-Americans, gosh, they have it tough and they deserve reparations and we should do everything we can.' No."[45] *Black. White.*, however, diverged from *Black Like Me* in ways that speak volumes about race in contemporary America. For one thing, the Wurgel-Marcotullis rarely experienced Griffin-esque anxiety while wearing black skin; they were too busy gleefully whooping it up at a black church service or bonding with members of a spoken-word poetry group. The Sparkses, by contrast, spent much of the series bored by their stints in whiteface. Ultimately the whole experiment has a *Waiting for Godot* air about it: anticipated "aha" moments—dramatic incidents of racism or white privilege—never quite materialize, because contemporary racism in Los Angeles operates in ways that are indeed insidious but far less flagrant and camera-ready than those the Jim Crow era delivered.

The most appalling example of the lasting appeal of skin dye sagas is the 1986 film *Soul Man*, in which the lead character, Mark Watson, dyes his skin black in order to obtain a scholarship to Harvard Law School.[46] The film was protested by the NAACP and panned by critics, who deemed it "an unpleasant, but apparently audience-reassuring, mix of crude racism and self-admiring liberalism."[47] Mark's decision to pass involves none of Griffin's soul searching; in fact, Mark never comes face-to-face with his own prejudice. "These are the 80s—the Cosby decade!" he tells his best friend, Gordon. "America loves black people!" Mark becomes even more thrilled with his new skin when he meets Sara Walker, a beautiful black law student who turns out to be a single mother. "I love the law, I love being black, I love this woman!" Mark exclaims. It takes Sara to make Mark, blithely indifferent to the racism he encounters, think twice about his skin change. Suddenly it is *her* scholarship that he has stolen, and at once Mark begins to ruminate. "I never thought all this would—," he tells Gordon, "—I never thought I'd fall in love with her. Shit, I never thought about anything."

That, in a nutshell, is the point of *Soul Man*. "Son, I want to give you your manhood," Mark is told by his father, explaining why he has disinherited him. And indeed by wearing black skin, Mark—like Griffin, Jeems, and Gerber—does become a man. The frat boy who cares only for money and blondes is suddenly—voila!—a socially conscious law student committed to an interracial relationship with a single mother. Like other skin-dye narratives, *Soul Man* is wrapped up in teaching the white boy a lesson, one that is spelled out by Watson's tough-love law professor, played by James Earl Jones, who tells him: "You must have learned a great deal more than you bargained for. You've learned what it feels like to be black." Mark shakes his head: "No, sir—I don't really know what it feels like. If I didn't like it, I could always get out. It's not the same, sir." Impressed with his protégé's insight, the professor nods sagely: "You've learned a great deal more than I thought."

Mark's journey reflects the by now familiar trajectory of skin-dye narratives, the fantasy that a stint in black skin can provide the white man with wisdom and manhood. Mark, like Griffin and Jeems, returns to whiteness but remains just a bit black. "When I got involved with [Sara] I was really white on the inside, although I was black on the outside," he reflects. "But now a part of me is black on the inside even though I'm white on the outside. I don't know, maybe I'm sorta gray on the inside—and the outside." Simply by wearing a black exterior, in other words, Mark acquires something of a black interior—which he retains even after his return to whiteness. To his best friend's dismay, Mark can no longer, alas, enjoy the Beach Boys. The film's final scene, in which Mark knocks out two racist students and wins the approval of a nearby black man, illustrates his position as both black and white. His act of domination is enabled by whiteness, and yet his empathy is born from a newly blackened "soul." *Soul Man*, which concludes by reuniting Mark with his black girlfriend, thus "blackens" its protagonist more than does "Mars Jeems" or *Black Like Me*; the happy interracial couple at the film's close represents the fantasy in which whites have become a bit more black and blacks a bit more white—helping us all to, as Rodney King would famously put it several years later, "just get along."

This fantasy of tolerance and empathy, however, is marred by the fact that neither Griffin (in the film version of *Black Like Me*) nor Mark Watson ever actually looks black, something that rabid critics of both films gleefully pointed out. The difficulty of presenting white-to-black passing on the big screen almost dooms such films from the start; the impact of both *Soul Man* and the film version of *Black Like Me* is diminished by their absurd-looking protagonists. *Watermelon Man* succeeds by cultivating an over-the-top tone, one that is perfectly suited to Cambridge's whiteface routine. *Gentleman's Agreement* retains its credibility because it concerns itself with more subtle physical differences than those between white and black. But the film version of *Black Like Me*, despite being based on a true story, is never believable because "Griffin" never fully dupes the viewer. Films about passing fetishize the passer by making the spectacle of race- or gender-based passing more engaging than the content of the film itself. Passing films, including the highly acclaimed *Boys Don't Cry* and the 2003 film version of Philip Roth's novel *The Human Stain*, in many respects end up being about the act of passing itself—whether or not it is performed successfully. This fact makes it difficult for *any* film about passing to live up to its potential, since plot and character become relegated, in the viewer's mind, to secondary matters. The most potent narratives of skin dye are written, not visual, because the written form affords readers a fuller sense of the doubling at work in the narrative. Reading *Black Like Me*, we can fully appreciate the contrast between the internal and the external Griffin, and we are permitted to envision a passing Griffin who looks believably black.

Despite spanning almost a century, the narratives I have looked at in this chapter remain largely of a piece. All are didactic and driven by fantasies about the white man walking in a black man's shoes—and *beside* the black man's shoes, since skin dye narratives about men hinge on an interracial homosocial exchange. Most narratives involve the trope of doubling, and all envision black and white as two separate entities divided purely by pigment, so that passing from one to the other merely involves the swapping of skin. This new skin is a passport to passing, allowing for a proximity to blackness that is critical to the enterprise, in which identity making is presented as an outside-in process. What separates the characters in this chapter from those of chapter 1 is that in order to be near black—literally and metaphorically—the figures in this chapter had to physically become black.

In his reading of various journalistic accounts of passing—from Griffin and Grace Halsell to Gunter Walraff, who passed as a Turkish immigrant in Germany, and Yoram Binur, an Israeli who passed as an Arab—Vron Ware is highly optimistic about the progressive role played by such narratives: "They offer the reader an extraordinary point of view, not of anything that can be called an authentic experience of being on the other side of the lethal line of color and culture, but of the callous, ignorant, and unfeeling actions of those who may not realize or care that they are helping to maintain a brutally unjust white supremacist system."[48] My own reading of such narratives is more cynical. Perhaps the reason for the lasting resonance of the skin dye genre lies in its inherent racial conservatism. Not only does it refuse to envision a cross-racial understanding that is not predicated on physical alteration, but also it sees white and black as existing in two entirely different realms of experience and/or physical space. It relies on a racial essentialism that transforms forays across racial lines into mere experiments from which whites can return unscathed. Even those forced into black skin end up reaping its benefits, making the genre more reflective of fantasy than anxiety. The genre can be a comfortable one for those who do not envision a blurred line between white and black—for those who see race as something that is, so to speak, skin deep.

3

Black Like She
Grace Halsell and the Sexuality of Passing

During the eighteenth and nineteenth centuries, miscegenation was broadly conceived in terms of its transformative power: it could potentially turn white babies black. In the popular imagination, however, more than the baby could be blackened by sexual proximity between black and white. In 1732 the *South Carolina Gazette* published a poem, "The Chameleon Lover," which envisioned miscegenationists as "imbib[ing] the blackness of their charmer's skin."[1] At least as far back as the eighteenth century, interracial relationships were credited with such "magical" powers: through repeated sex with a black partner, it was believed, whites could find themselves turning black.

This popular myth was shored up by a measure of historical truth. For example, in one twentieth-century study of black-white couples, a sociologist discovered a number of cases in which white partners in a mixed marriage had attempted to conceal their racial heritage and instead claimed membership in the black community.[2] Significantly, in most narratives about this sort of passing, it is the white woman, not the white man, who passes for black. From the Civil War on, most interracial mating was between black women and white men, but most interracial marriages were between black men and white women. According to a writer in 1924, such a marriage "condemned [white women] to bitter hatred and social ostracism among their race. They generally had no recourse but to associate with the colored people and become Negroes in all but color." In 1886 a North Carolina resident described the "low white women who cohabited with Negroes. Well I can remember, the many times when, with the inconsiderable curiosity of a child, I hurriedly climbed the front gate to get a good look at a shriveled old woman trudging down the lane, who, when young, I was told, had had her free Negro lover bled and drank some of his blood, so that she might swear she had Negro blood in her, and thus marry him without penalty." During the same era, two white girls were jailed for dressing in men's clothing and accompanying their black boyfriends to New Orleans, where they planned to marry them; perhaps the cross-dressing emphasized in the legal report of this case reflects displaced anxiety about another sort of transformation—a racial one—that could occur with such a marriage. As late as 1946 an article in *Negro Digest* declared:

> Most Negro-white marriages are between Negro men and white women, and usually the wife follows the husband into the colored community. In many instances she claims to be a light-skinned Negro, hoping thereby to overcome the aversion with which the majority of Negroes appear to regard interracial marriage. This is by far the easiest of all forms of passing, even if the woman happens to be a golden blonde. Few whites, or Negroes, either, for that matter, can imagine her saying she is a Negro if she isn't.[3]

It is intriguing that such accounts of white passing in the context of sex and marriage are primarily about women. In this chapter I consider the position of the female white passer in the context of interracial sex—not only because sex represents the most literal form of proximity but also because the transformative power attributed to such relationships seems to apply principally to white women. In *The Garies*, for instance, the white Mr. Garie is married to a light-skinned black woman; although he is stoned to death by a racist lynch mob—thus losing his life on account of his proximity to black people—he never, in a novel replete with sundry passing scenarios, actually passes as black. Proximity, as I have been arguing, is capable of turning white black, but the meaning of "proximity" has everything to do with gender.

Inherent to this chapter is the concept of sexual tourism, which involves an extension of one's sexual boundaries, exploration of new and "primitive" bodies in a sexual context. It is what bell hooks has called "eating the Other": "The direct objective was not simply to sexually possess the Other, it was to be changed in some way by the encounter."[4] Sexual tourism occurs when sex becomes not merely about pleasure but about appropriation—appropriation, in this context, of blackness itself. Yet while men and women engage in this sort of appropriative sexual tourism, the process, as we shall see, is imagined as racially transformative only for women.

Grace Halsell is not the only female white passer in this book—women are mentioned in chapters 1 and 5 as well—but because she sets herself up as the female "version" of a male enterprise (Griffin's experiment), she serves as a convenient case study in the broader gender dynamics of white passing. In dissecting these dynamics I follow the lead of Philip Brian Harper, whose work emphasizes how black passing narratives—in which, he argues, "the passer returns to 'the race'; she accedes to proper 'femininity'"—ultimately reinforce conservative race and gender roles.[5] This chapter also takes up where the last one, about the impact of skin swapping on men, left off. As I have shown, critics generally equate putting on blackface with putting on a masculine face.[6] These critics in fact create a narrative of blackface that is steeped in the phallic posturing of Norman Mailer's seminal 1957 essay "The White Negro," one that centers on the homosocial and sometimes homoerotic. My discussion of male skin dyers, from "Mars Jeems's Nightmare" to *Soul Man*, corroborates that male bonding plays a vital role in white passing narratives about men. But for female white passers, the homosocial becomes irrelevant; instead the heterosexual is crucial. In narratives about interracial love—which are so often concerned with cultural appropriation—white women acquire their "blackness" from the black men in their bed. This, I suggest, sexualizes the white passing narrative in unique and intriguing ways, and also makes myths about black men and white women central to popular narratives—written and visual—about interracial love. It is to these popular myths that I turn.

Black Man/White Woman

The first narrative about a white female passer came on the heels of *Black Like Me*. Ten years after Griffin's work was published, a Texan named Grace Halsell repeated Griffin's experiment, dyeing her skin black and traveling through Mississippi and Harlem. She published her "results" in a 1969 narrative, *Soul Sister*, which sold more than 1 million copies and was translated into six languages. *Soul Sister* is the story of a woman who didn't simply wear a black face but went on, in the 1970s, to wear the guise of a Mexican and a Native American as well. The story of Grace Halsell's racial and ethnic masquerade, which ended with her death in 2000, offers a fascinating glimpse of the intersection of whiteness and womanhood, and speaks volumes about the role of sexual tourism in white passing narratives.[7]

Before I turn to *Soul Sister*, I want to reconsider *Black Like Me* briefly in light of critical discussions of homosociality in the text. Although Griffin's narrative is persistently concerned with male bonding, this theme does not eclipse its heterosexual narrative. After Griffin shaves his head, he meets a "pleasant-faced Negro" who compliments his new look: "He said he understood the gals were really going for bald-headed men. 'They say that's a sure sign of being high-sexed.' I let him think I'd shaved my head for that reason." The follow-up to this brief interlude occurs as Griffin talks with Sterling Williams, the black shoeshine man. They are approached by a black woman, a widow who seems interested in Griffin. "'Why, how do you do?' she said to him, "with a magnificent smile that illuminated not only her face but the entire quarter. I bowed and returned the smile, spontaneously, because the radiance of her expression took me by surprise. 'Why, just fine. How do you do?'" As the widow takes her leave, Williams bursts into laughter and tells Griffin: "She liked you. You're in a fix now." He adds: "She ain't no slut. She's a widow looking for a mate, and you're well-dressed. She ain't going to pass up a chance like that." Dismayed, Griffin asks Williams to inform the widow that he is married: "Look—you know I can't fiddle around with things like that. It'll be no fun for her when this project gets known and she finds out I'm a white man." We never hear of the widow again, but Griffin later describes a scene in which his attempts to write a letter to his wife are thwarted by nagging feelings of alienation. "My conditioning as a Negro, and the immense sexual implications with which the racists in our culture bombard us, cut me off, even in my most intimate self, from any connection with my wife," he writes.[8] Scenes such as these, in which Griffin confronts his new relationship with women—black and white—form the beginnings of a heterosexual narrative in the text which Griffin never fleshes out. But if Griffin's work merely intimates possibilities of white passing by way of heterosexual involvement, Grace Halsell's *Soul Sister* boldly confronts it.

Writing in 1969, six years after the publication of *The Feminine Mystique*, Halsell seems a direct product of early feminism. She left her husband and pursued a career as a journalist, traveling the world on her own in search of good copy. Halsell begins *Soul Sister* by explaining her motive: Griffin's narrative deserved to be rewritten, ten years later, this time by a woman. She points out that "imagination, feeling" are what set her female perspective apart from that of male narrators: "What makes men different could be [a woman's] feeling rather than reason."[9] Halsell repeatedly employs gendered imagery to illustrate her undertaking. The secret process of changing her skin, for instance, becomes "somewhat like a pregnant woman wanting to have a child without too many people noticing the Before and After" (34); she later swallows her first skin-changing pill and writes that she felt it "as a pregnant woman would feel the seed within her" (46). But although she initially seems quite gender conscious, Halsell is at the same time loath to acknowledge the ways in which being a woman vitally affected her project. The jobs she accepted in Harlem and Mississippi—secretary, cleaning lady—are typecast by gender as much as, if not more than, race, yet Halsell attributes her maltreatment solely to the latter. She seems eager to adhere to Griffin's rather unrealistic goal of isolating race, apart from gender or class, as life's *über*-factor; like Griffin, she declares that she would change nothing about herself but skin color: "I wanted to find a personal answer to the question of precisely how whites treat a 'Mary Doe,' an individual with training and background, identical with mine, even using my own name" (18).[10]

Eager to walk in Griffin's shoes, Halsell allows Griffin himself to play a principal role in the early part of her narrative. As I showed in chapter 2, Griffin's text is structured around his experience of racial space. Much of the pain described in *Black Like Me* is literal: the discomfort of walking miles to find a bathroom or water fountain. Halsell, writing after Jim Crow has been dismantled, attempts to reimpose these separate spheres on her narrative in order to recreate Griffin's experience. For example, she spends all her time in New York in Harlem, as if to imply that blacks were confined solely to this space (which she deems, rather dramatically, "a black country" [60] and "Harlem-prison" [124]); Harlem thus becomes equivalent to the segregated water fountains of Griffin's narrative. Halsell seeks out Griffin's approval before she can undertake her journey and makes no attempt to mask the fact that she idealizes him. She describes a dinner spent with him, his daughter, and a black friend of Griffin's, in which Griffin sits "saintly and benign, a wellspring of faith and love that radiated in the eyes of the *black* painter and Mandy, the glowing *blond* child" (25). To Halsell, Griffin is both icon and fantasy. "That child might be his child, my child, our child," she muses, looking at Griffin and his daughter (25).

Griffin, however, is one in a long line of men who sit at the heart of *Soul Sister*. The text is as much about Halsell's sexual liberation as it is about her liberation from whiteness; her text is thus structured around Halsell's attempts to become closer to the Other by way of social, usually erotic bonds with black men. Although Griffin is the primary male authority figure in the early pages of her text, there are others. Halsell's father is a source of wisdom—"my father's injunction echoes for me . . . work to get what you want," she writes (40)—as are the three male doctors overseeing her experiment, to whom she persistently refers and defers.

But the most important heterosocial (and heterosexual) bonds that Halsell forms throughout *Soul Sister* are with black men. Unlike Griffin, who presents the black community as foreign to him prior to his skin change, Halsell has relationships with black men before she begins her experiment. She recounts, for instance, her visit to a black beach with her friend Roscoe Dixon: "By entering Roscoe's world, I had placed myself in his hands, among his people, at the site of his choosing. I felt strangely, freely, unabashedly liberated from conventional ideas and notions of race and reality. We had temporarily shattered the barriers imposed upon a white woman and a black man" (35). Dixon later tells her that his brother believed her to be part black, a fact that pleases her. Whereas Griffin describes his skin-darkening process in matter-of-fact tones, Halsell is hyperconscious of the change in her appearance and the ways in which it will affect her self-worth. She imagines herself "*black and ugly*, in lace-up working shoes and a dark, cheap cotton dress," all because she has been "brainwashed to believe that white ladies and pink ladies are naturally more attractive than caramel and chocolate ones" (30). Halsell, unlike Griffin, indulges her vanity and voices anxiety about becoming "*very black*," possibly for an entire year (34). She cannot separate becoming black from becoming unattractive to men— because men will be her passport to the world of the Other.

Upon arriving in Harlem, Halsell immediately calls her black friend Jim Hamilton. Ironically, Halsell first experiences racial judgment as a *white* woman: He refuses to help her because he takes issue with her experiment and her white liberal pose. After finding a place to stay, Halsell is given a ride and some words of comfort by Longus Moore, a café owner whom she describes as "a totally black Negro" (73). Her reaction to Moore's aid borders on hysterical:

> I came here to know you for what you are, you beast, you black, black, black man! And you are ugly to me. You are a nigger. And you feel sorry for me. You are pitying me, you are, Christ in heaven, you are loving me! It's not supposed to be like that! You're telling me you don't care if you will ever see me again, but that you will help me . . . no matter what I've done. You are my friend? God, how I need you, how I want you. (74)

Halsell goes on to say she feels "stripped naked, stripped bare of those myths I've worn like crown jewels—that white is right, that black is wrong" (74). Later in the narrative, Moore confesses his love for Halsell and asks her to marry him, which compels her to reveal her true identity. He then becomes her confidant, driving her about town on pseudo-dates to hot spots in Harlem. Halsell also dates two men in Harlem, both of whom she admits to sharing kisses with. Cliff, the ex-husband of an acquaintance of Halsell's, speaks harshly to her on their date but once inside her apartment becomes "a submissive, pleading, pliant figure, anxious to get what he wants through cajolery and concession" (115–16). Halsell never confronts her feelings for Cliff, admitting only, "Sexual complexes aside, I am saddened by Cliff's elaborate pretensions, his great desire to impress people" (116). She meets another man, John, at a Black Power bookstore and asks him to a Ray Charles show; she is then surprised when he wishes to go to bed with her and manages to "get by with a good-night kiss" (120).

Halsell's account of being a black woman in Harlem reads at times like a crass catalogue of sexual encounters. As she moves on to Mississippi, this theme continues. Seated in a bar, Halsell meets Floyd, a pimp who accompanies her for the night. Suspicious of Floyd's intentions, Halsell asks the janitor in her hotel about him; he warns her that she may be taken advantage of and then "wants me to stand close to his small, bony body, that is so emasculated in its crippled, aging condition" (151). After a brief stint as a cleaning lady for a white woman, Halsell confesses her story to Alex Waites, an NAACP freedom fighter, who arranges for her to stay with families in rural Mississippi and participate in civil rights activism. But the final episode in *Soul Sister* finds Halsell working, again, as a cleaning lady for a white family in Clarksdale. There her white boss attempts to rape her, begging for "black pussy," and Halsell, after barely escaping, ends her journey (211). The near-rape scene is significant (and tragic) in several respects. First, it overturns racist stereotypes: "I had gone with trembling heart to the ghetto, Harlem, fearful that a big black bogeyman might tear down the paper-thin door separating my 'white' body from his lustful desires. And now it had been a white, not a black, devil whose passions had overwhelmed him" (218). Second, it finds the white man hungry for the black Other, a grossly exaggerated version of Halsell's own need to become bonded with the Other by way of erotic (and social) encounters with black men. Halsell sets off on her journey with well-meaning naïveté, eager to "knock on their doors and say, black people let me in there with you!" (19). But she seems interested in knocking only on *male* doors.

The possibility of female companionship looms large in *Soul Sister* but is never realized. In Harlem, Halsell consistently sets herself apart from most of the women she encounters, though she empathizes with them. The "good top-level, intelligent, upper-middle-class" women at her job at Harlem Hospital, for instance, chastise and ostracize her because they "were holding up the standards, the values of the white system" (127, 128). Halsell is collegial toward several women in the memoir but rarely shares personal encounters with them. When she walks in on two women making love, she is shocked and frightened; lesbianism represents, in *Soul Sister*, the dangers of excessive female bonding.[11] The white women for whom she works either demean her or see her as a receptacle for dramatic confessions about their husbands' failings. They seem desperate to find companionship but unable to reach out to anyone, leaving them to spill their souls to the hired help. "We are two women in a house all day long," Halsell writes of her white employer, Mrs. Williams, "and I sense that she desperately wants to talk to me, but it can never be as an equal" (156). The few exchanges that Halsell does share with women, white or black, generally concern sex and/or relationships with men. The only black woman to whom Halsell does become close is Mrs. Tubbs, her host in the Mississippi Delta, who knows that Halsell is in fact white (which in all likelihood changed the dynamic between them). Halsell, in blackface, seeks to know the Other not via the homosocial but via the heterosexual, a fact that sets Halsell's narrative in line with Mariana Torgovnick's assertion in *Gone Primitive* that for many writers, the primitive is degenerative when associated with the female but regenerative when associated with the male.[12] For Halsell—and, as we shall see, for others—black women's "primitivity" is offensive and uncivilized, but the "primitive" black man holds the key to the regenerative world of the Other.

If men attain closeness to the racial Other by way of what Lott calls a "literal inhabiting of black bodies," Halsell, a woman, thus achieves a similar goal through a *sexual* inhabiting of black bodies.[13] The ultimate scenes of sexual tourism in *Soul Sister* occur during the text's two interludes, first in Puerto Rico, then in St. Thomas. She spends several weeks on each island sunning herself, taking her suntan far beyond acceptable standards of white beauty. In Puerto Rico she befriends Jim Hamilton, a black man from New York, as well as a Puerto Rican man who fondly calls her "'Negrita . . . negrita' (*black one*)" (52). While in the Virgin Islands, Halsell longingly admires the natives as "proud, self-assured, beautiful people" (135). Both scenes are set in tropical, erotic locales that are ripe for sexual tourism, and both sexualize Halsell's bond with the Other.

Throughout the 1970s Halsell engaged in a number of passing adventures, recorded in her 1996 autobiography *In Their Shoes*. Although her memoir, like *Soul Sister*, establishes a gender-conscious perspective (she titles the first section "Growing Up—Female") again Halsell seems hesitant to gaze on her passing excursions with a critical feminist eye. As in *Soul Sister*, her subjugated position (as a house servant) is as much a product of gender as of ethnicity or race; and as is true of her earlier experience with blackface, Halsell's ethnic play hinges on the presence of nonwhite men. After spending some time on a Navajo reservation, Halsell decides to pass as Bessie Yellowhair, a Navajo nanny for a family in Los Angeles. She borrows a Navajo woman's name and clothing and begins hitchhiking to L.A., taking her first ride from a white man. "Distressed to realize that he was not like me, not a Navajo, I did not trust him," she writes.[14] She escapes from his car after he makes sexual advances, a scene reminiscent of the final one in *Soul Sister*, but says: "I tried to understand why I was so shaken by the man's advances. I reminded myself that I always traveled alone" (143). White men lurk as a threat in Halsell's experiments, but nonwhite men are saviors or erotic objects. Halsell's stint as Bessie Yellowhair collapses once she can no longer tolerate being treated as a house servant, and she soon flees back to the safety of her white world. Halsell then passes twice as a Mexican (simply by speaking Spanish), first to swim the Rio Grande with "wetbacks" (her term) and then to cross El Punte with Mexican nannies. In both instances she finds solace in male companionship. Among the wetbacks she becomes close to is Cesar Guerrero Paz, who, she says, "accepted me as the poor of this world always seem to accept one another, at face value" (155). Her memory of him haunts her: "Since that time I think I have seen his face a thousand times" (161). During the year she spends in Mexico, Halsell befriends Eduardo Burriega, a U.S. citizen who is also a smuggler, and with whom Halsell, viewing herself as a liminal figure, identifies.

Crossing lines—ethnic, racial, or literal ones—continually sends Halsell into the arms of the male Other. Her passing, then, is contingent on sexual tourism, which itself relies on stereotypes about the masculine black as black buck; her passing is thus nourished by an exaggerated caricature of black culture. In order to pass, Halsell ultimately erects what W. T. Lhamon calls an "artificial nigger": a "Rorschach blot, on which people"—white people, that is—"flung their fantasies."[15]

All of Halsell's passing exploits, particularly those related in *In Their Shoes*, follow a similar rhythm: Halsell finds her way in to the world of the Other, dramatizes the danger she is in, then finds relief and safety upon reappropriating her white identity. This pattern is particularly evident in the border-crossing adventures, during which she becomes so carried away by the dangers ahead that "for the first time in an hour I realized that I was not really a fugitive in hiding" (176). The thrill of passing, of placing herself in a position of danger, seems to be Halsell's drug. She desires the rush of experiencing the Other's peril—but only from a position of safety. Whiteness can only be truly appreciated once the thrill of losing it becomes a (momentary) reality. Passing for black, in Halsell and in Griffin, allows its wearers to experience an exhilarating human emotion—fear—from a position of ultimate safety: whiteness.

The epigraph for *In Their Shoes* is from Whitman's *Song of the Open Road*. "Like Whitman," Halsell writes, "I am many persons in one. I feel that I am part black, part Bessie Yellowhair, part Mexican wetback; to put it in Whitman's grand phrase, 'I contain multitudes'" (2). The irony here is that Halsell's passing is not about discovering the Other but about discovering herself—in her words, "attempting to gain possession of myself" (2). The blackface episodes serve as a finishing school of sorts, and this is particularly reflected in the photo album section of *In Their Shoes*: behold Grace with her distinguished Texas family; Grace in a national rodeo; Grace interviewing celebrities on her first journalism gigs; and then Grace as Bessie Yellowhair, as a Mexican, in China and Lebanon. "Strangers became just like me—when I walked in their shoes," she writes in the book's epilogue (252). Blacks, Mexicans, Navajos—all are gateways through which Halsell passes on the road to her ultimate destination: self-knowledge. Like other narratives of skin dye, *Soul Sister* not only maintains sharp distinctions between black and white but also preserves the essential whiteness of its protagonist, who hopes to become a more enlightened, more nearly perfect white person by taking that whiteness off—at least for a little while.

Halsell's gender ends up shaping the narrative features of skin dye narratives in noteworthy ways. Like *Black Like Me*, *Soul Sister* is driven by the fantasy, not anxiety, of being black (though thrill and terror seem more intricately bonded in Halsell than in Griffin). In one respect Halsell, like other skin dyers, constructs identity as something that flows from the outside in; by persistently emphasizing the change in her appearance, not simply in becoming black but also in becoming Navajo and Mexican (in the latter case, language stands in for physical appearance), she implies that the clothes make the (wo)man. But at the same time, the sexual tourism at the crux of her text speaks to the fact that looking black is not enough. In order to feel black, Halsell must physically *feel* the black man; she both satisfies her erotic curiosity and acquires "authentic" blackness through sexual encounters with black men.

What this fact ultimately suggests is that in the eyes of white passers, "authentic" blackness lies with the black male, not the black female—a formulation that is, as I will show, borne out in contemporary hip-hop and urban popular culture more generally, which is forever asserting the authenticity of the black male persona.[16] It is for this reason that white passers, whether male or female, turn to black men, not black women, in order to acquire their authenticity as white passing for black. While traditional black passing narratives generally concern themselves with either women or (as in the case of the Ex–Coloured Man) feminized men, the white passing narrative rests on the extreme potency, the transformative power, of black masculinity. Halsell seeks out the "authentic" black experience, the one that will teach her how it truly *feels* to be black; and she does so through sexual encounters with black men. Because white women can take in the black man—the "true site" of blackness— narratives about them are almost always centered on sexual exchanges. This fact begins to explain why the most popular narrative of interracial sex involves the black man and the white woman, not vice versa. If interracial sex is about acquiring "authentic" blackness, so to speak, then the only interracial sex that matters—the only form of proximity capable of bestowing "authentic" blackness on a white person—must involve the black man. If "blackness" is contagious, in other words, then the black *male* is a pathogen. The black female might be a carrier who has been imagined, for centuries, as a hypersexed vixen: a source of fantasy fulfillment for the sexually subdued white man. But she is not "infectious" in the way that a black man is.[17]

By the time Halsell was writing, the black man–white woman scenario had become almost a fixture in both the public imagination and the public sphere. Interracial unions in the context of white appropriation of black culture flourished during the 1950s and 1960s, particularly within Beat culture. As the Beats sought out ways to appropriate the "hipness" of black men, they often turned to black and/or Mexican men and women for sexual exhilaration. In her memoir *How I Became Hettie Jones*, Hettie Jones (at that time Hettie Cohen) describes her visit to a jazz club with LeRoi Jones, who would become her husband: "I entered the Five Spot, and all these other new doors I opened with Roi, as another image—one half of the Blackman/whitewoman couple, that stereotype of lady and stud. This was unsettling. . . . All I wanted to do at the Five Spot was *listen*. Grachan Moncur told me I was the first white girl he had ever met who came for the music and not for the kicks."[18]

Though they dabbled in forms of sexual tourism with women of color, the men of the Beat movement ultimately locate "authentic" blackness in the black man. Mailer's essay "The White Negro," for instance, makes no mention of black womanhood. The "ménage-a-trois" he describes involves three boys: "the bohemian and the juvenile delinquent [coming] face to face with the Negro"; in the metaphorical "wedding of the white and the black it was the Negro"—the Negro *man*, we might add—"who brought the cultural dowry."[19] If, as Mailer writes, "jazz is orgasm, it is the music of orgasm, good orgasm and bad,"[20] and jazz is, for the Beats, associated with *men*, then the sexual ideal here involves not black women but black men. As a way of considering both a Beat-era sexual tourism that precedes Halsell and of exploring the flip side of her narrative—the white man and the black woman—I turn now to a text that, while not explicitly about white passing, is centered on the relationship between sex and appropriations of blackness: Jack Kerouac's novel *The Subterraneans*.

Black Woman/White Man

One cannot discuss Kerouac in this context without citing the famous passage from *On the Road* in which Sal wanders the streets "wishing I were a Negro, feeling that the best the white world had offered was not enough ecstasy for me, not enough life, joy, kicks, darkness, music, not enough night." Sal's relationship with Terry, a Mexican woman, triggers the same fantasy. Working in the fields with Terry, Sal imagines himself "like an old Negro cotton picker. . . . They thought I was a Mexican, of course; and in a way I am."[21] In what respects does Kerouac envision sexual liaisons as a viable way of acquiring authenticity?

Meditating on this question is Kerouac's 1958 novel *The Subterraneans*, which details his New York love affair with a black woman named Alene Lee in the guise of an affair between two members of the San Francisco underground: a white man, Leo Percepied, and a black woman, Mardou Fox. The style of the short novel, written as stream-of-consciousness prose poetry, is itself a kind of appropriative act; its cadences and improvisational feel—other than the couple's falling in and out of love, the book has no real plot—approximate the jazz that Kerouac prized. Despite its unenthusiastic reception (Henry Luce's conservative *Time* magazine review called Kerouac the "latrine laureate of Hobohemia"),[22] the novel sold twelve thousand copies upon publication and is a rich text that is often ignored by contemporary critics.

The Subterraneans is a poignantly honest novel about a white man's erotic encounter with a black body that is at once recognizably lovely and utterly unfamiliar. On first meeting Mardou, Leo admits to the allure that her color holds for him: "By God, I've got to get involved with that 'little woman' and maybe too because she was a Negro."[23] Pursuing Mardou, who is at first more interested in his beatnik friends than in him, Leo is hesitant and yet eager, appropriately for one who describes himself, in the novel's first passage, as "an unself-confident man, at the same time . . . an egomaniac" (1). He relates his "doubts" beautifully:

> Doubts, therefore, of, well, Mardou's Negro, naturally not only my mother but my sister whom I may have to live with someday and her husband a Southerner and everybody concerned, would be mortified to hell and have nothing to do with us—like it would preclude completely the possibility of living in the South, like in that Faulknerian Pillar homestead in the Old Granddad moonlight I'd so long envisioned for myself.[24] (45)

By loving Mardou, Leo becomes aware of his own whiteness in a new and profound way; he mentions his "fear of communicating WHITE images to her in our telepathies for fear she'll be (in her fun) reminded of our racial difference" (70). Leo is, after all, constantly reminded of that racial difference—and rarely lets the reader forget it either. The most tenderly honest moments in the novel are those in which Leo looks candidly at Mardou's black body: "I wake from the scream of beermares and see beside me the Negro woman with parted lips sleeping, and little bits of white pillow stuffing in her black hair, feel almost revulsion, realize what a beast I am for feeling anything near it, grape little sweetbody naked on the restless sheets of the nightbefore excitement" (17).

Leo is candid about his vulnerabilities. A man in his mid-thirties, he is significantly older than Mardou, and this age difference is palpable to him. Watching Mardou frolic with the other Beats, who remain on the fringes of the novel, Leo sees "for the first time their youthful playfulness which I in my scowlingness and writer-ness had not participated in and my old man-ness about which I kept telling myself 'You're old you old sonofabitch you're lucky to have such a young sweet thing'" (81). The novel is narrated by a writer who feels himself aging more each day, one whose masculinity remains fragile throughout. Often teased by his cohorts for "making yourself a reputation on the Beach as a big fag tugging at the shirts of well-known punks" (61), Leo, confronting other men who come on to Mardou, also laments "not being able to come right out and say, 'Lissen this is my girl, what are you talking about, if you want to try and make her you'll have to tangle with me, you understand that pops as well as I do'" (84–85). As a narrator, Leo is unafraid to paint himself from the most unflattering angles.

Yet it is precisely this insecurity that causes Leo to idealize Mardou, to turn to her in hopes of appropriating her youth, her hipness, her mad passion—in essence, her black womanhood. Mardou is so often a romanticized black Other whom Leo alternately wishes to be and to possess. She is "dark Mardou" (a phrase that serves almost as her epithet), the "tattered holy Negro Joan of Arc" who exudes a "snakelike charm" and at times resembles "the face on a beautiful porphyry mask found so long ago and Aztecan" (31, 11). She is "one of the most *enwomaned* women I've seen, a brunette of eternity incomprehensibly beautiful" as well as "the only girl I've ever known who could really understand bop" (51, 67). Invoking *On the Road*, Leo says that with Mardou by his side, he can make his "old dream of wanting to be vital, alive like a Negro or an Indian or a Denver Jap or a New York Puerto Rican come true" (70). And in perhaps the most essentializing moment in the text, Leo tells Mardou, "Honey what I see in your eyes is a lifetime of affection not only from the Indian in you but because as part Negro somehow you are the first, the essential woman, and therefore the most, most originally most fully affectionate and maternal" (94).[25]

Such passages have led critics to read *The Subterraneans* as a book about Leo's primitivism and essentialism—but to do so is to read only half the story.

Writing the text after their affair has ended, Leo looks back with a wise and wistful eye; his perceptions are thus a mélange of retrospective insight and heat-of-the-moment passion. His brutal honesty about his simultaneous attraction to and repulsion from Mardou, and especially about his fixation on her putatively "essential" blackness, are what lend *The Subterraneans* its stunning complexity. For as much as Leo attempts, throughout the novel, to capture Mardou in idealized terms—or to capture Mardou in any terms at all—she ultimately slips through the text, and through his hands. Even as Leo essentializes her, Mardou resists, and Leo allows her to do so. Almost every time Mardou's voice appears in the novel, it is to deconstruct one of Leo's idealized constructions. Leo brings Mardou to an intellectuals' party and listens as she "makes solemn statements about bop, like, 'I don't like bop, I really don't, it's like junk to me, too many junkies are bop men and I hear the junk in it.'— 'Well,' Mac adjusting glasses, 'that's interesting.'—And I go up and say, 'But you never like what you come from' (looking at Mardou).—'What do you mean?'— 'You're the child of bop,' or the children of bop, some such statement, which Mac and I agree on" (99). This short interaction keenly captures Leo's attempt to essentialize Mardou as a "child of bop," as one who, by virtue of being black, should *innately* relate to "her" music, but it also captures Mardou's resistance to being pinned down in such a way. Writing after the fact, Leo himself seems aware of his attempts to turn Mardou into the essential black woman and her refusal to play along with such efforts. In scene after scene Mardou bursts Leo's intellectual bubble and mocks his pretentiousness. When he launches into a lofty discussion of Wilhelm Reich's orgasm theory, Mardou keeps saying, "O don't pull that Reich on me in bed, I read his damn book, I don't want our relationship all pointed out and f——d up with what HE said" (47). Leo later muses on "how noisome, tiresome it must have been to her to have to appreciate all we were saying, to be amazed by the latest quip from the lips of the one and only, the newest manifestation of the same old dreary mystery of personality in the great KaJa" (100). Mardou's voice persistently enters the text in order to undermine Leo's.

To a great extent, readers of *The Subterraneans* never have the opportunity truly to see or hear Mardou; what we get instead are Leo's constructions of her, complemented by her deconstructions of these same elaborate constructions. If, as W. T. Lhamon writes, Kerouac "used the Negro as a metaphor of his needs"—in the way that for most artists during the 1950s, the "Negro" was a "Rorschach blot, on which people flung their fantasies"[26]—*The Subterraneans* is perhaps the only Kerouac novel that is self-conscious about this act of fantasy creation; the novel is ultimately *about* the kind of metaphor making and

Rorschach blot testing that Lhamon describes. Upon first meeting Mardou, Leo allows her voice a number of pages in which to tell her own story, a story of abuse and neglect and independence—"I had never heard such a story from such a soul except from the great men I had known in my youth," he says, "great heroes of America I'd been buddies with" (36)—but after this, Mardou's voice seems to fade in and out of the novel, ringing prominently at moments such as the ones I have cited, during which she undercuts Leo's lofty fabrications. "Men are so crazy, they want the essence, the woman is the essence, there it is right in their hands but they rush off erecting big abstract constructions . . . they rush off and have big wars and consider women as prizes instead of human beings, well man I may be in the middle of this shit but I don't want any part of it," says Mardou to Leo, who responds with a confession: "And so having the essence of her love now I erect big word constructions and thereby betray it really. . . . But I cannot in this confession betray the innermosts, the thighs, what the thighs contain—and yet why write?—the thighs contain the essence—yet tho there I should stay and from there I came and'll eventually return, still I have to rush off and construct construct—for nothing—for Baudelaire poems—" (16–17). Leo returns to this notion on the final page of the novel: "('Yes,' I thought, 'there's an essence, and that is your womb') 'and the man has it in his hand, but rushes off to build big constructions.' (I'd just read her the first few pages of *Finnegan's Wake* and explained them and where Finnegan is always putting up 'buildung supra buildung supra buildung' on the banks of the Liffey—dung!)" (110). Dung, indeed, is how Leo ultimately conceives of his portrait of Mardou, with its romanticizing and essentializing. Ultimately, *The Subterraneans* is about Leo's attempt to absorb the essence of black womanhood from Mardou and, later, to capture her very nature in words—yet failing miserably. Mardou resists the text not only because Leo's portrait of her is rife with contradictions, with simultaneous honesty and romantic illusion, but also because her undermining voice—a voice that mocks and thwarts Leo's "buildung supra buildung"—cannot be erased by Leo's authorial pen. *The Subterraneans* is the story of a white man who cannot ultimately appropriate his black lover's soul because he cannot help but destabilize his own visions of her as the site of "authentic blackness."

Leo, in fact, is never truly able to *possess* Mardou, in every sense of the word. On a literal level, Mardou always seems to "belong" to other men. When Leo first meets her, she is interested in Adam Moorad (Allen Ginsberg); Leo's later dream involving Mardou and Yuri Gligoric (Gregory Corso) plagues him until the end ("now I've got in full dragon bloom the monster of jealousy as green as in any cliché cartoon rising in my being," he says [86]). This dream serves almost as a self-fulfilling prophecy: Mardou does ultimately sleep with Yuri, confirming Leo's anxieties about his inability to ever own his love. Leo can never own Mardou's image, either, as he cannot ultimately capture her essence in words. And perhaps most important, he can never quite possess an understanding of Mardou; Leo's elaborate constructions bespeak an attempt to produce her out of his idealized notions of what blackness and womanhood should be, or what he would like them to be. Kerouac's novel details the undoing of both a relationship and a white man's effort to absorb the "blackness" of his lover's soul. The novel treats this subject with far more complexity and detail than does *On the Road*.[27]

The Subterraneans vividly illustrates the limitations of the black woman as "carrier": she cannot bestow the same authenticity on the white man that the black man can. The very fact that Kerouac deconstructs the relationship between the white man and the black woman but never does the same to that between black men and white men suggests that he sees the former relationship as ultimately unable to serve as a viable means of appropriation. Interestingly, what *is* a viable means of appropriation in Kerouac's text involves language. The jazz-style prosody of *The Subterraneans* gives a measure of "cool" to the text. Yet for the Beats, jazz is a masculine form of cool, embodied by the black jazzmen whom these white hipsters idolized.[28] Once again it is only the black man, bearer of the jazz that Kerouac's prose appropriates, who can provide Kerouac with the authenticity he so desires.

The Subterraneans is obviously a radically different sort of text from *Soul Sister*—though both are based on true stories, the former is a nuanced, artistic meditation and the latter a best-selling narrative aimed at a broad readership— but ultimately one affirms what the other implies: only the black man possesses the power to transfer his blackness, so to speak, onto whites.

Interracial Sex and the Big Screen

There is good reason to make the leap from Kerouac and Halsell to 1990s Hollywood: the decade witnessed the rise of hip-hop cinema, which included a spate of hip-hop themed films about interracial love. The theme was ushered in by Spike Lee's *Jungle Fever*, then later taken up in films such as *Zebrahead*, *Save the Last Dance*, and *Black and White*, among others. This fascination with interracial affairs seems to me to be tied to anxieties about the white appropriation of black culture, which was prevalent during the decade that witnessed the radical commercialization of hip-hop culture. The rise of white rappers, the heyday of the rock-rap fusion (personified by such acts as Limp Bizkit and Korn), and the ubiquity of hip-hop fashion—white suburbanites had not just their Adidas but their FUBU, Phat Farm, and Roca Wear—produced a great deal of discourse about appropriation and authenticity, and the interracial love film became part and parcel of that discourse. Not every film about black-white relationships is, of course, bound up with issues of authenticity. In *Jungle Fever*, for instance, the protagonists are driven not by a desire to appropriate or cross-identify but merely by an overwhelming curiosity ("You were curious about black, and I was curious about white," says Wesley Snipes's character to his Italian girlfriend).[29] But as we look back on several of these films, it becomes clear that the bulk of them indeed use the interracial love affair plot as a means of grappling with what has become known as the "wigger" phenomenon—slang for "white nigger," or the ways in which whites can (or cannot) potentially "become" black.

James Toback's *Black and White*, released in 2000, is a glaring example of a narrative that envisions interracial appropriation in terms of interracial sex. "What happens when you mix it up?" asked the provocative promotional tag line for the film, which tosses together a bevy of black and white characters and then lets us watch as they engage in sex, arguments, and murder (not necessarily in that order). With its star-studded cast of actors and rappers and its celebrity cameos, *Black and White* deals with the ways in which whites appropriate not blackness per se but black *masculinity*. The film's opening scene is designed to jar us. As a group of young black boys make their way through Central Park, laughing and spitting rhymes, they come upon a black man and two half-clad, young-looking white girls going at it in the woods to the tune of "Daddy's Little Girl." After treating us to a dollop of black and white flesh, Toback takes us to a townhouse where Charlie, one of the young white girls, arrives late for dinner. "I been at the *liberry*," she says to her scowling father, who corrects her pronunciation and asks that she remove her gold tooth.[30]

Cut to a scene in which Rich, the black man in the woods, arrives at a recording studio with his partner, Cigar. The two negotiate with a white record executive, who seems wary but interested in discovering what the rap duo can do for him. The film cross-cuts between Charlie's dinner table, at which she rails—in black "ghetto" slang—against her family's injunctions to "be a lady," and the white executive's studio, where Rich and Cigar negotiate with him. The message is clear: the two ways in which whites attempt to appropriate blackness involve sex and music.

Black and White's commentary on the music industry side of this equation is a crude cliché: white-dominated record labels control the reins (and wallets) of black rappers and singers. During the film's final moments, Rich and Cigar, having successfully made it as rappers, discuss the state of the industry. "Now it ain't no boundary," says Rich. "We all in it together, man: black people, white people, Asians—you know what I'm saying?—Indians, whoever. Nahmean? Looking on the TV seeing Japanese kids doing hip-hop and singing *your* song. There's a Japanese Cigar out there—you ever think of that?" Rich's words speak to the fact that in a contemporary global context, hip-hop and American urban culture are the country's biggest cultural export. Toback's main black characters, Rich and Cigar, are conceived as rappers in the film not only because they are rappers in real life (Oli "Power" Grant and Raekwon of the Wu-Tang Clan, respectively) but also because rap represents the primary way in which young whites seek to emulate blackness. Rap is also suffused with what Philip Brian Harper sees as the equation between authentic blackness and masculinity; for today's young white imagination, rappers are masculinity personified.

The point of *Black and White* is that everyone wants a piece of this black masculinity. The music industry executives want to market it for profit. Others want to milk it for sexual pleasure. Played by super-blonde supermodel Claudia Schiffer, Greta, a graduate student in anthropology writing her thesis about race, likes to share her bed with her ethnographic subjects: she lives with Dean, a college basketball player played by basketball star Allan Houston. The film's central drama centers on the efforts of Greta's ex-boyfriend Mark, a gambler turned cop, to indict Rich, rapper and thug about town, by way of Dean. Offering Dean $50,000 to fix his next game, Mark then uses the incident to blackmail Dean into ratting out his old friend Rich. Wielding this information as a means of seduction, Greta offers herself to Rich, who soon arranges to have Dean killed by his white lackey, Will. An entirely flat character, Greta is cold as ice and seemingly without any sort of dramatic motivation, save an all-consuming desire to be with a "real man." She left Mark for Dean when Mark abandoned his criminal ways; she left Dean for Rich when, as Mark tells her, she confronted weakness in Dean. And she leaves Rich, in the end, for the ultimate in black masculinity: Mike Tyson. Greta's man-hopping reflects the white woman's desire for the ultimate "real" man—a man who can only, of course, be black.

Charlie and her friends want a piece of Rich, too, not only because he turns them on but also because, as Charlie readily admits: "I want to be black. I want to get into the hip-hop thing." The crux of *Black and White* centers on the ways in which young "wiggers" use sexual tourism as a means of acquiring black legitimacy. "What do you think these white people really want from us, man?" Rich asks Dean. "You know what I'm talking about—white motherfuckers out here trying to imitate us, trying to dress black and all this shit, bitches throwing pussy all over. . . . I think they think they're gonna get some kinda life force or shit from fucking with us." Norman Mailer could not have said it more clearly (and he *did* say it, in 1959, describing the white man's quest for the ultimate orgasm). Of course, the acts of appropriation presented in the film are not entirely one-sided—Rich himself admits that with regard to Charlie, "I'm just trying to get a little of her information and see what I can do with it"—but *Black and White* is far more interested in what whites want from blacks than vice versa. The film's greatest flaw (and it has many) is that it makes Charlie and her friends hyper-aware of their desire to wear blackface. During a classroom discussion, which the young, with-it teacher kicks off with a quote he ascribes to Romantic painter Pierre Delacroix ("Young kids are always more given to examining what is wild than what is reasonable") and concludes with one from Iago ("I am not what I am"), Charlie and her friends sound like a page from an adolescent psychology textbook. "You don't want to be what people expect of your race. You know, like people say, 'Look, you're white, you have to be this way; you can't walk around and talk, whatever, Ebonics,'" says one girl. "What's wrong with choosing a style?" says another. Or as Charlie declares: "I'm a little kid, little kids are into phases. . . . I'm a kid in America. I can do whatever I want." These white high schoolers seem fully conscious of both their desire to "be black" and the transitory nature of this desire. As subjects of a documentary on the "wigger" phenomenon in America, they have no trouble admitting to Sam, the filmmaker who follows them around, that they are rebelling against their wealthy white parents, just as their parents rebelled against the elders of their own generation. The characters in *Black and White* wear their unconscious motivations on their sleeves, which ultimately makes the film painfully easy; the dynamics of contemporary black-white exchanges are far too complex and subconscious for such tidy explications. Instead of analyzing, Toback's film shocks. He substitutes depiction for discussion, announcement for analysis. As David Denby suggests in his review of *Black and White*, "perhaps material about race and ambivalence and the violence of attraction and distrust can't be resolved satisfactorily right now."[31]

The most glaringly uncritical aspect of the film is the way in which the "wigger" characters hope to acquire blackness by way of contact with black men, exactly as I have been describing throughout this chapter. The film is never short of explicit sexual scenes between black and white, and clearly what Charlie and her friends hope to swallow when they take in the black man is a little piece of his black essence—anything that will give them the authenticity they so desperately desire. Although we are treated to one sex scene in which Will, a white boy, is sandwiched between two black women, Will—like the women in the film—ultimately seeks legitimacy from black *men*. It is his pathetic need to be among Rich's posse that drives him to murder Dean, an event that sends him back into his wealthy father's open arms. *Black and White* is a film that locates authentic blackness in black men—specifically in black rappers—and thus allows its white "passers" to acquire this blackness by having sex with the "real thing."

This same ideology takes on a very different guise in the following year's *Save the Last Dance*, an MTV production—which Susan Wloszczyna in a review astutely called "a kind of *Guess Who's Coming to the Hip-Hop Club*"—about a white ballerina named Sara who, after her mother's death, is transplanted to inner-city Chicago to live with her estranged jazz musician father.[32] Struggling to fit in at an all-black school, Sara begins learning the ropes from Chenille, a black student who teaches her to say "slamming" instead of "cool." But Chenille is not a compelling enough link to the black world, so Sara becomes romantically involved with Derek, Chenille's strait-laced college-bound brother, who schools Sara in hip-hop dance 101. Sure enough, the film concludes with Sara winning acceptance to Julliard on the basis of her ability to incorporate hip-hop moves into her ballet routine, a moment that literalizes Sara's act of cultural crossover. Like *Black and White*, *Save the Last Dance* is both simplistic and cliché-laden; it evokes, in one fell swoop, *West Side Story*, *Flashdance*, and *Boyz in the Hood* (which presents the same conflict between the "good," college-bound black boy and the "bad," "thugged-out" black boy who is arrested in the end). And the film follows a by now familiar formula: white girl acquires—and materially and emotionally benefits from—blackness by way of sexual involvement with black boy. Of course, *Save the Last Dance* and *Black and White* are at opposite ends of the sexual spectrum. The latter hypersexualizes interracial sex, while the former desexualizes it (as Armond White put it in his scathing review of the film, "Plush-faced white girl Julia Stiles and her roundheaded black boyfriend Sean Patrick Thomas could grind all night and produce sexual sparks no more dangerous than Raggedy Ann and Andy dolls").[33] But these two approaches share the same underlying ideology: interracial sex is threatening to a white audience, and a film can either seize this threat and use it for titillating shock value, as *Black and White* does, or defuse this threat by making a film as neutered as *Save the Last Dance*.

Somewhere between these two approaches is the 1992 film *Zebrahead*, starring Michael Rapaport as Zack, a Jewish high school student in Detroit who has recently been dumped by his white girlfriend. The film's initial scenes establish interracial dating as a central theme. A group of black girls in the cafeteria discuss the types of men they would date. "I'd date an Italian boy, because he may look white, but he sure don't act white," says one.[34] Zack, it turns out, does not "act white" either. For one thing, he is Jewish, a fact emphasized at several points in the film. He is also a DJ who can sample James Brown and Puccini in the same set, and he comes from—gasp!—a single-parent home. His best friend, Dee, is black, and his father, a Casanova who surrounds himself with women in an attempt to get over the loss of his wife, owns a record store that has been in the family and on the cutting edge for decades; Zack's grandfather insists that "*we* broke out with Bebop; *we* did," and his father ceaselessly throws around such names as James Brown and Wilson Pickett.

The story takes off once Dee's cousin Niki moves to Detroit from East New York (a locale that presumably is meant to make her as "authentically black" as they come). Zack is immediately attracted to her, and on their first date she declares, "You're more on the homeboy side than on the white side." Zack replies: "This is Detroit; this is where I live. I may not live downtown, but it's still a predominately black city. This is me, though. This is who I am." Zack ultimately ends up vying for Niki's attentions with Nut, a stereotypical "truant black boy" who ends up killing Dee for being more loyal to Zack, a white boy, than to him. This chain of events does, in many ways, turn the film into a struggle between the "wigger" and the thug over who gets to *own* blackness, which seems, then, to be represented by Niki—a woman, not a man.

Yet the fact of the matter is that Zack does not need Niki for authentication because he is presented as equally "authentic," if not more so than she. Not only is his Jewishness highlighted as that which makes him not-quite-white, but also he is a respected DJ from a lower-middle-class family. As the new girl, Niki is in the same position as Sara of *Save the Last Dance*; Zack, giving her a tour of Detroit, reveals more to her than she does to him. Zack and Niki fight after he takes her to his white ex-girlfriend's party, where Niki overhears him telling his friends, "The blacker the berry, the sweeter the juice," but eventually it is Zack who gets the last word. "You're lucky," he shouts at her. "You were able to go to that party the other night and fit right in. I can't do that and I never could. You have a mother, and I can't remember mine . . . and you know how it is with my father." Zack's claim to blackness, so to speak, is acquired not through sex with Niki but through his friendship with Dee, a black man. The triangular relationship of Dee, Niki, and Zack suggests that the crucial exchange here is really between two *men*, one white and one black. Thus *Zebrahead*, like Kerouac's novel, does not present the black woman as capable of "transferring" blackness onto her white partner.

The same is true of Julie Dash's made-for-MTV film *Love Song* (2000). Set in New Orleans (and thus evoking Creole class pretensions), the film tells the story of Camille Livingston, the daughter of a black socialite, who becomes engaged to another wealthy black society boy, Calvin Dumas, but then falls in love with a white working-class musician, Billy Ryan. *Love Song* manifestly reverses expected class positions: here the black figure is wealthy and the white one is poor. Billy, who seems to have only black friends, shows Camille the "real" New Orleans, its smoky cafés and jazz joints—much as Zack shows Niki Detroit, and Derek reveals Chicago to Sara. As in *Zebrahead*, the white boy who falls for the black girl is in fact "blacker" than she—Billy is a highbrow version of a rapper, a respected blues musician in an all-black band—which means he does not have to appropriate anything from her. And that is a good thing, since the black woman seems never to be presented as a source of black "authenticity"—a position that, in all the narratives I have been discussing, is reserved for black *men*.[35]

Thus we see again how the American popular imagination is more captivated by the narrative of the black man and the white woman than it is by that of the white man and the black woman. Perhaps this is because whereas white men are permitted to dabble in the sexually "exotic," white women—bearers of the womb—pose the greater threat to the male public imagination when they do so. Or perhaps, as bell hooks proposes, it is just the opposite, and the white woman–black man scenario is actually *less* taboo to white audiences: "Since white women represent a powerless group when not allied with powerful white men, their marriage to black men is not a great threat to existing white patriarchal rule. In our patriarchal society if a wealthy white woman marries a black man, she legally adopts his status. Accordingly, a black woman who marries a white man adopts his status; she takes his name and their children are his heirs."[36] The hysterical, sometimes over-the-top quality of Halsell's text suggests that she believes the former to be true: interracial sex is indeed taboo, and violating this taboo is part of her overall attempt to violate the boundaries of whiteness.

Finally, though, there is something patently disquieting about the notion that passing as black, or cross-identifying as such, can be achieved through sexual proximity to blackness. That "something" is what is vexing about sexual tourism as whole: it reduces the Other to a territory worth tasting, traversing, and discarding. Reading *Soul Sister* today, one has a hard time *not* rendering judgment on Halsell's experiment, which is really a voyage of self-discovery. Its end—a desire to shed white privilege, to attain a kind of double consciousness—is noble, but the means to that end are ultimately self-defeating. They reduce and objectify the very people whom Halsell so desperately wants to elevate.

4

Contagious Beats
Passing, Autobiography, and Discourses of American Music

In 1926 the Salvation Army of Cincinnati received a court injunction to halt the construction of a movie theater next door to one of its homes for expectant mothers. It was not the sights emanating from this theater that so vexed Cincinnati residents but rather the *sounds* that might seep out of its doors. In a statement members declared that they were desirous of avoiding "the implanting of jazz emotions by such enforced proximity to a theater and jazz palace." Although today we might wonder just what a "jazz emotion" is, many Americans in the early part of the twentieth century knew all too well. "Jazz music causes drunkenness . . . by sending a continuous whirl of impressionable stimulations to the brain," declared Dr. Elliot Rawlings, a New York physician. "Reason and reflection are lost, and the actions of the persons are directed by the stronger animal passions." The Health Commissioner of Milwaukee agreed, explaining that jazz excited "the nervous system until a veritable hysterical frenzy is reached." A 1921 issue of *Ladies' Home Journal* stated that jazz music, in conjunction with the "crowd psychology" of "Negro dances," produces "an unwholesome excitement" in its listeners and went so far as to assert that on account of jazz, "the statistics of illegitimacy in this country show a great increase in recent years."[1]

In such critiques, which peaked in the 1920s but persisted until the 1940s, the meaning of "uncivilized" was overtly racialized. Dr. Florence Richards, medical director of a Philadelphia girls' high school, minced no words, remarking that "jazz's influence is as harmful and degrading to civilized races as it has always been among the savages from whom we borrowed it." It was not just any sort of hysteria that jazz could potentially unleash in its listeners; it was a distinctly racialized hysteria—since, after all, jazz was "black music." I have been arguing that an understanding of white passing hinges on ideas about proximity: by *being* near black—literally, socially, sexually—whites *become* near black. Early criticisms of jazz underscore yet another form of proximity to blackness that has transformative powers: listening to—or, even more so, playing—so-called black music. When critics and medical experts argued that the sound of jazz would bring out the barbarian in white listeners, they were essentially declaring that jazz could transform white to black. A *New York Times* article in 1922, for instance, lamented that black music would "get into the blood" of young whites and make white America like the "Negroes dancing in a Harlem cabaret . . . drunk with rhythm."[2] At the heart of Mrs. Max Obendorfer's claim, in an article for *Ladies' Home Journal* titled "Does Jazz Put the Sin in Syncopation?" that jazz "stimula[ted] the half-crazed barbarian to the vilest of deeds" lie cultural anxieties that stretch back to the late nineteenth century: What if jazz music, in its orgiastic frenzy, could turn white black? Such anxieties have long played themselves out in musical contexts. Beginning in the Reconstruction era, argues Ronald Radano, ideas about "black rhythm's 'infectious' nature" became widespread. In the 1890s, he writes, "ragtime addiction" became a recognized national phenomenon, akin to alcohol addiction. "Such imagined instabilities of an infecting and affecting hot rhythm suggest that the figurations of contagion were to be taken quite literally."[3]

In this chapter I explore the role of music as a potent agent of racial transformation. I return, in this regard, to the line between anxiety and fantasy. Whereas early censure of jazz reveals apprehensiveness about ways in which music can "blacken" its white listeners, this same claim becomes, for nonblack musicians playing what was broadly identified as "black music," a forceful fantasy. Whether in the context of jazz or hip-hop or rock 'n' roll, nonblack artists turned early misgivings into badges of pride, claiming that, yes, music can indeed turn them black—a fact they couldn't be more pleased about. Two autobiographical texts to which I turn in this chapter were written by musicians who, to use Nathan Huggins's words, "defected, became apostates . . . became Negroes"[4]: Mezz Mezzrow, the first famous white Negro and author of *Really the Blues*, and Johnny Otis, the legendary bandleader and musician who published his memoirs in *Upside Your Head! Rhythm and Blues on Central Avenue*. Although they span different decades as well as different coasts (Mezzrow moved between New York and Chicago, while Otis was firmly rooted in South Central Los Angeles), Mezzrow and Otis are of a piece. Their music, in a very literal sense, colored their lives. Both nonblack men passed as black (in their own eyes, at least); both engaged in cross-cultural identification within a musical context; both identified with blackness as a way of negotiating ethnic identities (Otis was Greek, Mezzrow a Russian Jew); both deliberately chose to resist the Americanization process and the whitening that comes with it. I focus on Mezzrow and Otis specifically because, simply put, they focus on themselves—on their personas as musicians and public speakers. Les Back and Vron Ware make a vital point when they argue that too often critics oversimplify the relationship of whites to "black" music, reducing the work of white musicians to imitation, slumming, or crude blackface. Their work on the interracial soul music scene in Muscle Shoals, Alabama, suggests that the white musicians "cannot be viewed as 'exceptional whites' or some version of modern black-face freaks without the burnt cork because they never 'crossed over'; they were never brought into focus. . . . [N]o one knew what they looked like; they only knew what they sounded like."[5] But Otis and Mezzrow—public figures who wrote books, men who were known as much for their personas as for their music—were not just heard but seen, in the same way that MTV-era artists have become not just musicians but *acts*. Like today's white rappers, Mezzrow and Otis reflected a kinship with "blackness" that was just as much visual as it was aural.

The comparison to white rappers here is deliberate; the final section of this chapter sets up a parallel between Mezzrow and Otis and white rapper Eminem, the contemporary personification of racial and musical crossover. All three genres—indeed, argues Barbara Browning, all African musical forms, which she rightly deems "infectious rhythms"—produced a wellspring of anxieties about a "blackening" pop culture and "were accompanied by equally 'contagious' dances, often characterized as dangerous, usually as overly sexually explicit, by white critics."[6] And all three genres defined their eras—the 1920s, the 1950s, and the 1990s—as moments when black culture hit the mainstream to an unprecedented extent. I have already discussed the 1920s and will discuss the 1990s in this chapter and the next. As for the 1950s, that decade completed and amplified the work that the 1920s had begun. It was the era in which, W. T. Lhamon argues, black culture "went national": it "crossed the Mason-Dixon line, jammed airwaves and stores and headlines, heavily influenced American literary forms and styles, commanded the attention of the Supreme Court, and involved itself with aspects of every extant form of art." Thanks to the public relations machine that was radio and television, the mid-fifties were "the precise moment when black culture should have become an apt symbol for the way millions of nonblacks wanted to be in the world."[7]

All three musical genres, too, are hybrid products. African, European, and American sounds resonate in jazz, for instance, while rap dips into African, African American, Caribbean, and Puerto Rican musical forms. Ironically, despite the hybridity of jazz and hip-hop, both have been defined as a site of authentic blackness and continue to be wrapped up in a rhetoric of authenticity. As Paul Gilroy writes:

> It is interesting that music has come to signify authenticity at the very moment when it has evolved into new styles that are inescapably hybrid and multiplex in character. Hip-hop was not an ethnically pure or particular African-American product but rather the mutant result of fusion and intermixture with Caribbean cultures from Jamaica and Puerto Rico. Its outer-national and intercultural origins are effectively concealed by powerful ethnocentric accounts of its history that see it merely as a direct descendent of jazz, soul, and blues.[8]

Perhaps America's fascination with musical crossover acts such as white jazzmen or white rappers stems from generalized cultural anxiety about the hybridity of American music—American culture, really—as a whole.

When it comes to music of any genre, authenticity is a highly charged issue. More than literary or visual art, music is generally seen as a barometer of "realness"—the most potent expression of selfhood, a mirror into the soul. This fact, which intimately binds the dancer and the dance, so to speak, encourages music fans to fixate on the authenticity of their favorite musicians; they must know whether they're real or "sellouts." Music associated with blackness, however, provokes particularly intense debate about authenticity because such music is popularly believed to come from deep within, from the "soul"; it has long been defined against the sterility, the inauthenticity, of "white" music. The ability to play a certain kind of music thus becomes a yardstick for measuring a musician's identity: if one can play "black" music, then one must, deep inside, posses a measure of blackness. The closer one's soul is to black people, the more "authentic" one's music—and identity—will be. In the context of jazz, rock 'n' roll, or hip-hop, then, music can change the beat of a white man's life.

Because it profiles musicians who pass, this chapter reflects a significant shift in the tenor of passing. Mezzrow and Otis cross-identified in a way that suggests their self-conscious appreciation of the African American musical aesthetic. Their passing, then, was more than skin deep. It reflected a depth of understanding about the fact that the essence of African American culture— the aesthetics of improvisation and "coolness," the ability to, as Ellison famously put it, "make life swing"—was distilled in African American music. For these men, to truly feel and play black music was, on a profound level, to truly feel black.

Johnny Otis's *Upside Your Head*

One day in 1956 a probation officer arrived at the home of Johnny Otis, the well-known musician and R&B promoter who had graced the cover of *Negro Achievements* magazine. Among his other accomplishments, Otis discovered and produced the first Chicano R&B sensation, Li'l Julian Herrera, the voice behind the local hit "Lonely Lonely Nights." The officer, recounts George Lipsitz in his introduction to Otis's *Upside Your Head*, asked Otis to help him locate a man named Ron Gregory, a name Otis was not familiar with. But when the officer pulled out a photo, Otis was in for a surprise: Li'l Julian Herrera was really Ron Gregory, a Hungarian Jew from the East Coast who had run away from home and been raised by a woman in the Boyle Heights section of Los Angeles. In an amusing turn of events, then, one of the first Chicanos to cross over into the black- and white-dominated world of R&B was actually a Hungarian Jew passing as Mexican. The irony of this anecdote runs deeper still, because Otis himself—one of the architects of L.A.'s black music scene, civil rights activist, pastor of a predominantly black church, and father of black-identified children—was not quite what he seemed to be either.

Born John Veliotes in 1921 to Greek immigrant parents, Otis grew up in an ethnically mixed but largely black neighborhood in Berkeley, California.[9] From his early days in church, Otis recounts, he identified more with the African American culture that surrounded him than with his own Greek American heritage. After dropping out of school to play drums in an all-black Oakland band and marrying his high school sweetheart, a black woman named Phyllis Walker, Otis eventually moved to Los Angeles, where he began an illustrious fifty-year career in blues, jazz, and R&B. As composer (his most famous piece is "Willie and the Hand Jive"), drummer, producer, radio DJ, promoter, civil rights activist, and preacher, Otis was involved with countless names in the history of blues, jazz, and R&B, from Count Basie to Big Mama Thornton and Esther Phillips; he was responsible for "discovering" such soul sensations as Jackie Wilson.[10] His antiracist activism led him twice to seek the Democratic Party's nomination for a seat in the California State Assembly and to publish a work on the 1968 Watts riots, *Listen to the Lambs*.

More a collection of poignant memories of a music scene than an autobiography, *Upside Your Head* chronicles in sketches and photographs Otis's journey from struggling blues drummer to vocal member of the African American community, one who ended up hosting California's weekly antiracist Pacifica Radio broadcasts and founding the Landmark Community Church, a nondenominational mixed-race church in southwest L.A. At the heart of this journey is another, more fundamental transformation, one that Otis scarcely addresses directly but which nonetheless sits at the forefront of his memoir. "I am concerned about my people . . . African Americans . . . who are held hostage by a hostile white majority," he writes.[11] How did Otis come to identify "my people" as the black community? In other words, how did a Greek boy grow up to become a black man?

The answer, Otis implies in *Upside Your Head*, lies in the music. A supporter of what he calls "unadulterated blues and jazz . . . in the true tradition of historic African American artistry . . . like Sarah, Ella, Roy Hamilton, or Charles Brown," Otis feels that whites simply cannot play the blues:

> When the music grows out of a unique way of life and it reflects the inside workings of a particular people, as the blues does, then it certainly follows that artists within that culture will function in a freer and more natural manner, and, no matter how skilled the emulator, he or she will never get it quite right. Eddie "Cleanhead" Vinson used to say that white performers, and particularly the singers, had the blues "Bassackwards." (107)

If only blacks can play jazz or blues—and Otis himself made a career out of playing this music—then it follows that Otis must be black; this is taken for granted throughout *Upside Your Head*. In his opening chapter Otis writes that the goal of his work is to "afford the reader a firsthand, insider's view of what it was like during that fascinating time when Los Angeles was giving birth to its rhythm and blues music style" (4). One would assume, reading this, that our narrator is an "insider"—a black man—especially since he consistently refers to himself as such. "I'm afraid we haven't preserved the traditional Black social wisdom," he states in an interview with several Central Avenue musicians, transcribed in *Upside Your Head*. "Our kids don't know how we are always in danger of disaster because of racism" (21). He describes Joe Louis as "our special hero, our personal sense of self-worth, our pride and joy, OUR BLACK SUPERMAN" (79). Otis experiences the evils of segregation while touring the South with his band mates: "Moving from town to town in our little raggedy school buses, having to go to the back door of restaurants to get something to eat, and being turned away at flea bag hotels and having to sleep in the freezing or sweltering bus—all this was hard to take. But the biggest hardship was

CONTAGIOUS BEATS

the funny hats and having to suffer through some of our bandleader's Uncle Tommish renditions such as 'Sonny Boy' or 'Shine'" (77). He shares moments of black pride, as when his tours included the Apollo Theater, when "we lived within the African-American communities, and as a result, were not subject to the kinds of racist pressure that we encountered elsewhere, especially in the Deep South" (88–89). Perhaps most important, Otis sees himself as an "authentic" black musician: "This authentic Black blues cultural element is the reason the Black bands were superior to the white bands. Many Black players may not have had the music lessons, the new musical instruments, and the technique of the whites, but *we* had that feeling" (40; emphasis added).

Yet despite his near-consistent use of "we" and his clear identification with the black community, there are recurring moments in *Upside Your Head* when Otis cannot help calling attention to his nonblack status. Otis remarks that his friends teasingly called him "hawk" on account of his "hawk nose" (74). His tours of the South often find him waxing romantic about the "soulfulness" of black culture in the voice of a white outsider—a voice that is at times reminiscent of Griffin's. During these moments, Otis slips into the third person when speaking of blacks:

> The whole flavor of traditional African American culture came to bear on their interpretations. The essence of traditional black singing and playing and the way the artistry was spun out . . . had to do with the way Black folks lived and were raised in their homes. The music grew out of the African American way of life. The way mama cooked, the Black English grandmother and grandfather spoke . . . the very special way the people danced, walked, laughed, cried, joked, got happy, shouted in church. (117)

In describing his Reno marriage to Phyllis, which "the state of California stymied . . . with an ugly, anti-miscegenation law" (59), Otis presents himself as both black and nonblack. The preacher who married the couple took Otis for black and, to Otis's dismay, launched into a racist diatribe about "you people" who "have the gift of singing and dancing, just as we excel in business and government" (59). Immediately after this incident, however, Otis describes his father's reluctant acceptance of Phyllis—"'Your mother sent me to annul the marriage, but I came to meet my new daughter,' he said in Greek, with tears in his eyes"—a poignant anecdote that highlights Otis's *nonblack* heritage (59). On page after page, "my people" refers to African Americans; yet in one of the text's final chapters, Otis vouches for his authenticity: "I have lived for over sixty years in the heart of the African American community, most of that time in the Los Angeles ghetto area. My wife, my children, and my grandchildren are Black" (151). Why in this instance does Otis not identify himself as black, since he does so at many other points in the text?

Upside Your Head, then, speaks from both sides of its mouth with regard to racial identity. On the one hand, Otis implies that the proximity to blackness that exists on so many levels of his life—he lived in a black neighborhood, married a black woman, and, most important, made a life and career in what he himself identifies as black music—enables him to adopt blackness and to pass as black. Yet on the other hand, he exhibits moments of anxiety about the authenticity of his passing and of his adopted identity as a black man.

It is through music that Otis resolves this tension. By shifting the focus of his memoir away from his personal life—about which he can be unexpectedly mum—and toward the music scene of which he was a part, Otis implies that his race is, in certain respects, the music itself. The nature of Otis's own racial identity is an elusive entity that haunts *Upside Your Head* but never ultimately surfaces; instead Otis defines himself through the music that has been his life's passion. With each page the memoir shifts further and further away from Otis himself. Section titles reflect this shift. Part one, "Central Avenue Breakdown," underscores the first key feature of Otis's identity: his neighborhood. Parts two through four, respectively titled "Rhythm and Blues," "The Musicians," and "The Music," forming the crux of the text, are concerned less with Otis himself than with his relationship to his music. The final two parts, "Preaching, Painting, and Plowing" and "The Los Angeles Rebellion and the Politics of Race," move even further away from Otis's personal story and instead focus on civil rights causes for which he fought.

For whites who identify as black, activism can provide a path out of the quagmire that is racial identity, a way of allowing thorny identity politics to be subsumed within public politics. In the nineteenth century, for instance, John Brown "wanted to be black—to look black and think black and act black (He may even have had his skin darkened on photographs to try to pass, in the opposite direction)"; abolitionist William Lloyd Garrison often told audiences that he came "as a black man" and "as one of you"; and Belgian journalist Jean-Charles Houzeau, editor of New Orleans's first black daily newspaper, "never sought to deny the rumor that I had African blood in my veins."[12] All three men, however, made personal issues of cross-identification beside the point; for them, public personas—causes—took center stage. Politics, a sense of historical consciousness shared with African Americans, plays this same self-defining role in Otis's life. But music, more than activism, becomes his way of eluding a neatly defined racial identity. Everything in *Upside Your Head*, even politics, comes down to music: "I find it impossible to separate a discussion of rhythm and blues from the social and political factors that bear on the African American people who invented the music," he writes (101). The most personal chapter of *Upside Your Head*, "Be-bop, Count Otis Matthews, and Me," substitutes a discussion of Otis's budding *racial* evolution with a description of his *musical* evolution: "Dropping all the pseudo-elitist notions about what was 'best' in music and who was modern and who was dated, helped to prepare me for my role in rhythm and blues" (55). Music serves as the defining feature of Otis's identity in *Upside Your Head* because music is the very embodiment of African American culture. In the music of his horn players, Otis hears, to quote this significant passage again, "the way mama cooked, the Black English grandmother and grandfather spoke . . . the very special way the people danced, walked, laughed, cried, joked, got happy, shouted in church. In the final analysis, what forms the texture and adds character to the music is the African American experience." To live black music, then, is to live all that critics have defined as the African American aesthetic: a "swinging" style of speech, of cooking, of dancing, of carrying oneself cool in the world.[13] Otis self-consciously fashions himself as the bearer of this tradition; his notes define him, and his notes are anything but white.

"Really" Mezz Mezzrow?

Otis is not alone in crafting his identity this way. When, in a 1968 interview, Chicago-born clarinetist Mezz Mezzrow asserted that "as a man thinks, so he is," he may have uttered his life's mantra.[14] After all, throughout his memoir *Really the Blues*—a jive-inflected story of the Chicago and New York jazz scenes from the 1920s to the 1940s which later influenced the "white Negroes" of the Beat movement—Mezzrow, son of Russian Jewish immigrants, informs readers that he indeed thinks like a black man. "I went in there green but I came out chocolate brown," he says of his days in the Pontiac Reform School, where he first encountered jazz.[15] While journeying back to Chicago from Pontiac, Mezz recalls an earlier journey that he and several Jewish friends had taken through Cape Girardeau, Missouri. "Dirty from riding the rails and dark-complexioned to begin with," Mezz recounts, he and his crew are denied service at a lunch counter because they are identified as black (17–18). Reflecting on his days at the Pontiac, Mezz then has a revelation, one that sets the tone for the rest of *Really the Blues*: "We were Jews, but in Cape Girardeau they had told us we were Negroes. Now, all of a sudden, I realized that I agreed with them. That's what I learned in Pontiac. The Southerners had called me a 'nigger-lover' there.

Solid. I not only loved those colored boys, but I was one of them—I felt closer to them than I felt to the whites, and I even got the same treatment they got" (18). Though he traveled the music circuit twenty years before Otis did, Mezzrow too writes a text about the music that changed not only his life but also his race. And he anchors it in an era—the 1920s—during which white passing became more about fantasy than anxiety.[16]

Unlike *Upside Your Head*, *Really the Blues* is self-consciously autobiographical. Mezz met journalist and critic Bernard Wolfe in a jazz club in 1942 and agreed to share his story; Wolfe and Mezzrow published the memoir in 1946, and Wolfe himself was then inspired to publish several pseudoscientific articles on a phenomenon he called "negrophilia." Some historical context is helpful in understanding Mezzrow's text. The position of whites in jazz history goes back to "Dixieland," the poor-white band music that grew up, during the 1890s, alongside New Orleans jazz.[17] But while Dixieland was generally loath to acknowledge its debt to black music, another prominent group of white jazzmen—the 1920s Chicago white jazz movement of which Mezzrow was sometimes a part—"innovated and rebelled," writes Burton Peretti, "by willingly becoming musically subordinate to a socially and culturally subordinate group": blacks. William Howland Kenney describes the "Chicagoans" as a "self-proclaimed inner circle of white true believers in jazz, surrounded, as they saw it, by a deadening middle-class world of crass commercialism."[18] He delineates three categories of white Chicago jazz musicians: those born in city neighborhoods (such as clarinetist Benny Goodman and drummer Vic Berton, as well as Mezzrow himself, who grew up on the Northwest Side), those born in the suburbs (drummer Dave Tough, clarinetist Bud Jacobson), and those born outside Chicago altogether (cornetist Bix Beiderbecke). The most famous group of Chicagoans came to be known as the Austin High Gang, a group of rebels who hailed from what Mezz describes as "a well-to-do suburb where all the days were Sabbaths, a sleepy-time neighborhood as big as a yawn and just about as lively, loaded with shade-trees and clipped lawns and a groggy-eyed population that never came out of its coma except to turn over" (103).

The geography of Chicago jazz underscores a crucial difference between Mezzrow's and Otis's literal positions in relation to black musicians. While Otis lived among blacks in a city that was not known for what we might call "musical tourism"—whites leaving their neighborhood in an effort to encounter "black" music—Mezzrow's Chicago was renowned for precisely that. Black musicians could not enter white clubs, but white jazzmen had the freedom to journey to the South Side and become schooled in the ways of "true" jazz. Much of *Really the Blues* details this literal and metaphorical journey between two very distinct spaces. Mezz calls his first visit to the South Side "my big night, the night I really began to live" (29), and he spends his early days commuting from North Side to South, even from nearby suburbs and towns (such as Burnham) to the South Side of Chicago. He was eager to become not a commuter, a tourist on the South Side, but a resident there. This same pattern followed him to New York, where he relocated during the late 1920s. Just as Carl Van Vechten led renowned "tours" to Harlem, during which white patrons could enjoy sexual and musical tourism, Mezz himself "dragged so many cats uptown, I got to be known as the 'link between the races' after a while" (208).

This geographical arrangement echoes the demarcated spaces of *Black Like Me*, in which Griffin draws a clear line between white and black worlds. Like Griffin's, Mezzrow's passing is bound up in literal boundary crossing, a theme that harks back to the birth of white passing, a product of anxieties about the elimination of literal and social space between black and white. White passing narratives are thus often involved in negotiating spaces between worlds, reversing the sort of literal movement from one (racialized) space to another that we find in black passing narratives: John Walden moves from North Carolina to South Carolina in *The House Behind the Cedars*; Mimi Daquin moves from Harlem to Greenwich Village in *Flight*. This movement from one space to another often serves to maintain racial distinctions in narratives that elsewhere call them into question. In *Really the Blues*, Mezz acquires "blackness" not only through music and sex (several of his wives were black) but also by traversing the boundaries between the white and black musical worlds. And yet the line between North and South Side Chicago, or uptown and downtown New York, seems a constant taunt to him, a perpetual reminder that although he may inhabit the black man's space, although he may play his music and marry his women, Mezz must forever cross a literal line in order to be with blacks—or to *be* black himself.[19]

Homosocial bonds are one way in which Mezzrow attempts to attain the authenticity that eludes him. Closeness to black men becomes a badge of authenticity for Mezz, as it does for other white male passers. Except for a brief mention here and there, women barely enter the text of *Really the Blues*; after all, writes Mezz, "women were a dime a dozen, but where could you find a good New Orleans jazz band?" (24). But Mezzrow's two father figures, Bix Beiderbecke and Louis Armstrong, loom large in the narrative. In many respects the text is a paean to Armstrong, in whose shadow Mezz humbly resides: "I hope [Armstrong] digs these records some day, and reads this book, too. They'll tell him all the things I just couldn't get my lips to say" (332–33). Additionally, Mezz never misses the chance to idealize his bonds with groups of black men, "the guys I felt were my real brothers, the colored musicians who made the music that sent me" (49). Of his friends in Harlem, Mezz recalls wistfully: "White guys in the same situation would be shooting each other up all over the place, trying to move in on each other. There was never a breath of competition between us. We were all real good friends" (229).

Like *Upside Your Head*, *Really the Blues* revolves around a quest for "realness" that is interrogated at every turn. Mezzrow and Otis appear both black and nonblack in their respective narratives; their status as successful passers is not resolved by either text. Yet this fact is only a starting point for an understanding of *Really the Blues* (and, in many respects, of *Upside Your Head*). First, Mezzrow's passing is not uniform throughout his memoir; on the contrary, it becomes more pronounced toward the end of the narrative. Although chapter 1 opens, as I have noted, with his transformation from "green" to "chocolate brown," Mezz spends much of the text speaking of a mere identification with what he sees as a black worldview, all the while circulating among blacks, whites, Italians, and Jews. It is only at the conclusion of *Really the Blues* that Mezz calculatingly engages in passing. In a Harlem jazz club he chides two girls trying to pass for white, who in turn accuse him of passing for white himself: "To this day those girls probably believe that I was passing. 'If you ain't one of us,' they argued, 'how in hell could you play that horn the way you do?' How I wished they were right" (204).[20] It is in Harlem that Mezz says his "education was completed . . . and I became a Negro" (210). Then, during a turning point in the text, when he is imprisoned at Rikers Island in New York, he declares himself colored to the warden, who "seemed a little relieved when he saw my nappy head," and enters his race as "Negro" (305). While in jail, Mezz is identified as black on two occasions, first by the Jewish musicians who "can't understand how come a colored guy digs the spirit of their music so good," and later by the judge who sends him back to jail because, as he puts it, "if I let you go you'll get right out with all the rest of your people and re-elect Roosevelt" (316, 319).

It is true that, like Otis, Mezzrow makes slippery use of self-reflexive pronouns in much of *Really the Blues*: sometimes blacks are "we" and sometimes "they," and Mezz alternately refers to himself, whether in his own voice or that of other figures in his narrative, as white, black, and Jewish. But perhaps this slipperiness is a product of the fact that Mezzrow's perception of himself changed over time. His passing, it seems, was a gradual enterprise, so that he did not start to pass as black until later in his life—which may be why the final pages of the text find a more strongly identified "black" Mezzrow than do the earlier pages. This is borne out by the articles about Mezzrow published after

Really the Blues made a stir, most notably an extended profile in *Ebony* titled "Case History of an Ex–White Man." The article calls Mezz "one of the few whites in the United States today passing for colored" and "in psychological makeup . . . completely a black man [who] proudly admits it." Since his stint at Rikers, the article continues, "he has given his race as Negro whenever asked," and he "denies that his [marriage to a black woman] is an interracial marriage. 'We're three of a kind,' he says sincerely." The birth of Mezzrow's son Milton Jr., the piece goes on, "marked the end of his search for a complete Negro identity. He had found himself in Harlem."[21] The article concludes with a mention of the two books that Mezz planned to write (but never did), both about the exploits of a white man passing for black. A 1951 article titled "Mezzrow Talks about the Old Jim Crow"—the very title authenticates his position as a black man—includes an anecdote about Mezzrow's being taken for "a Negro who's trying to pass the line."[22] It seems as if Mezz became more and more comfortable in his self-proclaimed "black" skin over time. And the more he came to envision himself as black, the more others followed suit.

It is through language—self-conscious mastery of African American vernacular—that Mezzrow most profoundly attempts to pass. He uses "jive to fashion a 'black' self on paper."[23] He may have been a mediocre cornet player, but Mezz was one heck of a jive talker. His identification with blackness is thus shored up by his ability to "signify." He proudly shows us, throughout *Really the Blues*, that he can talk the talk; he even provides the uninitiated with a "how to" manual: the memoir's appendix features an entire chapter "translated" into jive. This vernacular aspect of white passing harks back to *Pudd'nhead Wilson*, in which Chambers and Roxy are identified as black by way of their dialect. To be Other is to speak as Other, a sport Mezzrow relished.

As golden tongued as he is, however, Mezz underscores his verbal mimicry: "It's a fact—I wasn't putting my mind to it, but I'd started to use so many of the phrases and intonations of the Negro, I must have sounded like I was trying to pass for colored. . . . I was going on to twenty-seven, a Chicago-born Jew from Russian parents, and I'd hardly ever been south of the Capone district, but I sounded like I arrived from the levee last December" (111–12). Earlier in the text he humorously describes his sister's efforts to correct Bessie Smith's lyrics "until they sounded like some stuck-up jive from *McGuffy's Reader* instead of the real down-to-earth language of the blues," an anecdote that emphasizes the "proper" English on which he was raised (54). Such incidents suggest that despite the way in which his passing becomes more absolute as his narrative progresses, Mezzrow is at heart profoundly self-conscious about this struggle to be "really" a black man and "really" a jazzman. Gayle Wald discusses Mezzrow's inability to live up to an "authentic" black ideal, yet she fails to highlight just how eager Mezz himself is to underscore this fact. He writes unabashedly and poignantly of his own insecurities with regard to the color line:

> The race made me feel inferior, started me thinking that maybe I wasn't worth beans as a musician or any kind of artist, in spite of all my big ideas. The tremendous inventiveness, the spur-of-the-moment creativeness that I saw gushing out in all aspects of Harlem life, in the basketball games, the prize-fights, the cutting contests, the fast and furious games of rhyming and snagging on The Corner— it all dazzled me, made me doubt if I was even running with these boys. (239)

Mezz thus persistently highlights his own ambiguous racial status, his position as both "real" and "fake." Why?

Perhaps because throughout his life he remained entrenched in rhetoric about who had rights to jazz music. From the birth of the genre until well into Mezzrow's day, the question of whether anyone but African Americans could really play jazz was an incessant subject of debate among critics and musicians. "In a way, Mr. DuBois is right when he says that white musicians can play ragtime as well as Negro musicians; that is, white musicians can play exactly what is down on the paper," wrote James Weldon Johnson in his essay "The Poor White Musician." "But Negro musicians are able to put into the music something that can't be put on the paper, a certain abandon which seems to enter in the blood of the dancers, and that . . . is why Negro musicians are preferred." Eddie Condon, a white Chicagoan, agreed: "The Negro is born with rhythm. . . . We've got to learn it." Sidney Bechet, one of Mezz's idols, declared that white jazz "wasn't our music. . . . [I]t's awful hard for a man who isn't black to play a melody that's come deep out of black people"; he thus proclaimed that because Mezzrow "tried so hard to be something he isn't," the result was that "some of it would show up in his music, the idea of it would be wrong." Because, as Andrew Ross notes, during the Harlem Renaissance "black culture, and especially jazz, was cast as a vital and *natural* source of spontaneous, pre-civilized, anti-technological values—the 'music of the unconscious,' of uncontaminated and untutored feeling and emotion,'" the predominant view was that only blacks could truly play jazz and blues, because only they were in touch with this "primitivity."[24]

Such discourse left Mezz in a bind. On the one hand, as a committed jazz musician desperate to be accepted among the men he held in great esteem,

Mezz had to vouch for his authenticity—he had to pass. But on the other hand, as Henry Louis Gates puts it, "to pass is a sin against authenticity." [25] Mezz's purist bent left him little choice but to adopt a purist approach to the jazz debate, to assert that in fact only "real" blacks can play jazz. This accounts for his consistent need throughout *Really the Blues* to accentuate his *in*authenticity—for jazz is, in the eyes of the traditionalists with whom Mezz aligned himself, only for the black soul. The tension between these two ideologies is at the heart of his simultaneous self-presentation as both "real" and "fake"; it is the tension between the desire to *affirm* authenticity as a value and the longing to *be* authentic.

Mezz's entire vocabulary for speaking about jazz, after all, hinges on the gulf between "real" and "fake." In *Blues People*, LeRoi Jones noted that by the era of bop, when Wolfe and Mezzrow were writing *Really the Blues*, Dixieland revival groups were prevalent, whites had become the premier jazz critics, and there was much "senseless debate" about what "real" jazz was. [26] *Really the Blues*—from title to text—is a product of this rhetoric. Ultimately for Mezzrow "real" jazz is more than just a product of a black "soul." It hails from New Orleans ("the real jazz, like the real marihuana, comes from the bayou country," he says [92]; when Mezz makes it to New Orleans he proclaims that "for the first time in my life, you see, I had fallen all the way into the groove and I was playing real authentic jazz, and it was *right*—not Chicago, not Dixieland, not swing or jump or Debussy or Ravel" [294]). "Real" jazz is unwritten ("written music is like handcuffs . . . jazz and freedom are like synonyms" [125]) and performed by "insiders" ("whenever the outsiders pick up the jazzman's colloquialisms they kick them around until the words lose all their real fresh meaning" [142]). Most important, "real" jazz is never commercial, which means that "real" jazz musicians never have money in their pockets. In Mezzrow's eyes, the music industry operates in remarkably simple terms: "Somebody blows his guts out creating a new and authentic art form, then the unhip boys with shrewd commercial instincts come along and begin exploiting it, without bothering to learn it first. The result is that the public hears only the bastard version and goes crazy about it, figuring it's the real thing" (151). The general public, then, is a sucker; it "isn't hip enough," writes Mezzrow, "to separate what's authentic and what's phony" (352). Jazz is always, for Mezz, about "us" versus "them": "We were the keepers of the faith, the purists, the cats who stayed with it. The others were out to make money, not music," because to him, one can never make both (139). [27] He condemns Tin Pan Alley and big band music as poor copies of the real thing. The Holden Caulfield categories used here—Salinger's famous fictional adolescent tirelessly disparages the "phonies" of the world—

indicate why *Really the Blues*, with its binary divisions between real and fake, became gospel to one of the first great youth movements in America: the Beats. Jack Kerouac and Neal Cassady read Mezzrow in the 1950s and imitated his pose and prose; they were avid fans of *Really the Blues* and of Mezzrow himself, who lived, as Kerouac put it, on "the Great Negro sidewalk of the world."[28] As a whole, *Really the Blues* is a text fixated not simply on racial authenticity, on the way in which Mezzrow simultaneous passes and *poses*, but also on *musical* authenticity.[29]

Of course racial and musical authenticity are always, for Mezzrow, related. As I have noted, he is caught between affirming authenticity as a value, in which case he can never really pass and can never really play jazz, and affirming his own authenticity, in which case he must vouch for his legitimacy and speak of his passing. I want to suggest that ultimately, to escape this dilemma—he is uncomfortable passing yet also uncomfortable *not* passing—Mezz takes the same routes that Otis does. First, just as Otis comes to affirm the value of a multiracial milieu (at the end of *Upside Your Head* he boasts that his congregation is composed of blacks, whites, Latinos, Asians, and even several Jews and Buddhists), Mezz comes to idealize the mixed-race band. He speaks of organizing the "first important mixed-band recording dates that I know of" with Armstrong as the "idea of the millennium" (241); he becomes "the mixed-band king for a day" by getting such men as Benny Goodman and Pops Foster to collaborate (269), and later orchestrates a mixed band at Rikers. For both Mezzrow and Otis, then, the mixed-race setting becomes the ultimate one—perhaps because it allays their own racial anxieties. If the ideal music scene includes all sorts of players, then what does it matter what race they, Otis and Mezzrow, are anyway?

Mezzrow's second resolution to the problem of authenticity lies in the notion, equally applicable to Otis, that music can allow one to sidestep traditional lines of race altogether. While in Harlem, Mezz is struck by the wide appeal of jazz:

> Here was the phenomenon of jazz again. No matter who I played those records for—the Paris symphony or the Minsky house band, the turned-up noses in Park Avenue drawing rooms or the turned-down ones on the ghetto, the intelligentsia or the people who couldn't even read—I got the same response. "Wonderful!" they all shouted, knocked out by the beauty of this music, its pulse, its romance and soulfulness. . . . It taught me that all in all, what we got here is a real people's music. (202)

Jazz is the "glue" that holds Mezzrow's disparate circles of friends together. It is what makes Bix Beiderbecke, who "was born with harmony in his soul, and chords instead of corpuscles," a father to Mezz (81). "That's how it is," he writes, "when you play music with a man you understand and who understands you. . . . You speak the same language" (82). Jazz unites Mezz with the Austin High Gang, who Mezz says "vibrate" to the "tune" of the South Side "the way I did" (106). Throughout *Really the Blues*, jazz musicians—white, black, Italian, or Jewish—stand in a category of their own: "You can't blame them for walking around with a superior air, partly because they're plain lonely and partly because they know they've got hold of something good, a straight slant on things, and yet nobody understands it" (83). At various points in the text, Mezzrow's "we"—that slippery pronoun—refers only to the "race" of people known as jazz musicians. "Our music was called 'nigger music' and 'whorehouse music,'" he writes. "Jazz musicians were looked down on by the so-called respectable citizens as though they were toads that crawled out from under a rock" (61).

Later in his life Mezzrow continued to feel that only music could "crash the barriers of bias and hatred in racial matters and can help evoke a new civilization and culture which is needed, for to understand jazz you don't need to be technically minded and it's evident wherever I've been that people from all walks of life and colours of skin enjoy jazz in whatever form."[30] Music is, for Mezzrow and Otis, an answer to the ever-present question that is racial identity; it is the African American experience in its most distilled form. On account of its "ability to exceed the discursive force field of racial classification in American society," music becomes a way to hold one label—"musician"— above the traditional identity tags that neither Mezzrow nor Otis is completely comfortable wearing.[31] Both *Upside Your Head* and *Really the Blues* are texts about a unique sort of white passing: their authors fashion a race out of their livelihood.

Music and "Americanness"

In a certain respect, however, it is inaccurate to speak of Otis and Mezzrow as white-to-black passers because each identified as not-quite-white. Although he makes scarce mention of it in his work, Otis was raised in a traditional Greek home. Mezz, despite his claim that "being a Jew didn't mean a thing to me" and his doubt as to whether "we were a 'race,'" never seems to miss a chance to underscore his Jewish heritage (49, 390). Growing up on Chicago's Northwest Side, he is taunted for being Jewish. In jail he finds the posters he has put up sullied by swastikas. He shares a note from his father: "'Go anywhere you wish son,' he wrote, 'but always remember, *sei a mensch*.' That's the Yiddish for 'be a human being'" (188). Some critics have suggested that for immigrants, assimilation often took the form of African American identification;[32] others, however, propose that performance of or identification with blackness is, as Maria Damon puts it, "motivated not by the impulse to assimilate but by the impulse to resist."[33] My reading of *Really the Blues* is in line with this latter assessment, particularly because throughout his text Mezz seems consciously to create parallels between blacks and Jews. Not only are they lumped together by others—"You goddamn Jews and niggers are always duckin' work," says the deputy warden at the Pontiac Reform School (35)—but also in Mezzrow's eyes they share an innate understanding of jazz music, for him a most profound connection. Like *The Jazz Singer*, which sets up a parallel between jazz music and the Jewish "prayer" of a ghetto that, as the film puts it, "beats to a song older than civilization," *Really the Blues* often presents Jews and blacks as two races united by a common music—and by extension a common "soul."[34] Early in the text Mezzrow describes an "old Jewish man with a long beard and a little yomelkeh" in Chicago's Jewish ghetto listening to Blind Lemon Jefferson's *Black Snake Moan* and "shaking his head sadly, like he knew that evil black snake personally" (52). While at Rikers, Mezz—"a colored guy"—is asked to lead the Hebrew choir and is struck by the relationship between the two forms of music he might claim as his own: "I find out once more how music of different oppressed peoples blends together. Jewish or Hebrew religious music mostly minor, in a simple form, full of wailing and lament. When I add Negro inflections to it they fit so perfect, it thrills me. . . . I just sing 'Oh, oh, oh' over and over with the choir because I don't know the Hebrew chants, but I give it a weepy blues inflection and the guys are all happy about it" (316). The scene is ironic to the point of being comic: Mezzrow, a self-identified black man who was born a Jew, adds "black authenticity" to a Jewish choir.

The scene is also reminiscent of George Gershwin's tour of South Carolina with his friend DuBose Heyward, who wrote the novel on which Gershwin based *Porgy and Bess*. Heyward, a longtime resident of Charleston who called the trip more a homecoming than a visit, recalled an outing to a black church in which Gershwin took over, unasked, from the lead Negro "shouter" and led the congregation. The musical link between Jews and blacks, after all, runs deep. During the early decades of the twentieth century the two groups virtually created American popular music, engaging in a complicated love-hate dance during which Jews "capitalized on their ability to convey both closeness to the cultural stuff of 'Blackness' and distance from actual African Americans." Such appropriations, according to Jeffrey Melnick, enabled audiences to "have their cake and eat it too: not having to choose one or the other, spectators could consume Blackness as something which resided inside Jewishness."[35] Thus were born Tin Pan Alley legends: Irving Berlin signed himself "Cooney" and was rumored to have a "little colored boy" write all his songs; Sophie Tucker was taken by Europeans as black on the basis of her voice alone; Harold Arlen was supposedly called by Ethel Waters the "Negro-ist" white man she had ever known, and a songwriting colleague claimed Arlen was "really one of them." The black-Jewish musical exchange, to some extent, went both ways: Melnick notes several instances of black men who, during the 1920s, sang Yiddish songs.[36] Mezzrow's initial identification with blackness, then, is not tremendously extraordinary; by the 1920s, Melnick notes, "Jewish musical figures began actively to encourage interpretations of themselves which emphasized their natural sympathy for African American music and their (perhaps now voluntary) closeness to African Americans."[37]

In time, however, musicians such as Berlin famously began denying the black sources of their music and "whitening" their image. Melnick argues that the Jewish musicians' success lay in their ability to "assimilate and repackage Blackness," to create a "Jewish pastiche" that often masked the myriad sources from which their music sprouted. "It was understood on Broadway," Ann Douglas explains, that "you started black or ethnic and got whiter and more Wasp as, and if, success came your way."[38] Though he considers the ways in which Jews both likened themselves to and distanced themselves from blackness, Melnick, like Michael Rogin, ultimately reads performances of blackness (with or without actual blackface) as assimilating agents. As a potent example he cites the case of "Jewish Negro" and Mezzrow contemporary Artie Shaw. In his memoir *The Trouble with Cinderella*, Shaw, who grew up on New York's Lower East Side and then in New Haven, writes of being an "undesirable alien" in America, left with no choice but to erase his Otherness in the simplest way possible—by changing his name:

Art Shaw. Doesn't *sound* very "foreign." Certainly doesn't sound much like a Jewish kid, either, does it?

Well, what's he look like, maybe we can tell something that way? Dark hair, dark brown eyes, fairly regular features—could be almost anything, almost any nationality, Spanish, Italian, French, Russian, Greek, Armenian, damn near anything at all. In short, an American kid—may as well let it go at that. Although Shaw *sounds* Irish, wouldn't you say? Or maybe English? Anyway, what difference does it make? At least he's not a Jew or a "foreigner," so that's all right.[39]

The trajectory of Shaw's identity stands in sharp contrast to Mezzrow's: while Shaw grew whiter with time, Mezz grew blacker. As I see it, Mezzrow diverges from other Jewish (and ethnic) performers of black music by taking his adoption of blackness much further than they did. Whereas Gershwin's "Blackness" was, says Melnick, "temporary, detachable, and merely functional," Mezzrow's black identity was anything but.[40] Unlike the blackface wearers Rogin studies in *Blackface, White Noise*, or the musicians discussed by Melnick in *A Right to Sing the Blues*, Mezzrow ultimately accentuates, rather than erases, his Otherness—both as a Jew and as a black man. Mezz defiantly refuses to "whiten" with time. He indeed changes his name—but he changes it in order to align himself with another "Othered" race, that of the jazz musician. His fantasy is not one of assimilation or temporary appropriation; it is one of total passing.

In light of this fantasy, Mezzrow's attitude toward his own Jewishness is remarkably conflicted: he both negates and underscores it. This, I suggest, is so because, on the one hand, his fixation on authenticity leads him to distance himself from those Jewish musicians who sought to "water down" blackness. Since for many people "Negro" came to signify "real" jazz while "Jewish" implied "ersatz" (the former was, as Alain Locke put it, "primitively erotic" and the latter "decadently neurotic"), Mezzrow must align himself with those who play what is *really* the blues." But on the other hand, forging a link between Jews and blacks is another way in which Mezz authenticates his passing: his heritage, he implies, already "blackens" him in some way. While Jewish musicians like Bud Freeman identified with blacks yet still spoke of them as an Other—"It was not just their music that moved me but the whole picture of an oppressed people who appeared to be much happier than *we whites* who had everything," Freeman writes in his memoir *Crazeology*—Mezzrow uses his Jewishness to break down such binaries, highlighting his bond with blackness.[41] Such an act underscores his essential nonwhiteness and, ultimately, facilitates his crossing of the color line. Underscoring ethnic/nonwhite status, idealizing multiracial settings, mastering black vernacular in their memoirs, establishing music as a distillation of the African American race itself all are ways in which Otis and Mezzrow negotiate the myriad complexities of adopting a black identity.

Hip-Hop's Passing Beats

To turn from jazz and R&B to contemporary hip-hop involves a natural leap. Hip-hop is another innovation that revolutionized America's musical and racial landscape, and the discourse surrounding its white practitioners resoundingly echoes that of earlier eras.

Although rap music rose like a phoenix from the ashes of the South Bronx in the 1970s, it was not until the mid-1980s that white critics and audiences took notice and then became prime consumers of it. By the early 1990s whites and blacks alike were avidly lapping up one particular genre of hip-hop that made the cultural gatekeepers' hair stand on end: gangsta rap. Even though pundits had long leveled attacks on the genre of hip-hop, claiming, among other things, that it wasn't music at all ("Rap Is Crap," declared one *Los Angeles Times* headline), gangsta rap incited their venom like little else. "Rap seems to share many of the dangerous qualities of nicotine," wrote a black *Washington Post* editorialist in 1994. "It is addictive (or at least habituating); it is available in some particularly deleterious strains, and it is mood-altering." The column cites a study with deplorable findings: "Violent rap increases the consumer's tolerance of—and predisposition to—violence," while nonviolent rap "exacerbates the tendency toward materialism, reduces interest in academics and makes long-term success seem less likely."[42] *USA Today* also voiced concern about the persuasive power of hip-hop: "Without a new strategy to confront the roots of gangsterism and drive-bys—the absent opportunities and absent anchors and all-too-present drugs—a new generation will surely be seduced."[43] In an essay about rap censorship, Betty Houchin Winfield analyzes the overtly racialized quality of this seduction: "When rap music began appearing in the public consciousness by the mid-1980s, it represented a joining, gang-type of expression. The adult fear was that American youth would indeed 'join' and empathize with the black adolescents' urban experience."[44] The "American youth" about whom adults were—and continue to be—so concerned are, more often than not, white. As one *New York Times* letter writer stated in response to an early 1990s editorial attack on gangsta rap, "The perceived dangers of sex and politics in black music have been inventions fueled by white fear."[45] The more white youth shopped in the "rap" section of their local mall's record store, the more critics bemoaned the hazardous effects of the music. The implication is both clear and familiar: music has transformative power, and listening to "black" music can make whites behave in "black" ways. I do not mean to undermine legitimate studies exploring rap's effects—positive as well as negative—on young listeners. But I do want to underscore the hysterical nature of the discourse surrounding rap music in the late 1980s and 1990s, and especially the reliance of this rhetoric on metaphors of seduction and contagion. Such language echoes the discourse about musical "contagions" of other eras: jazz and rock 'n' roll.

Within this rhetoric a rift between "good" and "bad" black music is born: the former is (like the "good" black boy in such early-1990s hip-hop films as *Boyz in the 'Hood* and *Menace II Society*) titillating but ultimately tame, while the latter is too wild and "primitive" to be contained. More recently the binary has been neatly embodied in the contrast between the top-selling rappers Kanye West (college educated, middle class, and lyric centered) and 50 Cent (a larger-than-life caricature of all things gangsta). Crispin Sartwell gave voice to this dualism in the 1990s in a biting depiction of Tipper Gore, spokeswoman for (white) censorship:

> As Tipper defends our children, she does so in the blandest, most boring way; she appears in her pure whiteness. She becomes a pale spokeslady for pale "family values," the neutral ethical centerpoint on which we are all supposed to be agreed. She even claims a kind of nice appreciation for sixties black music, nice party dance music: We normal matrons aren't racist. We like black music, as long as it stays apolitical and doesn't offend us or corrupt our children. . . . White culture, in the person of Tipper Gore, can consume and enjoy black cultural production as long as it stays in its place.[46]

When Brent Staples, a black cultural critic, speaks of gangsta rap as "culturally poisonous," writing, "the last thing young people need is someone advising them to shoot first and talk later," he conjures up a malevolent blackness with the potential to infect both white and black listeners—an image that intensifies the rift between "good" and "bad" black music.[47]

Such rhetoric about contagion has fueled the cultural dialogue surrounding white rappers from Vanilla Ice to Fred Durst and Eminem. As critics waxed hysterical about the power of music to alter one's racial identity, whites trying to make it in hip-hop seized on the notion that listening to and producing black music could encroach on their racial status. Their efforts to authenticate themselves echo those of Otis and Mezzrow, and their esteem for authenticity, for "realness," is supreme. Fred Durst, of the multi-platinum rap/rock group Limp Bizkit, claimed he didn't care if black hip-hop fans bought his records, but "I just want 'em to go, 'hey, man, at least we know that guy's for real.'" Eminem told an interviewer, "I wasn't tryin' to be anything I'm not," explaining, "I just wanna be respected." Their fixation on authenticity often forces white rappers to take a hard-line stance about whether whites can truly make hip-hop—just as Mezzrow and Otis felt that jazz and blues could come only from a black soul. As MC Serch of 3rd Bass, a white rap group from the early 1990s, put it: "There's a lot of crackers that are making records that say, 'Yo, this ain't black music, it's just music.' *Eat a dick*. It's black music. We're now looking at a renaissance period for hip-hop. It's becoming global, so everyone's making it. That's fine, but don't open your mouth telling me, 'This ain't black music.' 'Cause you gotta respect it." If true hip-hop is "black music," where does that leave 3rd Bass? White rappers negotiate a contradiction: between an ambition to be "real" and a purist belief that "real" rap comes from black men.[48]

They do so by assertions of proximity to blackness. Geography has long played a vital role in hip-hop; rappers emphasize their attachments to particular cities, neighborhoods, and even blocks.[49] Growing up in a black neighborhood is thus a prerequisite for white rappers: it is what bestows an honorary "blackness" on them. Southern white rapper Paul Wall, for instance, claims hard-knock Houston as his breeding ground. Fred Durst grew up in Gastonia, North Carolina, and attended a predominantly black high school, where his black best friend's father introduced Durst to New York hip-hop. Durst began sporting his signature Adidas tracksuit and Yankees cap, joined a break dance crew composed of four black kids, and was often called "Nigger lover" by his high school classmates. Proof, a black rapper from Detroit, where Eminem grew up, calls himself Eminem's "boy for life" and told an interviewer to "keep in mind, he's always lived in black neighborhoods." Although he was raised in the suburbs, Kid Rock is often quick to point out that he was known for spinning records at the Mount Clemens housing projects in Detroit. Texan Vanilla Ice speaks of being a regular at an all-black club, City Lights, saying: "I was accepted there because I had so many friends that I knew that took me there. . . . I was embraced there, everybody knew me."[50] In fact, what ultimately deauthenticated Vanilla Ice—he went from crossover superstar to what Ice himself deemed the most hated man in hip-hop—were rumors that he had lied about his upbringing and the racial makeup of his high school. The implication is clear: had he indeed been close to blacks in high school, his validity as a rapper might have carried more weight. Similarly, for a brief moment in the early 1990s, L.A. rapper Boss was *the* female gangsta rapper on the scene, but her name made the headlines—and her reputation came undone—when word leaked that this self-proclaimed "gangsta bitch" was actually a well-educated young woman from the wealthy suburbs. Along the same lines, the "wannabe" white rappers in Danny Hoch's satirical 1999 film *Whiteboyz* can never claim authenticity, the film implies, for a simple reason: they live in all-white Iowa, and their only black friend, upper class and uptight, has even less "street cred" than they do.

Sexual liaisons with black women can be the feather in a white rapper's cap, but they are not fundamental; Eminem's on-again, off-again wife, for instance, is Kim Mathers: white, and a blonde. What *is* critical are bonds with black men. Just as Mezzrow valued his homosocial relationships and aligned himself with

Armstrong—an awe-inspiring black father figure—white rappers often associate themselves with a venerated black rapper or producer who can vouch for their authenticity. Eminem is Dr. Dre's right-hand man, and Fred Durst spoke in glowing terms about recording tracks with his idol, Method Man of the Wu-Tang Clan. Jewish rappers Blood of Abraham were aligned with Eazy-E of N.W.A., while MC Paul Barman was linked to De La Soul's Prince Paul. Paul Wall has been associated with two successful black rappers, Chamillionaire, his onetime partner in the Color Changin' Click, and Mike Jones, who introduced Wall to the public by giving the white rapper a verse on his first commercially distributed single, "Still Tippin.'" Bubba Sparxxx hit the scene in 2001 supported by producer Timbaland, who put his unmistakable musical stamp on Sparxxx's debut single, "Ugly." The setup is a fascinating reversal of both the master-slave dynamic and the black artist–white patron scenario that flourished during the Harlem Renaissance; it is the black elder statesmen of rap who serve as "patrons" now.

White rappers often surround themselves with a coterie of black friends and artists, as if to become black by association. Dr. Dre begat Eminem, and then Eminem begat 50 Cent by signing and ceaselessly promoting the blockbuster gangsta rapper. Detroit rock-rapper Kid Rock's shining moment came at the 1999 MTV Video Music Awards when he performed with Run-DMC by his side, causing host Chris Rock, who had previously joked about Kid Rock's authenticity by quipping that buff black rapper DMX—"the real thing"—could "steal Kid Rock's girl," to change his tune: "Maybe DMX *can't* steal Kid Rock's woman," he said with a chuckle, a remark that underscores the "realness" and the masculine status associated with proximity to "real" black rappers. Though rarely without Dre by his side, Eminem appears on the cover of his D-12 album, which he recorded together with his rapper friends from Detroit, literally surrounded by black rappers. Such proximity operates for white rappers just as it did for white jazzmen: it bestows a certain "blackness" upon them.

Interestingly, playing the black man's tune remains, as it was in Mezzrow's and Otis's day, a predominantly masculine enterprise. This is not to say that female crossover figures are not born of a lineage. They are: Sophie Tucker, a 1920s Broadway Yiddishe mama whom many, sight unseen, took for black; Teena Marie, deemed the "honorary soul sister" of the 1980s by *Vibe* magazine; 1970s singer Laura Nyro, about whom Patti LaBelle wrote, "She is a black woman in a white girl's body";[51] and of course white soul sister par excellence Janis Joplin. But when it comes to hip-hop, there has been smoke but no fire—female rappers, like Sarai or Lady Sovereign, who've been buzzed about but never saw their careers take off. I suggest that this is the case because current notions about men and women and crossover do not allow for a white woman who is as "authentically" hip-hop as Eminem proved himself to be—as authentically hip-hop, really, as the cultural guardians of all that is "true" hip-hop *require* him to be. Unlike white men, white women crossing race-inflected musical boundaries are generally excused when it comes to proving "street cred." When a white girl with attitude called herself Pink and delivered an album of pure R&B ("Got my own thing, got the ching-ching," she boasted in "Most Girls"), few suggested she wasn't "real" enough for the genre, or that she was engaged in cultural theft. When Christina Aguilera decided momentarily to go Latina, learning Spanish and recording "Mi Refleja," she didn't have to produce her "Boricua" pass; when she teamed up with rappers Li'l Kim or Redman and recorded hip-hop tracks, she didn't have to prove she was "down" enough to do that either. In 1990 N.W.A. rapper Eazy-E unleashed a white protégée named Tairrie B., who was deemed the Madonna of rap; in the blink of an eye she turned to heavy metal goddess. Princess Superstar began as a rapper and became part hip-hop, part dance-raver; former white rap trio Northern State turned femme punk with a dash of hip-hop. Pink morphed from R&B diva to punk rock chick, collaborating with hardcore outfit Rancid and sharing venues with rock act Linkin Park. Aguilera alternately displays the crooning of an alterna-chick ("Beautiful"), the prowess of a punk rocker ("Fighter," with guitar by Dave Navarro), the stiff sneer of a hip-hop diva complete with rap star collaborations ("Dirrty"), and the 1930s-style Hollywood glam of a swing-era diva ("Ain't No Other Man"). These crossover white women pull off the near impossible: they're musical chameleons, crossing generic boundaries in a way that makes them difficult to classify. Musically speaking, then, women have been too chameleon-like to embody "authentic" rap music, to represent it in the way that an Eminem does. There can be no female version of Eminem—call her "Feminem"—because tomorrow "Feminem" might wake up and be Metallica or John Mayer, and hardly anybody would feel surprised or betrayed by the transformation. For an album or even a track (Blondie's Debbie Harry, No Doubt's Gwen Stefani, Sonic Youth's Kim Gordon, and Fergie of the Black Eyed Peas have all dabbled in rap) white women are permitted to *feature* hip-hop; men, however, are expected to *live* it. For white women, hip-hop can be a style; for white men, it must be a *life* style.

Part of being true to Otherness means laying legitimate claim to it, and white male rappers do this differently than white jazzmen did. As self-identified black men with black wives, Mezzrow and Otis spoke of actual encounters with racism, and Mezzrow is derided on account of his Jewishness as well as his blackness. As a result, both men became active in antiracist causes,

Otis even asserting that his musical career was inherently political. In many respects hip-hop opens the door for similar antiracist efforts on the part of white rappers—yet white rappers are generally not socially or politically active, as Mezzrow and Otis were. When he first hit the scene, Eminem spoke often of his position as an underdog in the rap game, on which the *Rocky*-esque plot of his film *8 Mile* hinges: Can the much-maligned white boy rise to the occasion in an all-black world? Eminem thus turned his whiteness into a liability and, we might argue, engaged in fantasies of victimhood. Yet neither he nor any of his fellow white rappers has ever professed, as Mezzrow did, to have actually *become* black through proximity and music. No white rapper today would include himself in the African American "we" as liberally as both Mezzrow and Otis did. Instead, Eminem and his ilk legitimate their right to hip-hop by sporting "white trash" as a badge of pride that substitutes class for race. This white trash routine is inherently paradoxical: Eminem implies that he is so poor and so white he might as well be black. Bubba Sparxxx and Kid Rock, too, made much of their "white trash" identities, the latter rapping, on "Cowboy," "I ain't no G, I'm just a regular failure / I ain't straight outta Compton, I'm straight outta the trailer." Such tales of the trailer are the equivalent of Mezzrow's and Otis's confrontations with racism, establishing the artist's right to the music of the oppressed. It would be presumptuous for white rappers to claim racial discrimination as their own; instead they turn their class position into a kind of race, one that gives them license to speak of suffering. Some white rappers— the Boston troupe House of Pain, or Shamrock, winner of VH1's 2006 program *The (White) Rapper Show*—substitute Irishness for blackness. Others use Jewishness in this regard, much as Mezzrow did: Scott Storch, for instance, a prolific and pricey hip-hop producer, named his record label Tuff Jew. The Jews' role in early hip-hop, in fact, intriguingly parallels their role in early jazz and ragtime: Rick Rubin, the Long Island punk rocker who, together with rap impresario Russell Simmons, founded pioneering hip-hop label Def Jam; Lyor Cohen, who has headed a number of hip-hop labels including Def Jam; Jerry Heller, the former agent who co-founded Ruthless Records (with Eazy-E) and managed gangsta progenitors N.W.A.; the Beastie Boys, among the first rappers to serve up crossover hits; and 3rd Bass, among the first successful white rap acts, all were visionaries who appreciated the force of hip-hop well before mainstream white America did, and as a result were able to market it much the way Melnick says the Jews of the 1920s were able to "translate" early jazz for a broad audience.

If class or ethnicity serves as race for white rappers, so does rap music itself. Just as Mezzrow and Otis claim music as their race, white rappers speak of belonging to a "hip-hop nation." The very phrase turns hip-hop into not just a music but a culture and even, perhaps, a race. "If white kids can use hip-hop as a way to defy their racial destiny, that's a good thing," says Danny Hoch, the Jewish performance artist whose one-man show *Jails, Hospitals, and Hip-Hop* had him speaking alternately as a white man, a Puerto Rican, a black man, even a "wigger." Hoch essentially defines himself, racially speaking, through hip-hop: "My generation, the predominant culture was hip-hop, no matter where your grandparents came from. It was a common language that people could relate to." Hip-hop, Hoch says, is "a culture that came out of resistance— a kind of music, a style of dressing and talking, a way of viewing the world."[52] Hoch's definition of hip-hop culture suggests that hip-hop, like jazz and early rock 'n' roll, is the very crystallization of the African American aesthetic; the culture itself is embedded in the music. Like Mezzrow and Otis, then, non-black hip-hoppers see their music as their race and as a kind of cultural glue which holds them together, defining them as people and as musicians. They're not white; they're *hip-hop*.

5

Is Passing Passé in a "Post-Race" World?

Is passing passé? Evidence to the contrary abounds. Recent years have witnessed an upsurge in racial passing narratives, the theme remaining central to at least three highly touted novels—Danzy Senna's *Caucasia* (1998), Colson Whitehead's *The Intuitionist* (1999), and Philip Roth's *The Human Stain* (2000)—as well as to the screen adaptations of Roth's novel, starring Anthony Hopkins and Nicole Kidman (2003), and Walter Mosley's *Devil in a Blue Dress*, starring Denzel Washington (1995). Poet Clarence Major's *Come By Here: My Mother's Life* (2002) delivered a true-life passing saga; so did Brooke Kroeger's 2003 collection of case studies, *Passing: When People Can't Be Who They Are*, which prompted a National Public Radio program on passing and coincided with Brent Staples's series of editorials on the subject in the *New York Times*. Within the academy, new attention has been paid to "classic" passing narratives; once-ignored ones, including *The House Behind the Cedars*, are being revived; still others are being reread in the theoretical context of passing.[1] If, as critics have claimed, passing had become an outdated theme by the 1960s, what might we make of the growing contemporary interest in it?

"He who would enter the twenty-first century must come by way of me," wrote James Baldwin.[2] He meant it in the figurative sense, but I read it literally: an ever-growing number of white Americans have entered the twenty-first century wearing, in one form or another, blackness. The desire to sport some popular conception of "blackness"—to engage in what Ishmael Reed has called "cultural tanning"—has becoming one of the defining features of

youth culture, mocked by satirical films such as *Whiteboyz* (1999) and Warren Beatty's *Bulworth* (1998).[3] In a *New York Times* article I cited these films,
along with more recent ones such as *Malibu's Most Wanted* and *Bringing Down
the House* (both 2003), as evidence that "nouveau blackface, hip-hop-face, or
simply an 'act black' routine . . . is fast becoming an American comedic staple."
I argued that the "wigger" characters populating contemporary comedy "all
share the attitude that the racial amalgam is a fact of contemporary life. If you
can't beat it, parody it."[4] Interestingly, then, both blackface and black-to-white
passing have resurfaced in contemporary culture, whether highbrow or low.
We might read the former as a reaction to the latter: as mainstream American
culture imagines the comedic joys of performing blackness, a countercultural
voice emerges to remind us that in fact being black is not all punch lines and
laughter, that there is still much to tempt blacks to shed their blackness and
reap the benefits of whiteness.

   In addition to "passing" and "blackface," a third phrase dominated racial
discourse at the turn of the twenty-first century: "mixed race." In 1920 the U.S.
Census used "mulatto" as a racial category for the last time; in 2000 the category was reborn as "multiracial." The census sparked a revival of public interest in racial categories.[5] A survey of *New York Times* features over a series
of months in 2001, for instance, found that issues of biracialism haunted the
news. The front of the March 3 "Metro" section featured a story by Madison
Gray on Thomas Jefferson's multiracial descendants. Several months later the
"Week in Review" section was dedicated entirely to stories on, as the headline of Steven A. Holmes's article put it, "The Confusion over Who We Are."
"Multiracial Brazil" was the subject of an October piece by Larry Rohter, which
was preceded by numerous editorials about the mechanisms and findings of
the census.[6] In 2000 the *Times*'s year-long series "How Race Is Lived in America" included a number of pieces on biracial identity, and *Newsweek* devoted
its issue to "Redefining Race in America"; headlines included "The New Face
of Race"—complete with photos of multiracial individuals—as well as "What's
White, Anyway?" Memoirs about mixed-race identity—from Edward Ball's
Slaves in the Family to Rebecca Walker's *Black, White, and Jewish* and Judy
Scales-Trent's *Notes of a White Black Woman*—feed our fascination with the
white and black branches of America's family trees, while memoirs such as
Honky, about Dalton Conley's upbringing as the only white boy in the projects of New York's East Village, tap our interest in racial borrowing and cross-
cultural influence.[7] In an era of cultural mash-ups and globalized hybridity, an
era in which "rapidly developing communications technologies are facilitat-
ing transnational economic relationships, as well as global cultural exchange,"[8]

perhaps there is a growing awareness that, as Margo Jefferson wrote in the *Times*, we are all mulattoes now, in the sense that mulattoes "are gauges of the cultural complexities you choose—or choose not—to live with. You don't have to have parents of contrasting races to be a cultural mulatto. You have to stand apart from your heritage, study the forces (natural and unnatural) that made it, and then choose to become a part of whatever stirs and compels you, however foreign or distant."[9]

The revival of interest in—and increasing reality of—multiracial and multinational identities may further explain why black-to-white passing is suddenly relevant again. In the context of race, "authenticity" and "identity" have truly begun to unravel. First among academics and now among the masses, race has become the emperor's new clothes, a biological term without biological weight, and the public imagination has begun coming to grips with what Walter White—the blond-haired, blue-eyed "black" man who once ran the NAACP—called "the paradox of the color line": the fact that race is an idea, not a physical truth.[10] Nothing embodies this notion—that race is not seen but thought—like passing. If color is a thought, not a visual reality, why, after all, *can't* a Welshman named Anthony Hopkins play the onscreen Coleman Silk, American black turned Jew? And why can't Wentworth Miller, an actor of mixed heritage, play the young Silk? More broadly, why should someone whose father is black and whose mother is Jewish, who looks "white as snow" (as Coleman's mother describes him in the film), be bound to any single race? Recognizing the extent of multiracialism in America, the public is perhaps more open to seeing racial categories played with—and passing narratives represent the ultimate form of racial play. As Americans become reacquainted with their racially mixed heritages, and as we slowly begin to recognize how much cultural borrowing has shaped our intellectual landscape, we consume narratives about passing and multiracialism with avidity.

A more cynical analysis of this same phenomenon might propose that such narratives are a product of anxiety about, not acceptance of, current racial and ethnic ambiguities. The passing narrative flourishes, after all, during moments of unease about racial categories: Reconstruction left whites anxious about both miscegenation and the potency of the one-drop rule, while the new cultural capital of blackness in the 1920s made whites apprehensive about black influences on mainstream culture and blacks concerned about a potentially vanishing black population. The 1990s, like these two eras, gave rise to new conceptions of racial lines and widespread public dialogue about them. The late 1990s and the early years of the twenty-first century found us "dining at the ethnicity cafeteria," as one 2003 *Los Angeles Times* headline put it, and acknowledging that, as even conservative critic George Will admitted in the *Washington Post*, "race and ethnicity are increasingly understood to be not fixed but extremely fluid, hence dubious, scientific categories."[11] The rhetoric surrounding the census grows louder; evidence of our multiracial heritage abounds; a thriving not-quite-white population—Latinos—emerges to send racial categories into further disarray (as with the categories "Italian" and "white trash" in the 1890s and "Jew" in the 1920s); and Americans are left uncertain and perhaps uneasy about the future of the black/white divide. So passing rears its head again.

Ironically, public consciousness about multiracialism and cultural debt is also what makes passing quite a knotty subject to speak about in a contemporary context. If we are all of mixed heritage, then no one is *passing* as white or black; he or she is legitimately *claiming* whiteness or blackness. A true anti-essentialist framework must embrace the technical truth that passing makes no sense. Despite the legacy of the "one-drop rule," those who are both black *and* white are passing for black as much as they are passing for white. In *The Human Stain*, for instance, Coleman's white ancestry is written all over his face, so why can't he claim it? The more we come to accept the artificiality of that thing called race, the *less* we ought to speak of passing, since passing relies on firm racial categories and discernible lines between black and white. The more we turn "against race," to quote the title of Paul Gilroy's influential book, the more difficult it should be for us to envision a passing scenario that makes sense.[12] In an essay titled "Black Hair/Style Politics," Kobena Mercer sees hair as representative of the "creolizing cultures" of America:

> One cannot ignore how, alongside the commodification of electro and hip-hop, break-dancing and sportswear chic, some contemporary hairstyles among white youth maintain an ambiguous relationship with the stylizing practices of their black counterparts. Many use gels to effect sculptural forms, and in some inner-city areas white kids use the relaxer crème technology marketed to black kids in order to simulate the wet-look curly perm. So who, in this postmodern melee of semiotic appropriation and countervalorization, is imitating whom?[13]

How can we refer to passing at a time when "creolization" and "cross-cultural borrowing" seem more appropriate terms, and when "multiracialism" has become the catchword of the day? Can we, in particular, speak of white-to-black passing in today's cultural climate—a climate that is hyper-aware of racial borrowings and, specifically, of white cultural debt to blacks?

The fact is, when it comes to talking about race, most of us speak out of both sides of our mouths. We are against race, yes, but we also like our solid selves. How, after all, does one actually live in a racial free-for-all, a world in which all identity is, as Samira Kawash puts it, "not what we are but what we are passing for"?[14] Such a world runs contrary to our passion for security, for the type of identity comfort zone that even shifting subjects usually stake out in the end. More than anything else, today's passing fad is about the gulf between theory and practice. Yes, race is dead and passing along with it—but no, they're not. Theoretical jive about race as a "disproved" concept is, well, jive; good old Race, rigid and old hat, lives on in our hearts and minds. Slay something—blackness, whiteness, Latino-ness—in concept and you still haven't slain it in the flesh. And that is precisely why it is, after all, fruitful to speak of white-to-black passing in a contemporary context, as long as one develops the correct framework for doing so.

In chapter 4 I noted that a Mezz Mezzrow could never exist today, that no esteemed musician could get away with claiming blackness as audaciously as he did; I also considered the more subtle ways in which contemporary white rappers negotiate their crossover identities. In this chapter I return to this discussion in order to answer a broader question in light of contemporary discourse about passing, posing, and appropriation: How has white-to-black passing been reborn in recent narrative? I look not only at pop culture and the hip-hop scene but also at two memoirs that might be read as white-to-black passing stories: James McBride's *The Color of Water* and Gregory Howard Williams's *Life on the Color Line: The True Story of a White Boy Who Discovered He Was Black.* Each is a story of generational conflict in which the author's sense of racial identity clashes with that of a parent. To the child, race means one thing; to his parent, it means quite another—and therein lies the tension of these narratives, which tell their stories by very different means. The strategies employed by these two passing narratives reflect two ways in which passing has been envisioned in contemporary culture more generally.

Before analyzing the narratives, I want to consider cursorily two scenarios in which white-to-black passing exists today. The first involves a medium that has long been a vehicle for racial masquerade: radio. During the late 1940s and early 1950s, when rhythm and blues was being repackaged as rock 'n' roll, radio ruled the cultural sphere, and disembodied voices ran the radio—voices of men (and, every now and then, women) called disc jockeys. They replaced performance shows with records and talk. Loud and brash, they were the first live personalities on American airwaves. Coincidentally, "jockey" in 1940s parlance meant "trickster." And the greatest trick performed by the growing number of DJs involved race. Before television gave music an unequivocal race, radio left listeners wondering, "*Is* he or *isn't* he?" Ironically, while the few black DJs worked to sound as "white" as possible, white DJs—John Richbourg, Zenas "Daddy" Sears, Dewey Phillips, Gene Nobles, Hoss Allen, Alan Freed, and later Wolfman Jack—had black slang on the lips of every white and black teen in America. Visitors to the famed WLAC studios in Nashville were constantly shocked to discover that they had it all wrong: the most staid broadcasters were black, and the most jive-slanging, flamboyant ones were white.

This tradition lives on today, not only among DJs such as Los Angeles–based Theo or K-Sly—Asian Americans whom listeners still take for black—but also among blue-eyed soul singers such as Nikka Costa, Joss Stone, and Anastasia, who might be heard on the radio but rarely seen on television, and thus are easily taken for black. Passing for black by way of speech or dialect—as Chambers does in *Pudd'nhead Wilson*—can also occur in the context of the written word. In the 1940s, for instance, Vernon Sullivan, a self-proclaimed African American writer, wrote a series of raunchy, hard-boiled novels about black figures passing for white. His *I Spit on Your Graves* sold well in 1946 America, but little did the public know that "Sullivan" was actually Boris Vian: a white Frenchman who managed to pass as black not simply by picking up a pen but by using it to speak in black vernacular.

A second mode of contemporary white passing might be called the "would-be passing" scenario. Such narratives substitute not speech but socioeconomic status for skin color. In films such as *White Man's Burden* (1995) and, earlier, *The Jerk* (1979), protagonists are placed in the social and cultural shoes of a black man and left to negotiate their identities. *The Jerk*, one of Steve Martin's best films, opens with his most memorable line: "I was born a poor black child."[15] As Navin Johnson, Martin learns that he is white on his eighteenth birthday and sets out into the world to make sense of this fact. He returns, in the end, to his black mother and family, still without rhythm, still enjoying his white bread sandwiches and Twinkies, but more at home among blacks than whites. *White Man's Burden* takes place in an imagined America in which whites reside in inner-city ghettos and blacks make up the social elite. John Travolta plays Louis Pinnock, a white worker in, appropriately enough, a chocolate factory, whose life is torn apart by police brutality and acts of desperation.[16] Both films are would-be passing narratives in that they play with the hypothetical situation of a white man in a black man's shoes; they are versions of Griffin's experiment, but they allow culture and social status to stand in for skin color. Such narratives represent one way in which passing has been reconfigured in contemporary narrative: instead of having whites pass literally as black, they present whites passing for black in the cultural or socioeconomic sense. Like

Warren Beatty's Senator Bulworth, these protagonists adopt stereotypical trappings of blackness—clothing, dialect, social and economic position—as a way of adopting blackness itself.[17] At the same time, Beatty's, Martin's, and Travolta's characters make no real attempt to pass and remain very much white. Theirs are *almost*-passing narratives, but in fact narratives of cultural exchange.

Abolishing Whiteness and Th*e Color of Water*

James McBride subtitled *The Color of Water*, his 1996 memoir, *A Black Man's Tribute to His White Mother*, but the pat phrase—with its clear-cut racial categories—seems a poor fit for the text, in which race is anything but clear-cut. At once McBride's autobiography and a biography of his mother, Ruth McBride Jordan, *The Color of Water* is a poignant meditation on multiracial identity, particularly because of its complex and vivid portrait of Ruth herself, who comes alive, warts and all, in her son's stunning portrayal. A rabbi's daughter, born to Russian Jewish immigrants, she was raised in Virginia and fled to New York, where she successively married two black men, founded a Baptist church in Harlem, and raised twelve children. In many ways Ruth's story follows the lines of the would-be passing narratives I described earlier. She is a Jewish woman who is transformed by moving first to Harlem at a time when "Harlem was like magic," and then to Red Hook, Brooklyn, which "was beautiful in those days. It was integrated—Italians, Puerto Ricans, Jews, and blacks." Ruth's transformation is completed when she converts to Christianity after her mother's death—"That's when I decided to become a Christian and the Jew in me began to die," she says—and is symbolically finalized by the mourner's kaddish that her family says in her name: "When Jews say kaddish, they're not responsible for you anymore. You're dead to them. Saying kaddish and sitting shiva, that absolves them of any responsibility for you." Ruth is molded by her surroundings and becomes, in essence, black by proximity. McBride writes that "she actually preferred to be among the poor, the working-class poor of the Red Hook Housing Projects of Brooklyn," and "as a boy, I often found Mommy's ease among black people surprising."[18] In this respect Ruth's story follows a now familiar narrative. Living among black people, she absorbs their cultural identities. Like Grace Halsell, she imbibes the race of her two husbands (and, to some extent, of her sons). As the only nonblack among blacks, as one who sexually bonds with black men, Ruth—like Eminem or Dalton Conley—engages in racial crossover; she becomes, in Kobena Mercer's terms, a cultural creole.

Yet *The Color of Water* is more than a narrative of cultural exchange (as, for instance, Conley's *Honky* is) thanks to one crucial factor: Ruth is not a white person who is culturally black; she never acknowledges being white at all.[19] As the narrative begins, McBride presents his own quandary about his mother's race and identity, matters she "ignored," he writes. "I began to notice something about my mother, that she looked nothing like the other kids' mothers. In fact, she looked more like my kindergarten teacher, Mrs. Alexander, who was white" (12). Ruth's responses are cold and curt. "I do look like you. I'm your mother. You ask too many questions. Educate yourself. School is important," she snaps (13). To James's question about being black or white, she "snapped," "You're a human being. Educate yourself or you'll be a nobody!" (92). For many young children a mother is a larger-than-life object of awe, but to James and his siblings Ruth is a total enigma: "We traded information on Mommy the way people trade baseball cards at trade shows, offering bits and pieces fraught with gossip, nonsense, wisdom, and sometimes just plain foolishness" (21–22). His words describe the narrative itself, which is almost hermeneutic—a series of puzzle pieces meant to complete the mysterious picture that is Ruth's identity. If, as McBride writes, his mother's memory "was like a minefield, each recollection a potential booby trap, a bouncing Betty—the old land mines the Viet Cong used in the Vietnam War that never went off when you stepped on them but blew you to hell the moment you pulled your foot away" (253), then *The Color of Water* is a collection of mini-explosions that come together in the end to produce a stunning display.

The great mystery of the narrative, of course, revolves around race, which "was like the power of the moon in my house. It's what made the river flow, the ocean swell, and the tide rise, but it was a silent power, intractable, indomitable, indisputable, and thus completely ignorable" (94). What Ruth tries to ignore is her whiteness, which she not only never lays claim to but in fact actively denies. "By simultaneously bearing a white skin, nurturing a black identification, *and* remaining silent about the entire matter, Ruth prosecuted a repudiation of whiteness that also constituted . . . its very deconstruction as a normative identity," writes Philip Brian Harper.[20] When James asks her point-blank if she is white, Ruth claims only to be light-skinned:

> When Malcolm X talked about "the white devil" Mommy simply felt those references didn't apply to her. She viewed the civil rights achievements of black Americans with pride, as if they were her own. And she herself occasionally talked about "the white man" in the third person, as if she had nothing to do with him, and in fact she didn't, since most of her friends and social circle were black women from church. "What's the matter with these white folks?" she'd muse after reading some craziness in the *New York Daily News*. (32)

Ruth's adopted blackness is not without its contradictions, McBride tells us—"White folks, she felt, were implicitly evil toward blacks, yet she forced us to go to white schools to get the best education. Blacks could be trusted more, but anything involving blacks was probably slightly substandard" (29)—and it is by refusing to excise such contradictions from his narrative that McBride makes his portrait of Ruth so vibrant. For on the one hand, McBride acknowledges that Ruth has, in some way, succeeded in passing as black. He spends his childhood believing, if skeptically, that his mother is not-quite-white, and he declares at the end of the memoir that "she came over to the African-American side" (274). Yet at the same time he repeatedly calls attention, as he does in the book's subtitle, to his mother's nonblack status. Chapter 6, for instance, details his mother's excruciating singing voice, an anecdote clearly meant to set her apart from the other (black) parishioners in her church: "Up, up, and away she went, her shrill voice climbing higher and higher, reminding us of Curly of the Three Stooges. It sounded so horrible that I thought Rev. Owens, our minister, would get up from his seat and stop the song" (45). Ultimately, McBride writes, his mother remains a contradiction, which is poignantly captured by the skin cancer she becomes afflicted with late in life, a condition that, ironically, "affects mostly white people. To the very end, Mommy is a flying compilation of competing interests and conflicts, a black woman in white skin, with black children and a white woman's physical problem" (260).

It is in light of this paradox—Ruth's portrayal as both white and nonwhite, the presentation of whiteness as simultaneously mutable and intractable—that I read *The Color of Water* as a contemporary passing narrative. Like Mezzrow, Ruth will simply not own up to whiteness, and in this respect she passes as black (in her own eyes at least). Yet at the same time her whiteness is continually on display, as if both she and her son cannot help but call attention to it. This, I suggest, is as close to passing for black as whites can come today: they can adopt features of blackness, and they can repudiate whiteness, but part of repudiating whiteness involves owning up to this same whiteness. Being near-black gives them license to take on a black persona, but paradoxically, in order to claim blackness legitimately, they must simultaneously claim whiteness. We have come a long way from the nineteenth-century culture that envisioned whiteness as a singularly weak and vulnerable entity; contemporary culture—ever aware of the legacy of white privilege—acknowledges that whiteness can also be undeniably stubborn, a damned spot that is impossible to "out."

This paradox is evident in a movement that sprang up in the late 1990s among intellectuals and academics, among them Noel Ignatiev, who call themselves the "New Abolitionists." In their journal *Race Traitor*, they call on readers to "abolish the white race by any means necessary." Distinguishing themselves from anti-racists, the New Abolitionists aim to destroy the very concepts of race and of whiteness, which they recognize as a social construct that benefits a very particular "club" of people. "So-called whites must cease to exist as whites. To put it another way, they must commit suicide as whites to come alive as workers or youth or women or artists or whatever other identity will let them stop being the miserable, petulant, subordinated creatures they are now and become freely associated, developed human beings," Ignatiev exhorts in *Transition*. "Treason to whiteness is loyalty to humanity," an editorial in the anthology *Race Traitor* declares. "*Race Traitor* aims to dissolve the club [of whiteness], to break it apart, to explode it." How, we may ask, does one abolish one's own whiteness? Ignatiev highlights the importance of "violating the rules of whiteness," and *Race Traitor* is never short on confessionals about such violations. One white man, for instance, details the discouragement he faced when buying a black newspaper from a white shop owner in the South. He responds with "a profound act of racial sedition": "You must think I'm white," he tells her, and walks out of the shop, paper in hand.[21]

Being a race traitor rests on the same paradox that Ruth McBride Jordan personifies. A crucial part of abolishing whiteness involves recognizing its potency and its (socially constructed) presence. Only by bringing attention to one's whiteness, then, can one violate the rules of the "club." In order to dismantle whiteness, one must call attention to it as a powerful agent, which is why much New Abolitionism goes hand-in-hand with studies of whiteness. (Ignatiev, for instance, is the author of *How the Irish Became White*.) True race traitors must be, like Ruth McBride Jordan, simultaneously white and nonwhite; they must act in a "nonwhite" manner while owning up to the whiteness that causes others to treat them in particular, beneficial ways. They must recognize that whiteness is at one and the same time mutable, erasable—and stubbornly persistent. This is an irony that harks back to the epigraph in my introduction, about whites losing their whiteness: loss of whiteness today means confronting the ways in which one became, was constructed as, white in the first place. Losing and acquiring whiteness has, in other words, become one and the same thing.

This paradoxical act of avowing and disavowing—hinged on modern-day notions of whiteness as alterable and yet intractably durable—is also endemic to contemporary hip-hop. On the one hand, white rappers employ the rhetoric of proximity which I argue is the basis for white passing: having grown up among blacks, they have license to dress, speak, and perform in decidedly un-white ways. Yet in today's society, with its heightened awareness of cultural theft and racial crossover, proximity is powerful but not the transformative agent it once was. So in order to get away with publicly possessing and marketing a nonwhite persona, white rappers must repeatedly own up to their essential white status. They claim whiteness in words and disclaim it in action; their personas suggest "black" but their lyrics and interview comments tend to remind us that they are indeed white. Eminem, for instance, has said that he is tired of hearing his whiteness referred to ("I get offended when people come to me and ask me, 'So being a white rapper . . .' and 'Being that you're white . . .' and 'So growing up white . . .' and 'After being born white . . .' and white white white white is all I ever seem to hear—instead of the music," he told one journalist),[22] but his rhymes compulsively return to this same whiteness. "Y'all act like you've never seen a white person before," he begins one track. In another, "Some people only see that I'm white, ignoring skill / 'Cause I stand out like a green hat with an orange bill / But I'm not pissed / Y'all can't even see through the mist / How the fuck can I be white? / I don't even exist." In his most racially bold track, "White America," Eminem compares himself to Elvis and admits "if I was black I would've sold half." Everlast, a white rapper belonging to the group House of Pain, released a single titled "Whitey's Revenge," in which he censured Eminem with venom. MC Haystak titled his album *Car Fulla White Boyz*. Back in the Vanilla Ice era, Marky Mark's "So What Chu Sayin'?" was blunt: "I never claim to be Vanilla / I'm Irish American / and never did I claim to be African-American. . . . With respect to the Old School / that started this art form." Vanilla Ice himself angered fans at the 1991 MTV Video Music Awards by telling his detractors to "kiss my white ass." Struggling white rapper Johnny Blanco recorded "Fuck You, Whiteboy" because "I said to myself, 'Yo— because I rap, because I'm white, people are gonna dis me.' So I figured—before they dis me, I'll dis myself," he told me in an interview. "One of the funniest things about the Beastie Boys," writes Crispin Sartwell,

> is that they *sound white* even when (as on their early albums) they rap over black beats, and it seems to me that they *try* to sound *extremely* white. Vanilla Ice and even better white rap acts, such as House of Pain or Snow, try to sound black; the move is appropriative; it is slumming. But the Beastie Boys *show themselves as white* to (among others) black audiences and parody whiteness. This is an extremely transgressive stance, but they take it up with such light-hearted enthusiasm that it is irresistible.[23]

Much of this fixation on whiteness seems part of white hip-hop's strategic victim fantasy: perhaps in order to detract from the power and privilege that whiteness affords them, Eminem and other white rappers present themselves as underdogs in the rap game, repeatedly having to prove their skills in order to be accepted as legitimate.

This "I'm white"/"I'm not white" routine rears its head in other hip-hop-related contexts. William Wimsatt, graffiti artist and author of *Bomb the Suburbs* and *No More Prisons*, speaks as a member of "the hip-hop nation," but he also refers to himself as a "wigger," and was the founder of the "Cool Rich White Kids Foundation." Basketball player Jason Williams, famous for his "black" style of play, is nicknamed "White Chocolate," a title that underscores both his white essence and his black performance style. Even as these public figures wear the cloak of blackness, none of them can let us forget that he is a "white boy," lest he be accused of hip-hop's cardinal sin: inauthenticity. Ironically, to come close to passing as *black* today, one must also be self-consciously *white*.

Some white rappers have taken this emphasis on whiteness to an extreme, marketing themselves not as would-be blacks but as emphatically white. Black-influenced artists such as MC Paul Barman and Beck represent what might be called the "nouveau nerd" trend: adorned in faded corduroys and vintage T-shirts, they wear their self-conscious, scrawny techno-geekiness with pride. They are caricatures of whiteness, grotesque exaggerations of the uncool. The on-line Wikipedia made their personas official, defining "Nerdcore hip hop, or geeksta rap" as "a subgenre of hip hop music that is performed by nerds or geeks, and is characterized by themes and subject matter considered to be of general interest to nerds."[24]

In chapter 4 I proposed yet another feature of white rappers' adopted black identities: their aligning of ethnic upbringings with racialized ones. In *The Color of Water*, much of what makes Ruth nonwhite is her Jewishness, which is fundamental to the memoir's plot and structure. The text is designed so that McBride's upbringing as a mixed-race child is equated with his mother's experience as a Jew in the segregated South, then as a white woman in Harlem and Brooklyn. The author deftly handles the transitions between the two narratives and life stories. These transitions are sometimes overt (a chapter on Ruth's brother Sam is followed by one on James's siblings; a chapter titled "Shul" is followed by one titled "School") and sometimes subtle (in chapter 11 Ruth dances in a school show; in chapter 10 James dances at a party), but they underscore a parallel between the discrimination faced by Ruth as a Jew—she is called "Christ killer" and attends neither the black nor the white school in her Virginia hometown—and by James as an African American. Ruth, McBride writes, "never spoke about Jewish people as white. She spoke about them as

Jews, which made them somehow different. It was a feeling every single one of us took into adulthood, that Jews were different from white people somehow. Later as an adult when I heard folks talk of the love/hate relationship between blacks and Jews I understood it to the bone" (87). McBride captures the "curious blend of Jewish-European and African-American distrust and paranoia" that his parents brought into their home (28).

On the one hand, he sets Ruth up as the product of a classic Jewish immigrant family; her tyrannical father and kind but silently suffering mother are reminiscent of the parent figures in works ranging from *The Jazz Singer* to Anzia Yezierska's *Bread Givers*. But on the other hand, her larger-than-life matriarchal power also evokes the African American mother figure. McBride's choice of imagery in describing his mother's "madwalk," for instance, has suggestive racial overtones: "the bowlegged strut that meant thunder and lightning was coming—body pitched forward, jaw jutted out, hands balled into tight fists, nose red, stomping like Cab Calloway with the Billy Eckstein band blowing full blast behind him" (102). Ruth's persona as the almighty matriarch evokes both Jewish lore and African American tradition; it is one way in which McBride merges the two cultures in his work. Jewishness thus acts as a kind of third race in *The Color of Water*; it is that which makes Ruth not quite white, not quite black, though she is also not quite Jewish. At the same time, because it is equated with blackness, Jewishness blackens Ruth. It is Al Jolson's burnt cork in *The Jazz Singer*, which darkens him on the one hand and whitens him on the other.[25]

In *The Color of Water* this tension is reflected in a theme that plays a critical role in all passing narratives: the generation gap. In black-to-white passing stories family is, for the passer, a bête noire: a racial skeleton in the closet. Black passers can be "outed" via a darker parent (as in *Imitation of Life*) or sibling (as in *Plum Bun*); their narratives are thus wrapped up in the erasure, and eventual reclaiming, of family bonds. Ruth McBride, by contrast, is caught up in the opposite scenario: her passing depends, from the very beginning, on the *assertion* of family bonds, on her black husbands and dark-skinned children. Her son, too, is eager not to eradicate family history but to unravel it. What, he must know, is his mother's "true" race? The narrative, however, presents two different answers to this question, because it puts forth clashing conceptions of race. In Ruth's eyes, she has never really been white at all—since she grew up in an era when Jews in the Jim Crow South were not white. It was a time, we might say, when race could mean not simply "black" or "white" but "gray"; it was a moment when, to refer to Karen Brodkin Sacks's *How the Jews Became White Folks*, Jews were on the brink of becoming "white folks" but were not quite there yet. But some twenty years later—during James McBride's childhood—Jews had grown whiter. He came of age at a time when racial lines were drawn differently, when one was black or white but never gray, and those who were not aligned with one or the other of the two colors were doomed to instability. In alternating between his mother's story and his own, McBride sets two narratives containing clashing conceptions of race alongside each other. In one, race is a sliding, multifaceted signifier; in the other, it is a black and white affair. At the crux of the narrative is the dilemma of generational conflict—and in many respects this is the dilemma of the contemporary moment as a whole. As we historicize race more than ever before, how do we sort through the myriad definitions that remain at odds with one other? How can the younger generation, with its own notions of racial identity, make sense of older, now outdated ideas about race? Is Ruth Jewish or is she white? In one narrative (Ruth's), she is the former; in another (James's), she is the latter; in the complete narrative—*The Color of Water* as a whole—she is both. The only strategy, it seems, is to let past and present, one generation and another, sit side by side.

Passing as Black, Passing as White: *Life on the Color Line*

Gregory Howard Williams's *Life on the Color Line: The True Story of a White Boy Who Discovered He Was Black* begins as a traditional passing story—though not Williams's own story. The figure initially most critical to the text is Williams's father, Tony. The memoir begins with a description of the Open House Café in Virginia, where in 1950 Gregory (known as Billy) and his brother Mike are at home, described by Tony Williams as "the best location in the country, right smack-dab in the middle of the Eastern Seaboard, and less than five miles away from the number one tourist attraction in America." In these opening pages, details are critical. We read that Mike's middle name is "Alain . . . for Dr. Alain Locke, the first African-American Rhodes scholar, though I didn't learn about him till much later." We learn little about Billy's mother but a great deal about the charm and charisma of his father, whose "ease and camaraderie with employees and patrons"—of both races—"enhanced the popularity of the Open House Café"; at one point, Tony defies segregation laws to serve a front-room meal gratis to a black war veteran. Tony's curious relationship to race and segregation is further heightened during a brawl between soldiers at the café in which he is stabbed. As his wife phones for an ambulance, Tony's partner calls out, " 'Mary, I hope you told them this was a white man stabbed, and they don't think it's a nigger cut up down here in Gum Springs!' Just as I began to fear that the police had mistaken my daddy for a colored man," Williams goes on, "I heard the wail of a siren in the parking lot." [26]

Tony Williams becomes, like Ruth McBride Jordan, an enigma to his son, who suspects that there is a secret to be discovered. During a conversation with his maternal grandmother about the feud between his father and uncle Frank, Billy,

> sensing that the secret was almost within my grasp . . . moved closer and tried again.
>
> "I bet he don't like my dad 'cause he's Italian."
>
> "Italian, my fanny," Grandma responded. Squinting through her thick rimless glasses, she snarled, "Frank works with some real Italian boys on his ship. They even showed him how to make genuine spaghetti. That ain't the reason, Mr. Smarty Pants."
>
> "Well, what is it?" I demanded in exasperation.
>
> "I ain't saying!" she hissed, her pink round face turning bright red as she planted her hands on her hips. "If you don't understand it now, you will one of these days." (17)

Of course Tony's secret does eventually come out. Caught in a downward economic spiral and abandoned by his wife, Tony reveals to his family that Miss Sallie, the black woman who works for him at the tavern, is in fact his mother. The family will be moving, he continues, to Muncie, Indiana, where they will live with his aunt Bess in the black section of town. Billy, of course, is beside himself with shock and denial:

> I didn't understand Dad. I knew I wasn't colored, and neither was he. My skin was white. All of us are white, I said to myself. But for the first time, I had to admit Dad didn't exactly look white. His deeply tanned skin puzzled me as I sat there trying to classify my own father. Goose bumps covered my arms as I realized that whatever he was, I was. I took a deep breath. I couldn't make any mistakes. I looked closer. His heavy lips and dark brown eyes didn't make him colored, I concluded. . . . He was darker than most whites, but Mom said he was Italian. That was why my baby brother had such dark skin and curly hair. Mom told us to be proud of our Italian heritage! That's it, I decided. He was Italian. I leaned back against the seat, satisfied. Yet the unsettling image of Miss Sallie flashed before me like a neon sign. Colored! Colored! Colored! (33–34)

As Tony continues to describe the road ahead—"You're the same today that you were yesterday. But people in Indiana will treat you differently"—Billy, glaring at his father, allows the news to sink in: "I saw my father as I had never seen him before. The veil dropped from his face and features. Before my eyes he was transformed from a swarthy Italian to his true self—a high-yellow mulatto. My father was a Negro! We were colored! After ten years in Virginia on the white side of the color line, I knew what that meant" (34).

The scene, complete with its use of the veil metaphor, is a standard one in passing narratives from *Pudd'nhead Wilson* to *An Imperative Duty*: the protagonist must suddenly confront his or her newly revealed black identity. This scene in *Life on the Color Line*, however, marks an interesting turning point in the memoir: it is the moment at which the narrative becomes one about Billy's identity, not his father's, as Billy comes to the realization that if his father is "colored," then so is he. The paternal mystery is soon solved: we learn that Tony's father was a plantation owner and his mother a black slave with some Native American ancestry, and that Tony himself once wrote progressive speeches for pro-black Muncie politicians. Once this enigma is resolved, the text shifts from father to son and becomes Billy's passing story.

But what kind of passing narrative is it? At first it seems to be a white-to-black one. In a chapter titled "Learning How to Be Niggers," Billy and Mike come to grips with their new identities. "With the growing list of honey, brown, and chocolate relatives, it was becoming harder to perceive myself as white," he writes (51). Tony lays out the ground rules: "Colored families live on this side of Madison, and crackers on the other. Stay outta there. If the crackers learn you're colored, they'll beat the hell out of you. You gotta be careful here, too. Coloreds don't like half-breeds, either" (38). Like the Ex–Coloured Man, Billy must learn how to "be" black—and, also like Johnson's fictional persona, he often seems to be *passing* as such. In one scene he ends up in a fight with a boy who calls him a "white motherfucker," to which he replies, "I ain't white! I ain't white!" and "pounded him again and again in the chest" (119). When his father taunts him, Billy insists: "Why do you call me white? I'm not white. And Mike's not a nigger" (156). Mike's principal refuses to believe that he lives in the black section of town, "till Aunt Bess waved him down and told him we was colored boys" (47). Billy learns to identify with the various shades of brown on his block. In many respects, then, the memoir is indeed a white-to-black passing narrative.

Yet at many other moments, Billy (like Mike) passes for white. His father registers him as white in school, where he plans to tell others that Aunt Bess is his maid. The truth is soon out, however, and Billy must answer to whites who call him a "nigger" and blacks who call him a "cracker." In the bus station Billy and his father attempt to sit in the whites-only waiting room but cannot pass as white. In the dating pool Billy finds himself in "shark-infested waters":

"Muncie would not permit me to date white girls, and apparently couldn't tolerate seeing me with black girls either. Muncie's white community would only be satisfied with an inconspicuous and unobtrusive eunuch. My very existence made people uncomfortable and shattered too many racial taboos" (166).

Is Billy passing for white or for black? Is *Life on the Color Line* a white-to-black passing narrative or a black-to-white one? It is, in the end, both. We can read the memoir as a traditional passing-as-white narrative, especially during the moments when Billy begins dating his blonde high-school girlfriend, Sara Whitney, whom he eventually marries. Yet at the same time, *Life on the Color Line* is a story about passing for black, about how a "white boy discovered he was"—and learned how to be—"black." "I am grateful to have been able to view the world from a place few men or women have stood," Williams writes at the close of his memoir. "I realize now that I am bound to live out my life in the middle of society and hope that I can be a bridge between races, shouldering the heavy burden that almost destroyed my youth" (284). Williams's words echo those of Mezzrow, who spoke of being just this sort of bridge between races. But Williams's story also seems particularly appropriate for an era fixated on the notion of "mixed race" identity, and on that specter of blackness that mars all of our illusions about "pure" white identities. His is a passing narrative for our own day: he is not passing as white, nor is he passing as black; he is passing as both black *and* white. Our passing narratives thus reflect growing acceptance of the fact that because race is indeed a construct, and racial categories are not as rigid as we once believed them to be, then any racial identity involves passing. Out of this notion is born a narrative like Williams's, a text that simultaneously fits the mold of the traditional black-to-white passing story as well as the white-to-black one.

Haunting this very contemporary narrative, in which race is never easy to define, is a second mini-narrative: the narrative that Williams's father insists on. Tony is the memoir's gadfly; he returns to the story—and to his son's life—in order to insist that Greg's identity is as simple as whiteness can be. For Tony, Greg is white because it is most beneficial for him to be so. Greg, however, sees himself as not-quite-white because of the complexity of his cultural heritage. As in *The Color of Water*, then, generational conflict rears its head. Competing narratives within a single text—in one, race is literally a black and white issue, while in another, race is anything but—reflect the instability of race as a concept. The current moment is host to opposing ideas about what it means to be "raced," and this opposition is split along generational lines. Coming to grips with race today means grappling with the ways in which our parents made sense of racial lines. It is thus no accident that both Williams and McBride write texts that feature competing narratives; they write at a moment when no single narrative about race dominates, when we struggle to make sense of conflicting racial narratives and find that no one narrative is a perfect fit after all.

Danzy Senna's 1998 novel *Caucasia* can also be read in this light. A modern-day *Plum Bun*, *Caucasia* tells the story of two half-black, half-white sisters who are separated as children. The dark-skinned Cole goes off to Brazil with their African American father, while light-skinned Birdie accompanies their white mother to New Hampshire, where she passes as Jewish. The central tension of the novel involves Birdie's struggle with her own racial identity. Growing up in Boston in the 1970s with Cole by her side, she learns to prove her "blackness"; in small-town New Hampshire she must learn the rules of being a white American teenager, frosted lipstick and all. When reunited with her sister and father at the end of the novel, Birdie sees her family transformed. The Afrocentric father who once ignored her because of her light skin has written a tract on the illusory nature of race. "He's right, you know," Cole says of her father's theory. "'About [race] being all constructed. But'—she turned to me, looking at me intently—'that doesn't mean it doesn't exist.'" [27] Cole's words could very well come from a contemporary academic. She succinctly voices an accepted wisdom about race: the color line, as Kawash puts it, "must be addressed doubly, as both the origin of an absolutely real division and as the product of an utterly false and impossible distinction." [28] Race is thus very real and very false, and as a result any racial identity involves some form of passing. Birdie's passing is thus a passing for white *and* a passing for black; like *Life on the Color Line*, *Caucasia* is a narrative that can be read in light of both modes of passing. Both narratives reflect one way to write about passing in a "post-race" world: instead of writing a white-to-black passing story or a black-to-white one, authors may write a single text that is, at one and the same moment, both.

Such an approach to the passing narrative is not new; at least two earlier texts can be read in a similar fashion. Ralph Ellison's posthumously published *Juneteenth* traces the race-baiting Senator Sunraider's origins back to his illegitimate birth and upbringing in the home of Reverend Hickman, who named him Bliss. The novel is most overtly a traditional black-to-white passing narrative; Bliss passes not only from black into white but also from religion into secularism, appropriating the rhetoric of Hickman's sermons for his own political glory. As the fragments unfold, we learn that Bliss's white mother, Janey, named Robert Hickman, the Reverend's brother, as her child's father. But is Janey, a shrewish, ghostlike figure in the text, a seeming construct of Bliss's unconscious, a reliable source? Ellison does not close off the possibility that Bliss's father could in fact have been white. If so, Bliss's story is of white-to-black passing *as well as* black-to-white passing. Perhaps the scene in which Bliss attacks a blackfaced clown is symbolic of Bliss's own blackface performance: "I hit and hit, trying to make all the blackness go away. . . . [T]he blackness was all over the back of my hands."[29] We might read *Juneteenth*, then, as a narrative that begins as a traditional passing story and slowly comes undone. Bliss, perhaps, is passing for both white *and* black.

Langston Hughes's 1945 short story "Who's Passing for Who?" also employs such a strategy. Caleb Johnson—"colored social worker, who was always dragging around with him some nondescript white person or two, inviting them to dinner, showing them Harlem . . . much to the displeasure of whatever friends of his might be out that evening for fun, not sociology"—arrives at a Harlem bar with a white couple in tow, whom he introduces to the narrator. An hour into the conversation, the couple admit that they are actually black and have been passing as white for the past fifteen years. "All at once we dropped our professionally self-conscious 'Negro' manners, became natural, ate fish, and talked and kidded freely like colored folks do when there are no white folks around," the narrator says, a remark that seems ironic in light of his earlier claim that he and his highbrow literary coterie, all of whom "considered ourselves too broad-minded to be bothered with questions of color[,] . . . liked people of any race who smoked incessantly, drank liberally, wore complexion and morality as loose garments, and made fun of anyone who didn't do likewise." Later that evening, however, the joke is on the pretentious narrator and his friends. The couple make a second confession: they are in fact white, passing as blacks passing for white. "We didn't say a thing. We just stood there on the corner in Harlem dumbfounded, not knowing now *which* way we'd been fooled. Were they really white—passing for colored? Or colored—passing for white?"[30] This same question applies to the story as a whole: Is it a black-to-white passing narrative or a white-to-black one? Again the answer seems to be that it is *both*. Perhaps this earlier mode of passing narrative, which we might call the dual-passing story, has been revived in recent years because it is well suited to contemporary culture, with its emphasis on multiracialism and the artificiality of race.

I have suggested two strategies used by passing narratives in a "post-race" world: one involves adopting blackness by simultaneously disavowing and claiming whiteness, while another puts two modes of passing into effect concurrently. In both narratives, generational conflict fuels the competing narratives within a single text: James's narrative in *The Color of Water* (in which race is about black and white) clashes with his mother's (in which race is about black, white, and Jewish), while *Life on the Color Line* offers one narrative in which Greg passes for white and another (fueled largely by his father) in which he passes for black. It is worth noting, too, that a number of the generic features laid out in earlier chapters can be found in the contemporary narratives. The motif of doubles is present in *Life on the Color Line*. Billy's upward mobility—he becomes a professor of law and marries a beautiful blonde—is contrasted with his brother Mike's downward spiral into alcoholism, jail, and eventual blindness. At least in the eyes of his father, who repeatedly calls Mike a "nigger," Billy is the whiter of the two brothers; such light/dark doubling lends structure to many "classic" passing narratives.

The role of geography as a racial signifier remains a constant in white passing narratives, particularly contemporary ones. Both *The Color of Water* and *Life on the Color Line* are kinetic texts in which the protagonist's move from one *space* to another signifies a move from one *race* to another. The fantasy, which began as anxiety, that *being* near black *makes one* near black is still very much in effect today—but it must present itself in new and complex ways that jibe with the contemporary racial climate. Proximity is still potent—figures ranging from Eminem to McBride and Williams are still initiated into "blackness" through physical proximity to the neighborhood, the housing project, and the homosocial bonding that occurs in such spaces (or, in the case of Halsell and others, the sexual bonding they experience there)—but it can no longer stand alone. The more conscious we are of appropriation and imitation, the more complex and varied aare our passing narratives, and the more proximity becomes one of several steps in any racial transformation. It is when *near* black becomes *near(ly)* black that geography ends and racial myth begins.

Epilogue
Hits and Misses of a Racial Free-for-All

Not all white-to-black passing scenarios make for poignant memoirs or become gripping films. Some make headlines and become talk show fodder. In 1988 the *New York Times* reported on Philip and Paul Malone, "fair-haired, fair complexioned" twins who applied for jobs as firefighters in Boston in 1975 but were rejected because of low civil service test scores. They reapplied two years later and were hired—not because their scores had changed but because their race presumably had. As they explained twenty years later when they applied for promotions and faced a barrage of questions about their initial applications, after their mother had allegedly showed them a sepia-toned photograph of their "black" great-grandmother, the Malones had answered "black" to the question about race on the forms the second time, and they were hired as affirmative action applicants. Their claim was never substantiated, and the Malones lost their jobs.[1]

In 1983, forty-one-year-old Mark Stebbins won election to the city council in Stockton, California, a city with a population of 169,000, 37 percent of whom were black and 46 percent Hispanic. Although he billed himself throughout his campaign as a black politician, Stebbins had, the newspapers reported, "curly light brown hair, blue eyes, white skin, and, according to his birth certificate, white parents." Shortly after Stebbins's victory, a black councilman—named, ironically enough, Ralph White—took him to task for fraud and demanded a recall; Stebbins, in protest, declared that because he "felt" black, because he was "more at home among blacks than whites," and because his wife was black, he qualified as black himself. The public didn't agree; Stebbins lost his seat in the recall.[2]

Law professor Randall Kennedy cites both of these cases as examples of racial autonomy gone awry. He does not, however, allow them to impinge on his fundamental opposition to race-based classification systems. "I, for one," he writes, "believe it would be better to tolerate some racial fraud, or even a considerable amount of it, under a regime of racial self-identification than to allow affirmative-action programs to be policed via the imposition on individuals of racial identity tests."[3] Kennedy's argument—the choose your own race approach—raises critical questions about the enterprise of white passing and white crossover. One cannot read an entire book about whites who adopt or appropriate black identities without asking, at its conclusion, is it fair? It is time to pose explicitly the question I have been insinuating all along: How do we render value judgments on the figures in these narratives, whites who claim blackness? As Kobena Mercer puts it: "At what point do such identifications result in an imitative masquerade of white ethnicity? At what point do they result in ethical and political alliances? How do we tell the difference?" In a pointed attack on the white Negro in 1957, Seymour Krim meditated along similar lines: "How 'Negro' should white musicians and jazz-lovers allow themselves to become? Can they maintain a balance of self-identity even while loving the music? And more important, does it follow that to be influenced by the music you have to adopt Negro values[?] . . . Further, does just loving the music mean that immediately you become part Negro, as it were, turn your back on your own inheritance?"[4]

I want to conclude this book by casting a wide net and laying out the philosophical implications of Mercer's and Krim's incisive questions and Kennedy's argument about racial identification. First, do some whites indeed possess a stronger claim to "black" culture, especially music, than others? Are some modes of appropriation more "authentic," appropriate, or legitimate than others? Second, is passing for black inevitably grounded in racist stereotypes about whiteness as sterile and blackness as primitive/authentic, or can it be a complex, progressive act? When is white-to-black passing taking things too far—or not taking them far enough?

The Stebbins and Malone cases serve as a worthwhile point of entry into such quandaries. The Malones, after all, are a case study in what is *wrong* with claiming blackness when one lacks either the outward appearance or the family tree to shore up that claim. They—like the growing number of college applicants taking DNA tests in the hopes of discovering reasons to check the "black" or "Hispanic" boxes on their applications—reflect two fundamentally wrongheaded approaches to race.[5] First, their motives were material. They used blackness as a means to an end, an object to be consumed, an accessory to be featured and then cast off when it was no longer lucrative or useful. The same can be said of two additional approaches to crossover identification: Grace Halsell's sexual tourism, discussed in chapter 3, and scenarios in which racial crossover is merely a superficial adolescent phase. "Born theoretically white," Leslie Fiedler wrote of Americans in 1964, "we are permitted to pass our childhood as imaginary Indians, our adolescence as imaginary Negroes, and only then are expected to settle down to being what we really are: white once more."[6] Being a "wigger" today, says David Roediger in his article "*Guineas, Wiggers,* and the Dramas of Racialized Culture," is often associated with adolescence in that a "wigger" is essentially an adolescent, two-dimensional projection of the Other, built of reified ideas about blackness and stereotypes that are more caricature than reality. Such a model would de-authenticate many: the over-the-top teenagers in *Black and White*; Elvis and countless other black performers whose youthful identities were born of black cultural influence but soon became whitewashed; today's young Japanese hip-hop fans—Joe Wood aptly dubbed them "yellow Negroes"—at clubs and record stores named Harlem and Sounds of Blackness, who feature a style called *burapan*: outsized FUBU clothing, crimped hair, skin darkened with the aid of tanning booths and makeup.[7] But this category would exclude Otis and Mezzrow and Ruth McBride Jordan, who self-identified as black for the bulk of their lives and were anything but Johnny-come-latelys, fleetingly consuming blackness.

The Malones' claim to blackness also hinges on scientifically problematic notions of race and the "one-drop rule." Biologically speaking, race is becoming an increasingly bankrupt concept. Even the scientifically challenged, however, can recognize that possessing one or two relatives with any traceable amount of black ancestry hardly makes for a sound reason to reconfigure one's racial status—unless we cling to the archaic racist notion that the slightest tinge of black "blood" has potent transformative powers. In this light, Stebbins's claim to black identity carries more weight than the Malones': Like Otis or Ruth McBride, his crossover identification and passing hinge on culture, not biology. To lay claim to a race through cultural identification, as opposed to "biology," is to apprehend something progressive: "race" is not a scientific reality but a very real social one.

The contrast between, on the one hand, Stebbins, Mezzrow, Otis, and McBride, and on the other the "wiggers" of the world, crystallizes something else I have been suggesting throughout this book: that believable, estimable white passers lay claim to blackness by reason of their identification with a culture—a time-honored African American aesthetic. Although scholars such as Walter Benn Michaels reject the notion of "black culture" as always and ever essentialist—one is not black because one does "black" things, Benn Michaels famously argued; one does "black" things because one has already been designated as essentially black—there is a longstanding tradition of critics, from James Weldon Johnson, Ralph Ellison, and Albert Murray to contemporary academics such as Joel Dinerstein and Gena Dagel Caponi, who defend and/or define the "black" in "black culture." "The African American aesthetic," Caponi writes, "is a set of techniques and practices—a technology of stylization—that recur over time and across different forms of cultural expression." Music is the "key" to that aesthetic, she explains; it is "the fulcrum of African culture and the expression that sustained African aesthetic principles in the Americas."[8] Caponi goes on to talk about such cultural "technologies" as African dance, vernacular traditions including signifyin(g), and the aesthetic of the "cool." I propose that admirable white passers rely on an understanding of and an identification with elements of this African American aesthetic: Mezzrow's vernacular, for instance; Otis's music; Ruth McBride Jordan's lifelong experience of Otherness, first as a Jew and then as the mother and wife of African Americans. Their cross-identification is predicated on a genuine understanding and enactment of black culture. It is also accompanied by an awareness of the complexity of adopted African American identities: however black they may be, all concede being at least partly white. In discussing Eric Clapton's identification with Robert Johnson, George Lipsitz is wary of artists whose identification with the Other is steeped in romanticized visions of that Other, and I would suggest that for the most part, heroic passers such as Mezzrow and Otis heed his warning: "If we are going to be honest about the words we share—and the worlds we share—we have to face the harsh facts that divide us as well as the fond hopes that might one day unite us. Romanticism gives us a wishbone, but combating racism requires us to display some backbone."[9]

Eminem, too, steers clear of romanticizing the blacks and the black culture with which he identifies and—by remaining constantly alert to white privilege, in lyrics and in interviews—deliberately calls attention to that which not only unites him with but also separates him from the Other. His art form, meanwhile, is a stunning incarnation of the hip-hop aesthetic, a modern rendition of the "cool" tradition that runs through African American art. "It is cool to sweeten hurt with song and motion; it is hot to concentrate upon the pain," writes Robert Farris Thompson.[10] In an essay about Lester Young, Joel Dinerstein suggests that cool is "an ideal state of balance, a calm but engaged state of mind between the emotional poles of 'hot' (excited, aggressive, intense, hostile) and 'cold' (unfeeling, efficient, mechanistic)—in other words, a relaxed 'intensity.'" Of the four "core African American cool concepts" that Dinerstein lays out, the fourth is most vitally hip-hop: "to be emotionally expressive within an artistic frame of restraint."[11] Rappers never speak their pain; they rhyme it. Rakim, the Notorious B.I.G., Jay-Z, 50 Cent, and so on and so forth— their subject matter is hot as hell, but their delivery is cool as ice. Likewise, Eminem delivers his emotionally fraught lyrics about his mother, his wife, and his trailer park traumas in a tone that is often comical and aggressive, but never overly emotive. He is hip-hop because he is cool to the maximum.

Despite the fact that we can distinguish between those who lay claim to a culture and those who lay claim to a caricature, there are still vexing issues at stake in laying cultural claim to another race. When the Malones were asked to support their claims of being black, the Personnel Administrator for the Commonwealth of Massachusetts cited these criteria: applicants can claim blackness "(1) by visual observation of their features; (2) by appropriate documentary evidence, such as birth certificates, establishing black ancestry; or (3) by evidence that they or their families hold themselves out to be Black and are considered to be Black in the community."[12] The definition of race is ludicrously loose here, as if deliberately attempting to sidestep theoretical quagmires altogether: "race" can be biological (2) or cultural (3); it can be external (1) or internal (2, 3). But one has to admit that in the real world, racial identification is a dual-faceted, practical process; it involves taking into consideration how one classifies oneself (by any combination of ancestry, appearance, and culture) and how one is classified by others (by appearance and social coding). If "blackness" is a social construct, then the ability to be socially construed as black ought to play at least some role in any justifiable claim to that label. As Stebbins's opponent, Ralph White, told the *Times* reporter, "Whites can have a concern for blacks, but they don't know what it's like to have a door slammed in their face."[13] For all that we might support McBride Jordan or Mezzrow or Otis or abolitionist John Brown in their claims to the "black box," so to speak, we have to acknowledge the one considerable way in which they *cannot* be justly deemed black: outwardly. And when it comes to an entity—race—that is at least partly a matter of external appearances that have been deemed to mean something far greater than just the way a person looks, outsides make a world of difference.

The fact is, cross-cultural identification raises knotty questions because the issue of cultural ownership is itself knotty. Nowadays there are, generally speaking, two approaches to that hotly debated issue, which most vividly rears its head in the context of discourse about popular music. In one approach—

call it the "happy hybridity" model—culture is celebrated as an interracial, international mash-up, and a genre of music such as Brazil's Baile Funk might be celebrated for embodying what Sasha Frere-Jones in the *New Yorker* called "the intricate connecting, borrowing, and trading that are the essence of popular music."[14] In the "happy hybridity" model, white passers or cross-identifiers are par for the course, natural outgrowths of contemporary cook-up culture.

But in another model—call it the "onerous ownership" model—they are villains: cultural pirates or thieves. *The Source* magazine, for instance—for a time the preeminent hip-hop publication—avidly protested Eminem's success, claiming in an on-line open letter that the white rapper was "being used as a tool by the corporate machine to steal hip-hop and make it their own." The magazine took a hard-and-fast stance on cultural ownership: "Just like generations past, when Jazz and Rock 'n' Roll were lost, it seems that hip hop culture is being snatched right out from under us."[15] A 2003 *Ebony* headline—"White Stars are Ripping Off Rap and R&B"—also embodies the "onerous ownership" approach to culture.[16] Clearly this approach has its theoretical problems. Does inventing something necessarily give one rights to it—especially when that invention (hip-hop) is a product of other inventions (reggae, disco, funk, spoken-word poetry)? Even if it does, don't copyrights eventually expire? In the end, the history of music is a game of cultural Ping-Pong between races and genres: a rapper may be influenced by a 1970s rocker, who was influenced by an R&B act, who learned rhythm from a jazz musician, who was influenced by a classical pianist, and so on. Hip-hop as a genre was at least partly born of Jamaican toasting—but the art of Jamaican toasting was itself an imitation of American radio DJs in the 1940s and 1950s, who chatted garrulously over the songs they broadcasted. The anxiety of cultural transmission runs deep.

But at the same time, too many chapters in American cultural history prove the perils of the "happy hybridity" model; one cannot forget that our cultural back-and-forth has rarely been governed by fair trade laws. Take, for instance, the case of radio pioneer Vernon Winslow. Born to a privileged black family in Chicago, he attended Chicago's Art Institute and moved to Louisiana, where he wrote a "Jive-Lingo" column for the *Louisiana Weekly* under the pen name "Poppa Stoppa." Jive, as he called it, didn't come naturally to his highbrow tongue; it was a masquerade that he stepped up a notch when a local white radio station, WMJR, asked him to adapt his column for an on-air show in the late 1940s. There was one caveat: since Winslow was black and the radio station was white, he was to write the show's transcript, but white DJs would read it on the air. Under his tutelage these white boys were transformed into "Poppa Stoppas," expert at delivering Winslow originals like "Wham, bam, thank you, ma'am" and "Look at the gold tooth, Ruth." All ran smoothly until one fateful broadcast, when the Poppa Stoppa of the day failed to show up for work. Panicked, Winslow went on the air and delivered his own jive routine. He was promptly fired. It was one thing for whites to go on the radio and talk black but quite another for a black man to do the same.

Ultimately, Winslow's story has a happy ending: he turned to advertising, earned new radio sponsors, was reborn on the air as Doctor Daddy-O, and became the toast of New Orleans. But his saga markedly reflects the uneven power relations at work in what I have described as the game of cultural Ping-Pong that has defined American—and, really, the essence of postcolonial—culture. It is a marvelous example of what Homi Bhabha has called "colonial mimicry," that is,

> the desire for a reformed, recognizable Other, *as a subject of a difference that is almost the same, but not quite.* Which is to say, that the discourse of mimicry is constructed around an ambivalence; in order to be effective, mimicry must continually produce its slippage, its excess, its difference. . . . [M]imicry emerges as the representation of a difference that is itself a process of disavowal. Mimicry is, thus, the sign of a double articulation; a complex strategy of reform, regulation and discipline, which "appropriates" the Other as it visualizes power.[17]

Mimicry reflects the vexed power dynamics at the heart of subject-Other relations. Reebee Garofalo has tidily summed up the historical reality of most musical exchanges between black and white with the phrase "black roots, white fruits."[18] Even though hip-hop may yet defy this pattern—it has come of age, after all, in a culture hyperconscious of the anxieties of influence—the music scene has long been governed by inequities: credit has simply not been given where it was due. This is true literally, in that black artists never received the same rewards as white performers who covered their songs, and metaphorically, for thanks to the cover song phenomenon, by the third generation of fans, rock's black roots were obscured in the public imagination by its white fruits. This is a fact that still rankles. In 2004, for instance, the Associated Press reported on the controversy surrounding Miller Brewing Company's "50th Anniversary of Rock 'n' Roll" beer cans—which featured not a single black artist.[19] I myself interviewed Japanese DJs in Tokyo who had no clue that their music was *not* a Japanese invention; having absorbed hip-hop and black American pop culture so thoroughly, they rapped in Japanese and claimed that there was nothing uniquely African American about it. They are passers in denial, and living examples of the trickle-down effect: first-generation crossover performers conceive of their art form—and their own racial identities—very differently than their heirs do.

Ultimately, I propose a theoretical balance between happy hybridity and onerous ownership, recognizing, as Ronald Radano does, that "black music is patently intermusical as it is intermediated and, finally, interracial," while at the same time conceding that, first, being widely acknowledged as an essentially black cultural product does, in some respects, qualify something (for example, certain genres of music) as just that, and second, the interraciality of which Radano speaks has long been tainted by a legacy of inequality.[20] For this reason I support George Lipsitz's demand that cross-racial "explorations have to be carried out with a self-conscious understanding of unequal power relations." His critique of David Byrne's and Paul Simon's appropriation of "ethnic" music is based on "their unwillingness to examine their own relationship to power or to allow for reciprocal subjectivities between and among cultures. . . . They obscure power relations in the present as well as the enduring consequences of past acts of subordination and suppression. Most important, they define delight in difference as a process organized around exotic images from overseas, with no corollary inspection of their own identities."[21] Lipsitz, in other words, would likely approve of Mezzrow, who, while appropriating blackness, never ceased scrutinizing his own identity as a Jew and as a white man, with all the power privileges that entailed. In lyrics and interviews, Eminem and other self-consciously white rappers have done the same ("If I was black, I would've sold half," Eminem raps in "White America."). Even Elvis did a decent job in this regard. "Let's face it," Presley told *Jet* in 1957, addressing his rhythm and blues influences, "nobody can sing that kind of music like colored people. I can't sing it like Fats Domino can. I know that."[22] Vanilla Ice, by contrast, famously never credited friend and producer Mario Johnson, aka Chocolate, for lyrics and music on his hit "Ice Ice Baby." Burton Peretti draws a distinction between Dixieland musicians, who denied the black sources of their music, and the Chicago jazz musicians who "approached black culture with such openness and repaid it with comparable gratitude, praise, and emulation."[23] "Correct" appropriation, I propose, is not about cultural copyrighting but about cultural footnoting, giving literal and metaphorical homage where homage is due.

To pay homage is to "out" American culture as the mulatto that it is. America's closeted identity, so to speak, is that of a hybrid, and yet all along America has fashioned a public face that is, to paraphrase George Schuyler in *Black No More*, utterly without any black branches on its family tree. This country has long been steeped in what Lipsitz has called a "possessive investment in whiteness," which "prevents us from facing the present openly and honestly."[24] I would add that the possessive investment in whiteness prevents us from contending with our crossbred *past* honestly as well. Cross-identifiers have an opportunity to protest the possessive investment in whiteness—in the way that Ruth McBride Jordan does—as long as they embody what Peter McLaren deems "postcolonial hybridity." "To choose blackness or brownness merely as a way to escape the stigma of whiteness and to avoid responsibility for owning whiteness is still very much an act of whiteness," he writes. "To choose blackness or brownness as a way of politically misidentifying with white privilege is, on the other hand, an act of transgression, a traitorous act that reveals a fidelity to the struggle for justice."[25]

To pay homage is, finally, to give thought to issues of influence and power, privilege and positionality—and that process is what lends white-to-black passing its greatest potential as a progressive act. In comparing the musical career of Elvis to that of Jerry Lieber and Mike Stoller—two Jewish songwriters who grew up among blacks in the 1940s and wrote songs, such as "Charlie Brown" and "Yakety Yak," that were inflected with black dialect—Nelson George writes that while Elvis "never put the time into developing his interpretation of blackness," Lieber and Stoller's songs "constituted the thinking white man's equivalent of Presley's gyrations." George, in other words, finds it laudable to *interpret* blackness but not to *imitate* it. LeRoi Jones puts forward a similar proposition in *Blues People*, in describing the music of the white Chicago jazzmen. "The result of this cultural 'breakdown' was not always mere imitation," he writes, explaining that it often resulted in the evolution of different jazz *styles*—one "white," one "black."[26]

The process of interpretation that George and Jones lay out here is akin to the process of paying homage that I described earlier. Both compel white passers or cross-identifiers to engage in self-conscious scrutiny of their raced place in the cultural sphere. And such scrutiny cultivates a certain double-consciousness in crossover whites, a precious, profound double consciousness that means refusing to take race for granted; it means being aware of both how one sees the world and how the world sees one. White passing and cross-racial identifications can be tremendously progressive acts, but only when they are persistently self-reflexive in this way, when they result in an exploration of blackness, whiteness, and the power dynamics forever at play between the two.[27] This is quite often the case with contemporary white rappers, who have encouraged whites, for perhaps the first time, to begin speaking of themselves *as whites*. On VH1's *The (White) Rapper Show*, which aired in early 2007, the white rappers never ceased offering reverence to hip-hop history and persistently alluded to their own whiteness; one rapper's stage name—John Brown—even called attention to his role not as an ur–black artist but as a white artist existing within a nonwhite legacy and standing in protest to white hegemony. As Roediger writes, the growth of hip-hop culture means that "to an unprecedented extent white youth are listening to an explicit critique, often an unsparing critique, of 'white' society."[28] This is meaningful indeed, and it is the sweetest fruit that cultural crossover can bear. With their essentialist leanings and their forays into exoticism, white passers have their glaring flaws. But at their best—from Griffin and Mezzrow to Houzeau, Otis, McBride Jordan, and even Halsell—they have the power to cultivate double consciousness not just within themselves but within a culture that is too often mired in the rigid racial thinking and stubborn color blindness that are the legacy of America's literal and figurative color line.

NOTES

INTRODUCTION

1. George Bourne, *Picture of Slavery* (Middletown, Conn.: Edwin Hunt, 1834), 88.

2. Joel Williamson, *New People: Miscegenation and Mulattoes in the United States* (New York: Free Press, 1980), 51.

3. Josephine Schuyler, "Seventeen Years of Mixed Marriage," *Negro Digest*, July 1946, 65.

4. Philip Brian Harper, "Passing for What? Racial Masquerade and the Demands of Upward Mobility," *Callaloo* 21.2 (1998): 382.

5. For more on the role of the dupe in passing, see Amy Robinson, "It Takes One to Know One: Passing and Communities of Common Interest," *Critical Inquiry* 20 (1994): 715–36.

6. Carlyle Van Thompson, *The Tragic Black Buck: Racial Masquerading in the American Literary Imagination* (New York: Peter Lang, 2004), 3.

7. Harryette Mullen, "Optic White: Blackness and the Production of Whiteness," *Diacritics* 24.2–3 (1994): 77.

8. Houzeau was a civil rights activist, natural scientist, and journalist who served as editor of the *New Orleans Tribune* until 1868. In addition to being taken for black, he also passed as a Mexican in order to avoid arrest for aiding in the escape of slaves and Unionists during the Civil War. For more on the fascinating life of Houzeau, see his memoir, with David C. Rankin's introduction, Jean-Charles Houzeau, *My Passage at the New Orleans Tribune*, ed. David C. Rankin and trans. Gerard F. Denault (Baton Rouge: Louisiana State University Press, 2001), 84.

9. These two scenarios can be separated along the lines of Kate Baldwin's distinction between becoming "black," which refers to appearance, and becoming "Negro," which implies second-class citizenship and the social roles that come along with it. Kate Baldwin, "Black Like Who? Cross-Testing the Real Lines of John Howard Griffin's *Black Like Me*," *Cultural Critique* 40 (Fall 1998): 103–43.

10. In its interest in cultural definitions of whiteness, my work is allied with the mission of "whiteness studies," which is flourishing in fields ranging from cultural studies to law. David Roediger is best known for his pioneering work in white studies, especially *The Wages of Whiteness* (London: Verso, 1991), *Towards the Abolition of Whiteness* (London: Verso, 1994), and his anthology *Black on White: Black Writers on What It Means to Be White* (New York: Schocken, 1998). Noel Ignatiev, *How the Irish Became White* (New York: Routledge, 1995), is another crucial work in the field, as is Richard Dyer, *White* (London: Routledge, 1997). For a good overview, see Les Back and Vron Ware's introduction to their book *Out of Whiteness* (Chicago: University of Chicago Press, 2001), and Ruth Frankenberg's introduction to her anthology *Displacing Whiteness* (Durham: Duke University Press, 1997).

11. Samira Kawash, *Dislocating the Color Line: Identity, Hybridity, and Singularity in African-American Literature* (Stanford: Stanford University Press, 1997), 8.

12. Kevin J. Mumford, *Interzones: Black/White Sex Districts in Chicago and New York in the Early Twentieth Century* (New York: Columbia University Press, 1997), 141.

13. Barbara Browning, *Infectious Rhythm: Metaphors of Contagion and the Spread of African Culture* (New York: Routledge, 1998), 6–7.

14. Maria Carla Sanchez and Linda Schlossberg write that "passing can be experienced as a source of radical pleasure or intense danger; it can function as a badge of shame or a source of pride." Maria Carla Sanchez and Linda Schlossberg, eds., introduction to *Passing: Identity and Interpretation in Sexuality, Race, and Religion* (New York: New York University Press, 2001), 3. Also see Eric Lott's oft-cited discussion of blackface, an act he reads as a product of both admiration and appropriation, desire and repulsion. Eric Lott, *Love and Theft: Blackface Minstrelsy and the American Working Class* (New York: Oxford University Press, 1995).

15. Elaine Ginsberg argues for the former and Juda Bennett suggests the latter. See Elaine Ginsberg, ed., introduction to *Passing and the Fictions of Identity* (Durham: Duke University Press, 1996), 3; Juda Bennett, *The Passing Figure* (New York: Peter Lang, 1996), 36.

16. Ralph Ellison, "What America Would Be Like without Blacks," in *The Collected Essays of Ralph Ellison*, ed. John F. Callahan (New York: Modern Library, 1995), 580. James Baldwin, too, aptly said of Americans that "no other people has ever been so deeply involved in the lives of black men, and vice versa." James Baldwin, *Notes of a Native Son* (1955; reprint, Boston: Beacon Press, 1984), 175.

17. James Weldon Johnson, *The Autobiography of an Ex-Coloured Man* (1927; reprint, New York: Vintage, 1989), 21. Along these lines, Samira Kawash, in *Dislocating the Color Line*, reads the Ex-Coloured Man as one who "cannot *be* black or white; his appearance as black or white is produced through the imitation of the blackness or whiteness of others" (147).

18. Michael Omi and Howard Winant, *Racial Formation in the United States from the 1960s to the 1980s* (New York: Routledge, 1986), 68.

19. See, for instance, Kawash, *Dislocating the Color Line*; Bennett, *The Passing Figure*; Ginsberg, *Passing and the Fictions of Identity*, an anthology that includes only one essay on white passing; and Sanchez and Schlossberg, *Passing*. Brooke Kroeger's excellent *Passing: When People Can't Be Who They Are* (New York: Public Affairs, 2003) devotes one brief but rich chapter to a white woman who unwittingly passes as black.

20. Susan Gubar and Michael Rogin have similarly differentiated between black passing and blackface; see Susan Gubar, *Racechanges: White Skin, Black Face in American Culture* (New York: Oxford University Press, 1997), 44–45; Michael Rogin, *Blackface, White Noise: Jewish Immigrants in the Hollywood Melting Pot* (Berkeley: University of California Press, 1996), 124.

21. I am grateful to Joel Dinerstein for this phrase.

22. James Baldwin, *Nobody Knows My Name* (1961; reprint, New York: Vintage, 1993), 230–31.

23. Gayle Wald, *Crossing the Line: Racial Passing in Twentieth-Century American Literature and Culture* (Durham: Duke University Press, 2000), 16.

24. Black passing narratives have indeed flourished in nonfiction formats—consider Walter White's memoir, *A Man Called White*, for instance—but it took some time until they did so. Not until well into the twentieth century, long after Jim Crow was dismantled, did black passers speak out and deliver their confessionals. White passing narratives, by contrast, have long been rooted in nonfiction.

25. Priscilla Wald, in *Constituting Americans: Cultural Anxiety and Narrative Form* (Durham: Duke University Press, 1995), makes much of Freud's uncanny: "Intrinsic to the narrative of identity is the ongoing possibility of a return to its own genesis in the uncanny (the unrecognizable self)—in its efforts, that is, to establish continuity where there has been a rupture" (10).

26. Ann Douglas, *Terrible Honesty: Mongrel Manhattan in the 1920s* (New York: Noonday, 1995), 77.

27. James Weldon Johnson, "American Negro Spirituals," in *Signifyin(g), Sanctifyin', and Slam Dunking: A Reader in African American Expressive Culture*, ed. Gena Dagel Caponi (Amherst: University of Massachusetts Press, 1999), 70.

28. Kevin Mumford, *Interzones: Black/White Sex Districts in Chicago and New York in the Early Twentieth Century* (New York: Columbia University Press, 1997), 30.

29. Mel Watkins, *On the Real Side: Laughing, Lying, and Signifying: The Underground Tradition of African-American Humor* (New York: Simon & Schuster, 1994), 207.

30. Mumford, *Interzones*, 35.

31. Ibid., 143.

32. Richard Slotkin, *Regeneration through Violence* (Middletown, Conn.: Wesleyan University Press, 1973), 110–12.

33. See chap. 5 of Philip Brian Harper, *Are We Not Men? Masculine Anxiety and the Problem of African-American Identity* (New York: Oxford University Press, 1996), and Valerie Smith, "Reading the Intersection of Race and Gender in Narratives of Passing," *Diacritics* 24.2–3 (Summer–Fall 1994): 43–57.

34. I take the phrase from Paul Spickard, *Mixed Blood: Intermarriage and Ethnic Identity in Twentieth-Century America* (Madison: University of Wisconsin Press, 1989), 338.

35. See Shirlee Taylor Haizlip, *The Sweeter the Juice* (New York: Simon & Schuster, 1994), and Judy Scales-Trent, *Notes of a White Black Woman* (University Park: Pennsylvania State University Press, 1995).

36. Walter Benn Michaels addresses this paradox cogently in *Our America* (Durham: Duke University Press, 1995) and "Autobiography of an Ex–White Man," *Transition* 73 (1997): 122–43. The *Newsweek* issue is from 18 September 2000.

37. James McBride, *The Color of Water: A Black Man's Tribute to His White Mother* (New York: Riverhead, 1996), 16.

38. Kobena Mercer, *Welcome to the Jungle: New Positions in Black Cultural Studies* (New York: Routledge, 1994), 216.

39. "Even though he seemed to be down with us in the beginning, it appears that Eminem may be becoming a part of a dangerous, corruptive cycle that promotes the blatant theft of a culture from the community that created it. Willingly or not, he is being used as a tool by the corporate machine to steal hip-hop and make it their own. Not since Jazz and Rock'n Roll has a culture influenced so many people, so quickly, worldwide, the way hip-hop has done, that the powers-that-be felt threatened enough to take it from us." Gotti, *The Source* on-line magazine, http://www.daveyd.com/commentarysourcevseminem.html (accessed 22 December 2007).

40. LeRoi Jones, *Blues People* (1963; reprint, New York: William Morrow, 1999), 86.

1. WHITE PANIC AND WHITE PASSING

1. Cited in *George Bourne and The Book and Slavery Irreconcilable*, by John W. Christie and Dwight L. Dumond (Wilmington, Del: The Historical Society of Delaware, 1969), 109.

2. In the first chapter of *Mulatto America*, Stephen Talty meticulously unearths the little-known history of white slavery in America. Stephen Talty, *Mulatto America: At the Crossroads of Black and White Culture: A Social History* (New York: HarperCollins, 2003).

3. Edward S. Abdy, *Journal of a Residence and Tour in North America from 1833 to August 1834*, vol. 2 (London, 1835), 9–10; Joel Williamson, *New People: Miscegenation and Mulattoes in the United States* (New York: Free Press, 1980), 69; James Hugo Johnston, *Race Relations in Virginia and Miscegenation in the South, 1776–1860* (Amherst: University of Massachusetts Press, 1970), 209; Martha Hodes, *White Women, Black Men* (New Haven: Yale University Press, 1997), 29. For another slave-era case of what could be seen as white passing, see E. Franklin Frazier, *The Negro Family in the United States* (Chicago: University of Chicago Press, 1966), 87–89, which describes the case of two white women who identified with the black race in order not to be separated from their black half-sisters. Virginia Dominguez, in *White by Definition: Social Classification in Creole Louisiana* (New Brunswick, N.J.: Rutgers University Press, 1986), describes a 1956 case, *Green v. The City of New York*, in which a black couple could not adopt their daughter unless her race was changed on her birth certificate from white to colored.

4. Frantz Fanon, *Black Skin, White Masks* (New York: Grove Press, 1967), 155.

5. William and Ellen Craft, *Running a Thousand Miles for Freedom: The Escape of William and Ellen Craft from Slavery* (1860; reprint, Baton Rouge: Louisiana State University Press, 1999), 4; hereafter cited by page number in the text.

6. William Wells Brown, *Clotel* (1853), in *Three Classic African-American Novels*, ed. William Andrews (New York: Penguin, 1990), 121; hereafter cited by page number in the text.

7. Nancy Bentley notes this in her discussion of Richard Hildreth's *Archy Moore* in "White Slaves: The Mulatto Hero in Antebellum Fiction," in *Subjects and Citizens: Nation, Race, and Gender from Oroonoko to Anita Hill*, ed. Michael Moon and Cathy Davidson (Durham: Duke University Press, 1995), 195–216. Discussions of white slavery also pervade early feminist rhetoric, in which women often compared themselves to slaves; see Karen Sanchez-Eppler, "Bodily Bonds: The Intersecting Rhetorics of Feminism and Abolition," *Representations* 24 (Fall 1998): 49; and Russ Castronovo, "Incidents in the Life of a White Woman," *American Literary History* 10.2 (Summer 1998): 237–65.

8. Frank Webb, *The Garies and Their Friends* (1857; reprint, New York: Arno Press, 1969), 188.

9. George Washington Cable, "Salome Muller, The White Slave," in *Strange True Stories of Louisiana* (New York: Charles Scribner's Sons, 1889), 164; hereafter cited by page number in the text.

10. David Roediger, *The Wages of Whiteness* (London: Verso, 1991), 169. That

whites could be imagined as slaves without losing their whiteness is further indi-
cated by the fact that a number of antebellum racial theorists argued that indeed
whites could be slaves. Men such as Judge William Harper in South Carolina, for
instance, argued that slavery was not about racial inferiority but about social inferiority, which could apply to whites as well as blacks. George Frederickson, *The
Black Image in the White Mind* (New York: Harper & Row, 1971), 59. Harper, in
1835, argued that "it may be well and proper that a man of worth, honesty, industry, and respectability, should have the rank of a white man, while a vagabond
of the same degree of blood should be confined to the inferior caste. It is hardly
necessary to say that a slave cannot be a white man." Williamson, *New People*,
18. Talty analyzes the rhetoric of those, such as George Fitzhugh, who proposed
that socioeconomic conditions, not race, ought to be the criteria for enslavement.
Talty, *Mulatto America*, 21.

11. Naomi Zack, *Race and Mixed Race* (Philadelphia: Temple University Press,
1993), 82.

12. It is worth noting that one pre-Reconstruction scenario involving white
passing *did* blur racial lines quite a bit: cases of maroonage, as described by Peter
Linebaugh and Marcus Rediker in *The Many-Headed Hydra: Sailors, Slaves, Com-
moners, and the Hidden History of the Revolutionary Atlantic* (Boston: Beacon,
2000). The white maroons often adopted black identities. I thank Robin Kelley
for this reference.

13. Grace Elizabeth Hale, *Making Whiteness: The Culture of Segregation in the
South,1890–1940* (New York: Pantheon, 1998), 296.

14. C. Vann Woodward, *The Strange Career of Jim Crow* (New York: Oxford
University Press, 1966), 43.

15. Lawrence J. Friedman, *The White Savage: Racial Fantasies in the Postbellum South* (Englewood Cliffs, N.J.: Prentice-Hall, 1970), 86, 122. See also Josiah
C. Nott, *The Negro Race: Its Ethnology and History* (1866), in *Racial Determinism and the Fear of Miscegenation Pre-1900: Race and the Negro Problem*, ed. John
David Smith (New York: Garland Publishing, 1993), 1–28.

16. Nott, *The Negro Race*, 11.

17. Watson F. Quinby, *Mongrelism* (1876), in Smith, *Racial Determinism and the
Fear of Miscegenation Pre-1900* (New York: Garland, 1993), 394; G. W.Cable, *The
Silent South, Together With the Freedman's Case in Equity and the Covict Lease
System* (New York: Charles Scribner's Sons, 1899), 56; Eric Lott, *Love and Theft:
Blackface Minstrelsy and the American Working Class* (New York: Oxford University Press, 1995), 57. Martha Hodes notes that prior to Emancipation, intermarriage and interracial liaisons were more tolerated, and only after the Civil War
did they become a tremendous threat to whites. This underscores my point that
whites truly began to fear a loss of whiteness after the breakdown of the free/slave
distinction. Hodes, *White Women, Black Men*.

18. Williamson, *New People*, 108.

19. Ibid.

20. Ronald Takaki, *Iron Cages: Race and Culture in Nineteenth-Century America* (New York: Alfred A. Knopf, 1979), 31–32.

21. Claude Nolen, *The Negro's Image in the South* (Lexington: University of Kentucky Press, 1967), 191.

22. Leon Litwack, *Been in the Storm So Long: The Aftermath of Slavery* (New York: Alfred A. Knopf, 1979), 351.

23. Noel Ignatiev, *How the Irish Became White* (New York: Routledge, 1995).

24. Woodward, *Strange Career of Jim Crow*, 50.

25. W. J. Cash, *The Mind of the South* (New York: Doubleday, 1954), 119.

26. As Constance Penley explains, "If you *are* white trash, then you must engage in the never-ending labor of distinguishing yourself, of codifying your behavior so as to clearly signify a difference from blackness that will, in spite of everything, express some minuscule, if pathetic, measure of your culture's superiority." Constance Penley, "Crackers and Whackers: The White Trashing of Porn," in *White Trash: Race and Class in America*, ed. Annalee Newitz and Matt Wray (New York: Routledge, 1997), 90.

27. Nolen, *The Negro's Image in the South*, 171–73; John Higham, *Strangers in the Land: Patterns of American Nativism, 1860–1925* (Westport, Conn.: Greenwood Press, 1963), 66. David Roediger refers to the Italians of the late nineteenth century as members of the "not-yet-white population"; see Part II of *Towards the Abolition of Whiteness* (London: Verso, 1994).

28. Cathy Boeckmann, *A Question of Character: Scientific Racism and the Genres of American Fiction, 1892–1912* (Tuscaloosa: University of Alabama Press, 2000), 6; Louis Menand, *The Metaphysical Club* (New York: Farrar, Straus and Giroux, 2001), 123. Useful discussions of the relationship between Darwin and racial science include chapter 6 of *The Metaphysical Club*; Boeckmann's introduction to *A Question of Character*; and Charles Martin, *The White African-American Body* (New Brunswick, N.J.: Rutgers University Press, 2002), particularly 133–36.

29. Mary Douglas, *Purity and Danger* (1966; reprint, London: Routledge, 1995), 54, 140.

30. Also relevant to ideas about germs, contagion, and racial purity is early-twentieth-century rhetoric about the "immigrant menace." See Alan Kraut, *Silent Travelers: Germs, Genes, and the Immigrant Menace* (Baltimore: Johns Hopkins University Press, 1994).

31. Susan Gubar, *Racechanges: White Skin, Black Face in American Culture* (New York: Oxford University Press, 1997), 45.

32. *Sally Miller v. Louis Belmonti*, Supreme Court of Louisiana, Eastern District, New Orleans (July 1845).

33. Takaki, *Iron Cages*, 209.

34. Alice Hall Petry sees Cable's use of documentation as his way of "challenging the boundaries of fiction and non-fiction in ways that anticipate Joyce, Dos Passos, and the metafictionists of our own time." See Alice Hall Petry, "The Limits of Truth in Cable's 'Salome Muller,'" *Papers on Language and Literature* 27.1 (Winter 1991): 2–31.

35. Samira Kawash, *Dislocating the Color Line: Identity, Hybridity, and Singularity in African-American Literature* (Stanford: Stanford University Press, 1997), 147.

36. Shelly Fisher Fishkin, "Race and Culture at the Century's End: A Social Context for *Pudd'nhead Wilson*," in *Essays in Arts and Sciences* 19 (May 1990): 17. One aspect of the novel indicating that Twain was working anachronistically with postbellum ideologies about race is the fact, pointed out by Barbara Ladd, that in antebellum America, Tom and Roxy would have been legally white (according to Missouri law in 1855); in postbellum America the one-drop rule would have been applied more stringently, making the pair black. Barbara Ladd, *Nationalism and the Color Line in George W. Cable, Mark Twain, and William Faulkner* (Baton Rouge: Louisiana State University Press, 1996), 118–19.

37. This is Ladd's argument in *Nationalism and the Color Line*, 101.

38. Hershel Parker, *Flawed Texts and Verbal Icons* (Evanston: Northwestern University Press, 1984), 143.

39. Myra Jehlen, for instance, dismisses his role in the novel entirely, claiming that "although Chambers is sadly disadvantaged by his years of servitude, his debility has too little force to motivate the novel; nothing much comes from it or is expected to." Myra Jehlen, "The Ties That Bind: Race and Sex in *Pudd'nhead Wilson*," in *Mark Twain's Pudd'nhead Wilson*, ed. Susan Gillman and Forrest G. Robinson (Durham: Duke University Press, 1990), 107. Eric Sundquist, in his discussion of radical racial rhetoric and the novel, discusses Tom's imitation of whiteness but says nothing about Chambers's imitation of blackness. Eric Lott, in considering the role of blackface in *Pudd'nhead Wilson*, offers a detailed analysis of Tom but no mention of Chambers, who is perhaps the most salient blackface wearer in the novel. See Eric Sundquist, "Mark Twain and Homer Plessy," *Representations* 24 (Fall 1988): 102–28; Eric Lott, "Mr. Clemens and Jim Crow: Twain, Race, and Blackface," in *The Cambridge Companion to Mark Twain*, ed. Forrest G. Robinson (Cambridge: Cambridge University Press, 1995), 129–52.

40. Mark Twain, *Pudd'nhead Wilson* (1894; reprint, New York: Norton, 1994), 18–19; hereafter cited by page in the text.

41. Herman Melville, "Benito Cereno," in *Great Short Works of Herman Melville*, ed. Werner Berthoff (New York: Harper & Row 1969), 250.

42. I disagree with Myra Jehlen, who sees Chambers as feminized by being enslaved. Jehlen, "The Ties That Bind," 112.

43. See Linda A. Morris, "Beneath the Veil: Clothing, Race, and Gender in

Mark Twain's *Pudd'nhead Wilson*," *Studies in American Fiction* 27.1 (1999): 37–52; and Marjorie Garber, *Vested Interests* (New York: Routledge, 1992), 290–92.

44. Cited in Harryette Mullen, "Optic White: Blackness and the Production of Whiteness," *Diacritics* 24.2–3 (1994): 83.

45. Richard Slotkin, *Regeneration through Violence* (Middletown, Conn.: Wesleyan University Press, 1973), 54.

46. Warren Hedges, "If Uncle Tom Is White, Should We Call Him 'Auntie'? Race and Sexuality in Postbellum U.S. Fiction," in *Whiteness: A Critical Reader*, ed. Mike Hill (New York: New York University Press, 1997), 231.

47. Other "accidental" passers include the protagonists of William Dean Howells's *An Imperative Duty* and Francis E. Harper's *Iola Leroy*.

48. See James Weldon Johnson, *The Autobiography of an Ex-Coloured Man* (1927; reprint, New York: Vintage, 1989); Walter White, *Flight* (1926; reprint, Baton Rouge: Louisiana State University Press, 1998). The third potential passer in *Pudd'nhead Wilson* is, of course, Roxy. She stands as a specter of miscegenation in the novel and, as Arthur Pettit puts it, as the "most poignant example in Mark Twain's writing of his conviction that the greater crime of the South was not miscegenation, but the white Southerners' unwillingness to admit that mulattoes were, after all, the products of their own lust." Arthur G. Pettit, "The Black and White Curse: Miscegenation and *Pudd'nhead Wilson*," in *Pudd'nhead Wilson* (New York: Norton, 1980), 358. As Lott asserts, all narratives dealing with white appropriations of blackness return to miscegenation (*Love and Theft*, 57). Cable's mention of Salome's mulatto children brings such mixing to the foreground of his story. For Twain, miscegenation anxiety is embodied in Roxy, the white black woman, the beautiful and proud slave mother.

49. For more on this, see Parker, *Flawed Texts and Verbal Icons*.

50. Sundquist, "Mark Twain and Homer Plessy," 122.

51. Both Michael Rogin and Sarah Chinn have made much of this clue, writing at length about the crucial role of fingerprinting in the novel. Chinn sets up an interesting parallel between palm reading and fingerprinting in the novel, arguing that the novel is about the shift from one mode of identification to another, thus dramatizing, she claims, a trend in scientific inquiry in the United States at the end of the nineteenth century from embodied to disembodied (i.e., quantifiable). Also see John S. Whitley's claim that Twain's novel parodies detective fiction. Charles Martin argues that the fingerprinting motif parodies notions of racial essences. Michael Rogin, "Francis Galton and Mark Twain: The Natal Autograph in *Pudd'nhead Wilson*," in Gillman and Robinson, *Mark Twain's Pudd'nhead Wilson*, 73–85; Sarah Chinn, *Technology and the Logic of American Racism* (London: Continuum, 2000); John Whitley, "Mark Twain and the Limits of Detection," *Journal of American Studies* 21.1 (April 1987): 55–70; Martin, *The White African-American Body*, 138.

52. As Rogin, in linking fingerprints to eugenics, explains, the book's "mother story, scientifically reducing identity to natal autograph, establishes a fixed racial character against the power of play." Rogin, "Francis Galton and Mark Twain," 85.

53. Franco Moretti, *Signs Taken for Wonders* (London: Verso, 1983), 135.

54. Priscilla Wald reads a similar tension in narratives that explore "the overlapping and sometimes contradictory cultural practices through which personhood is formulated." Priscilla Wald, *Constituting Americans: Cultural Anxiety and Narrative Form* (Durham: Duke University Press, 1995), 113. Her readings of various texts, particularly Frederick Douglass's autobiography, highlight "the risky, complicated, and engaging strategies through which [these texts] confronted cultural anxieties: in order to be psychologically unsettling, they had to be formally unsettled" (113). In other words, she looks at the same tension between ideology (read: anxiety) and genre that cuts to the heart of Twain's and Cable's work. Wald makes the Freudian uncanny central to "national narratives of identity," which express anxiety about the relationship between the self that has been expressed in the text and the one that has been *suppressed* by it: "Intrinsic to the narrative of identity is the ongoing possibility of a return to its own genesis in the uncanny (the unrecognizable self)—its efforts, that is, to establish continuity where there has been a rupture" (10). The doubling that I have cited as a crucial trope in white passing narratives manifests this same use of the uncanny. In white slaves, the familiar (whiteness) converges with the unfamiliar (slavery). Chambers and Salome stand as uncanny reflections of their narrative "twins," Tom and Madame Karl. They are mirror images gone awry, familiar partners made unfamiliar by a twist of race.

55. Francis E. W. Harper, *Iola Leroy, or Shadows Uplifted* (1892; reprint, College Park, Md.: McGrath Publishing, 1969), 203, 234.

56. William Pickens, "The Vengeance of the Gods," in *The Vengeance of the Gods and Three Other Stories of Real American Color Line Life* (1922; reprint, New York: AMS Press, 1975), 11–86; hereafter cited by page number in the text.

57. For more on Pickens, see Sheldon Avery, *Up from Washington: William Pickens and the Negro Struggle for Equality, 1900–1954* (Newark: University of Delaware Press, 1989).

2. DY(E)ING TO BE BLACK

1. Jane Gaines, *Fire and Desire: Mixed-Race Movies in the Silent Era* (Chicago: University of Chicago Press, 2001).

2. Michael Awkward, *Negotiating Difference: Race, Gender, and the Politics of Positionality* (Chicago: University of Chicago Press, 1995), 19.

3. Ibid, 80–81.

4. Robert Montgomery Bird, *Sheppard Lee* (New York: Harper, 1836), 156; hereafter cited by page number in the text.

5. As Paul Petrie explains, Chesnutt subtly sought to "soften white resistance to accepting African-Americans as equals" and was therefore engaged in "re-deploying the generic conventions of white racist plantation-dialect fiction for racially progressive purposes." Paul Petrie, "Charles W. Chesnutt, *The Conjure Woman*, and the Racial Limits of Literary Meditation," *Studies in American Fiction* 27.2 (1999): 185, 183–84. For more on Chesnutt's radical reworking of the plantation genre tradition, see Robert Nowatzki, "'Passing' in a White Genre: Charles W. Chesnutt's Negotiations of the Plantation Tradition in *The Conjure Woman*," *American Literary Realism* 27.2 (Winter 1995): 20–36; Charles Duncan, "The White and the Black: Charles W. Chesnutt's Narrator-Protagonists and the Limits of Authorship," *Journal of Narrative Technique* 28.2 (Winter 1995): 111–33; Sandra Molineaux, "Expanding the Collective Memory: Charles W. Chesnutt's *The Conjure Woman Tales*," in *Memory, Narrative, Identity*, ed. Amrijit Singh, Joseph Skerrett, and Robert Hogan (Boston: Northeastern University Press, 1994), 164–76; Eugene Terry, "The Shadow of Slavery in Charles Chesnutt's *The Conjure Woman*," *Ethnic Groups* 4.1–2 (1982): 104–25; Valerie Babb, "Subversion and Repatriation in *The Conjure Woman*," *Southern Quarterly* 25.2 (Winter 1987): 66–75; Lorne Fienberg, "Charles W. Chesnutt and Uncle Julius: Black Storytellers at the Crossroads," *Studies in American Fiction* 15.2 (Autumn 1987): 161–73. For a book-length study of Chesnutt's progressivism, see William L. Andrews, *The Literary Career of Charles W. Chesnutt* (Baton Rouge: Louisiana State University Press, 1980), which also argues that Chesnutt employs the plantation tradition for subversive purposes. Eric Sundquist, in *To Wake the Nations: Race in the Making of American Literature* (Cambridge: Harvard University Press, 1993), discusses Chesnutt in the context of the Uncle Remus stories, and Richard Brodhead places his tales in a broader literary context in *Cultures of Letters: Scenes of Reading and Writing in Nineteenth-Century America* (Chicago: University of Chicago Press, 1993).

6. Cited in Petrie, "Charles W. Chesnutt, *The Conjure Woman*, and the Racial Limits of Literary Meditation," 84.

7. Charles W. Chesnutt, "Mars Jeems's Nightmare," in *Conjure Tales and Stories of the Color Line* (1899; reprint, New York: Penguin, 2000), 26; hereafter cited by page number in the text.

8. This reading would place "Mars Jeems's Nightmare" in line with "The Wife of His Youth," an earlier story by Chesnutt in which a light-skinned black man comes to terms with the dark-skinned woman he married as a slave.

9. Sundquist, *To Wake the Nations*, 328.

10. Like black-to-white passing narratives, she remarks, Chesnutt's tale "attests to the very same values of whiteness and rightness, blackness and backness." Susan Gubar, *Racechanges: White Skin, Black Face in American Culture* (New York: Oxford University Press, 1997), 25.

11. Sundquist, *To Wake the Nations*, 296.

12. Richard Slotkin, *Regeneration through Violence* (Middletown, Conn.: Wesleyan University Press 1973), 110. Slotkin's portrait of Mary Rowlandson is applicable not only to Jeems but also, as we will see, to all who experiment with black skin: "She has partaken of the Indian's world, their bread and wine; she has devoured it as it would have devoured her. She has become (for a while) Indian-like in her behavior; she gained insight into the Indian heart and lived intimately with the Indians" (112).

13. Gubar, *RaceChanges*, 174–75.

14. Charles W. Chesnutt, *The House Behind the Cedars* (1900; reprint, New York: Penguin, 1993), 113.

15. Harper notes that the domestication of black passers serves to feminize them, which is why, he argues, black passing narratives cannot envision "the very possibility of black masculinity." Philip Brian Harper, *Are We Not Men? Masculine Anxiety and the Problem of African-American Identity* (New York: Oxford University Press, 1996), 126. He cites *The Autobiography of an Ex–Coloured Man* as an example of this phenomenon, and might also have discussed *The House Behind the Cedars*, in which John Walden, a widower, feels unnatural affection for his sister.

16. Nella Larsen, *Passing* (1929; reprint, New Brunswick: Rutgers University Press, 1986), 206.

17. James Weldon Johnson, *The Autobiography of an Ex–Coloured Man* (1927; reprint, New York: Penguin, 1990)), 126.

18. George Schuyler, *Black No More* (1931; reprint, Boston: Northeastern University Press, 1989), 14; hereafter cited by page number in the text.

19. Review of *Black Like Me* by John Howard Griffin, *Time*, 28 March 1960, 90.

20. Eric Lott, "White Like Me: Racial Cross Dressing and the Construction of American Whiteness," in *Cultures of U.S. Imperialism*, ed. Amy Kaplan and Donald E. Pease (Durham: Duke University Press, 1993), 474–95. Gayle Wald, *Crossing the Line: Racial Passing in Twentieth-Century American Literature and Culture* (Durham: Duke University Press, 2000), 164, 180. Kate Baldwin makes mention of Griffin's dualism but focuses on placing Griffin's experiment in the context of the cold war, which made Griffin invested in "promoting a rhetoric of racial equality based in national (read: god-fearing) citizenship." Kate Baldwin, "Black Like Who? Cross-Testing the 'Real' Lines of John Howard Griffin's *Black Like Me*," *Cultural Critique* 40 (Fall 1998): 117.

21. John Howard Griffin, *Black Like Me* (New York: Signet, 1962), 16; hereafter cited by page number in the text.

22. In Howells's *Imperative Duty* and Walter White's *Flight*, for instance.

23. Samira Kawash, *Dislocating the Color Line: Identity, Hybridity, and Singularity in African-American Literature* (Stanford: Stanford University Press, 1997), 9.

24. Hugh Smythe, "It's Like This," *Saturday Review*, 9 December 1961, 53–54.

25. *Black Like Me*, dir. Carl Lerner, Hilltop Company, 1969. Brendan Gill in the *New Yorker* called the film "tardy and misguided," attacking the screenplay writers for "scarcely troubl[ing] to disguise from us that it's a tract." *Newsweek* declared: "Horton's agonizing discovery of all the clichés of the past 300 years makes *Black Like Me* obscenely embarrassing. For a while, one almost expects him to burst into 'Mammy' a la Jolson. Alas! No such relief." Brendan Gill, "Danger! Virtue at Work," *New Yorker*, 23 May 1964, 151–52; *Time*, 28 March 1960, 90.

26. *A Double Life*, dir. George Cukor, Universal Pictures, 1947.

27. Judith Halberstam, *Skin Shows* (Durham: Duke University Press, 1995), 7.

28. The first, *Crossfire*, was released in July 1947. *Gentleman's Agreement*, dir. Elia Kazan, 20th Century Fox, 1947.

29. Kate Baldwin in "Black Like Who?" reads the cold war context as central to *Black Like Me*. In *Gentleman's Agreement*, Phil closes his article by stating, "Equality and freedom remain still the only choice for wholeness and soundness in a man or in a nation."

30. As Fanon points out, the Jew "can sometimes go unnoticed. . . . The Jew is disliked from the moment he is tracked down. But in my case everything takes on a new *guise*. I am given no chance; I am overdetermined from without. I am the slave not of the 'idea' that others have of me but of my own appearance." Frantz Fanon, *Black Skin, White Masks* (New York: Grove Press, 1967), 115.

31. Elliot Cohen, "Mr. Zanuck's *Gentleman's Agreement*: Reflections on Hollywood's Second Film about Anti-Semitism," *Commentary*, January 1948, 51.

32. Daniel Itzkovitz, "Passing Like Me: Jewish Chameleonism and the Politics of Race," in *Passing: Identity and Interpretation in Sexuality, Race, and Religion*, ed. Maria Carla Sanchez and Linda Schlossberg (New York: New York University Press, 2001), 45.

33. Frank Webb, *The Garies and Their Friends* (1857; reprint, New York: Arno Press, 1969), 192–93.

34. Waldo Frank, *Memoirs* (Amherst: University of Massachusetts Press, 1973), 103.

35. Ibid., 107, 105.

36. Daniel Itzkovitz discusses the Frank-Toomer trip in "Passing Like Me."

37. Bruce Cook, "What Is It Like to Be a Negro?" *Commonweal*, 27 October 1961, 129.

38. Bradford Daniel and John Howard Griffin, "Why They Can't Wait: An Interview with a White Negro," *Progressive*, July 1964, 15; emphasis added.

39. Walter Benn Michaels, "Autobiography of an Ex–White Man," *Transition* 73 (1997) 133, 129; Schuyler cited in James A. Miller, foreword to Schuyler, *Black No More*, 4; Awkward, *Negotiating Difference*, 195. For a thorough reading of the simultaneous essentialism and anti-essentialism at work in *Black No More*, see Stacy Morgan, "The Strange and Wonderful Workings of Science: Race Science

and Essentialism in George Schuyler's *Black No More*," *College Language Association Journal* 42.3 (March 1999): 331–52.

40. *Watermelon Man*, dir. Melvin Van Peebles, Columbia Pictures, 1970.

41. A contemporary film that is equally interesting in this regard is *Putney Swope*, dir. Robert Downey Sr., Herald Pictures, 1969, in which Swope acquires a black consciousness that is really a black *power* consciousness. Amusingly, Swope's voice in the film is actually that of a white man passing for black: Downey dubbed his own voice into the film because he felt that the original actor's voice was not "black" enough.

42. *Silver Streak*, dir. Arthur Hiller, 20th Century Fox, 1976.

43. Armistead Maupin, *Tales of the City* (New York: Harper & Row, 1978).

44. Joshua Solomon, "Skin Deep," *Washington Post*, 30 October 1994, C1.

45. Felicia R. Lee, "Confronting America's Racial Divide, in Blackface and White," *New York Times*, 16 February 2006. http://www.nytimes.com/2006/02/16/arts/16race.html (accessed 15 February 2008).

46. *Soul Man*, dir. Steve Miner, Balcor Films, 1986.

47. Cited in Margaret Walters, review of *Soul Man*, *Listener*, 26 February 1987, 30. See also Richard Schickel's review in *Time*, 24 November 1986, 98, which mentions *Gentleman's Agreement*.

48. Vron Ware, *Beyond the Pale: White Women, Racism, and History* (London: Verso, 1992), 93.

3. BLACK LIKE SHE

1. "The Chameleon Lover," *South Carolina Gazette*, 1732, cited in Richard Godbeer, *Sexual Revolution in Early America* (Baltimore: Johns Hopkins University Press, 2002), 211.

2. Joel Williamson, *New People: Miscegenation and Mulattoes in the United States* (New York: Free Press, 1980), 16; Louis Wirth and Herbert Goldhamer, "The Hybrid and the Problem of Miscegenation," in *Characteristics of the American Negro*, ed. Otto Klineberg (New York: Harper & Brothers Publishers, 1944), 303.

3. Alrutheus Ambush Taylor, *The Negro in South Carolina during Reconstruction* (New York: Russell and Russell, 1969), 11; James Hugo Johnston, *Race Relations in Virginia and Miscegenation in the South, 1776–1860* (Amherst: University of Massachusetts Press, 1970), 265; New Orleans Freedmen's Bureau Court Register, vol. 137 (14 March 1867); Herbert Ashbury, "Who Is a Negro?" *Negro Digest*, October 1946, 6.

4. bell hooks, "Eating the Other," in *Black Looks: Race and Representation* (Boston: South End Press, 1992), 24. Justin Edwards points out that Jazz Age Harlem was often depicted as an erotic space, much like the South Pacific Islands in the previous century. Sexual tourism in the 1920s did not necessarily involve travel; it became possible right on 125th Street or, even more easily, right in one's own

bed—as long as it was shared with a black person. Justin D. Edwards, "Carl Van Vechten's Sexual Tourism in Jazz Age Harlem," in *American Modernism across the Arts*, ed. Jay Bochner and Justin D. Edwards (New York: Peter Lang, 1999), 167–84. "Interracial sex is a way that fragmented persons try to make themselves whole," writes Crispin Sartwell. "White people want not only black bodies but black music, black religion, black food, black culture (all of which are sexualized in one way or another in the white imaginary), as a way to rediscover what in themselves has been lost to themselves by their oppression." Crispin Sartwell, *Act Like You Know: African-American Autobiography and White Identity* (Chicago: University of Chicago Press, 1998), 108.

5. Philip Brian Harper, *Are We Not Men? Masculine Anxiety and the Problem of African-American Identity* (New York: Oxford University Press, 1996), 126.

6. In various contexts, Eric Lott and Gayle Wald discuss the ways in which blackface performance was a form of cross-racial homosocial bonding. See especially Eric Lott, *Love and Theft: Blackface Minstrelsy and the American Working Class* (New York: Oxford University Press, 1995) Andrew Ross similarly reads the white Negro as a masculine phenomenon. See Andrew Ross, "Hip, and the Long Front of Color," in *No Respect: Intellectuals and Popular Culture* (New York: Routledge, 1989), 65–101.

7. Since Halsell's experiment involves skin dye, it also contains some of the narrative features described in chapter 2. Notably, Halsell imagines herself permanently "blackened" by her experience. In a later book she recounts responding to a colleague's racist remark by asserting, "I am black, you know." Cited in Les Back and Vron Ware, *Out of Whiteness* (Chicago: University of Chicago Press, 2001), 79.

8. John Howard Griffin, *Black Like Me* (New York: Signet, 1962), 18, 30, 70.

9. Grace Halsell, *Soul Sister* (Greenwich, Conn.: Fawcett Books, 1969), 16; hereafter cited by page in the text.

10. Halsell's conflation of gender and race may perhaps reflect the ways in which 1970s feminism modeled itself on the civil rights movement (just as the nineteenth-century feminist movement mirrored abolitionism). For more on the relationship between the feminist and civil rights movements, see Vron Ware, *Beyond the Pale: White Women, Racism, and History* (London: Verso, 1992). Another text that treats the intersection of whiteness, womanhood, and race is Ruth Frankenberg, *White Women, Race Matters: The Social Construction of Whiteness* (Minneapolis: University of Minnesota Press, 1993).

11. The same is true of a contemporaneous text dealing, in a more subtle fashion, with female whiteness: *The Bell Jar* by Sylvia Plath.

12. Mariana Torgovnick, *Gone Primitive: Savage Intellects, Modern Lives* (Chicago: University of Chicago Press, 1990).

13. Eric Lott, "Racial Cross-Dressing and the Construction of American White-

ness," in *The Cultural Studies Reader*, ed. Simon During (New York: Routledge, 1999), 242.

14. Grace Halsell, *In Their Shoes* (Fort Worth: Texas Christian University Press, 1996), 14; hereafter cited by page number in the text.

15. W. T. Lhamon, *Deliberate Speed: The Origins of a Cultural Style in the American 1950s* (Washington, D.C.: Smithsonian Institution Press, 1990), 90.

16. In his discussion of black pop music and cultural crossover, Harper suggests that the barometer of a black musical group's "authenticity" lies in its relationship with "the street," which is coded as a masculine realm. "Contemporary video dance not only *refers* to the masculine-oriented street-cultural forms from which it derives, it thereby actually helps to constitute as 'authentic' the potently *masculinist* cultural presentations through which the street context is figured." Harper, *Are We Not Men?* 96. Similarly, in *Am I Black Enough for You?* Todd Boyd notes the association between gangsta rappers and "authentic" blackness, which, "especially in the form of hardened black masculinity, has become a significant commodity in contemporary popular culture." Todd Boyd, *Am I Black Enough for You? Popular Culture from the 'Hood and Beyond* (Bloomington: Indiana University Press, 1997), 63. For more on constructions of black masculinity, see Joseph L. White and James H. Cones, eds., *Black Man Emerging* (New York: W. H. Freeman, 1999); Daniel Black, *Dismantling Black Manhood* (New York: Garland, 1997); Robert Staples, *Black Masculinity* (San Francisco: Black Scholar Press, 1982); Marcellus Blount and George P. Cunningham, eds., *Representing Black Men* (New York: Routledge, 1996); Hazel Carby, *Race Men* (Cambridge: Harvard University Press, 1998).

17. Even Frantz Fanon is unable to conceive of the white man's desire for the black woman. In *Black Skin, White Masks* (New York: Grove Press, 1967), he describes both the man of color's desire for the white woman and the woman of color's desire for the white man in terms of their longing for whiteness ("I marry white culture, white beauty, white whiteness" [63]); he later describes the white woman's desire for the black man in terms of her rape fantasies and projections, but nowhere in *Black Skin White Masks* does Fanon say anything about the white man's desire for the black woman. It is as if such a scenario is either uninteresting or inconceivable to Fanon and his audience.

18. Hettie Jones, *How I Became Hettie Jones* (New York: Grove Press, 1990), 35.

19. Norman Mailer, "The White Negro," in *Advertisements for Myself* (New York: Putnam, 1959), 340.

20. Ibid., 314–15.

21. Jack Kerouac, *On the Road* (1955; reprint, New York: Penguin, 1976), 180. James Baldwin bitingly dismisses this passage as "absolute nonsense, of course, objectively considered, and offensive nonsense at that; I would hate to be in Kerouac's shoes if he should ever be mad enough to read this aloud from the

stage of Harlem's Apollo Theater." James Baldwin, *Nobody Knows My Name* (1961; reprint, New York: Vintage, 1993), 230.

22. Henry Luce, "The Blazing & The Beat." http://www.time.com/time/magazine/article/0,9171,863041–2,00.html (accessed 22 December 2007)

23. Jack Kerouac, *The Subterraneans* (New York: Grove Press, 1958), 2; hereafter cited by page number in the text.

24. This passage reflects Kerouac's own anxieties about Alene, whom he once tried to pass off as Indian to his friends. Ellis Amburn, *Subterranean Kerouac* (New York: St. Martin's, 1998), 193.

25. For another look at Kerouac's tendency to essentialize his nonwhite lovers, see his 1955 novel *Tristessa*, a fictional account of an actual affair with a Mexican woman, Esperanza Villanueva.

26. Lhamon, *Deliberate Speed*, 72, 90.

27. The same cannot be said of the 1959 film version of *The Subterraneans*, produced by MGM (dir. Ranald MacDougall). While the ads promised that the film would portray "love among the bohemians," it seems to have had a very odd conception of what "bohemian" meant: Mardou becomes a white girl played by Leslie Caron (of *Lili* and *Gigi*), and Leo is played by the wholesome, Waspy George Peppard. The film closes as Leo embraces Mardou and says, "You cook, I'll write." Kerouac, obviously, was horrified.

28. For more on the relationship between black masculinity and the concept of "cool," see Marlene Connor, *What Is Cool? Understanding Black Manhood in America* (New York: Crown Publishers, 1995). For more on the relationship between the Beats, jazz, and "cool," see Lewis MacAdams, *Birth of the Cool* (New York: Free Press, 2001). For American concepts of "cool" more generally, see Peter Stearns, *American Cool: Constructing a Twentieth-Century Emotional Style* (New York: New York University Press, 1994), and Thomas Frank, *The Conquest of Cool* (Chicago: University of Chicago Press, 1997).

29. *Jungle Fever*, dir. Spike Lee, 40 Acres & A Mule Filmworks, 1991.

30. *Black and White*, dir. James Toback, Bigel/Mailer Films and Palm Pictures, 1999.

31. David Denby, "Opposites Attract," *New Yorker*, 10 April 2000, 99.

32. *Save the Last Dance*, dir. Thomas Carter, MTV, 2001; Susan Wloszczyna, "Rap-Era Romance Falters," *USA Today*, 12 January 2001, E5.

33. Armond White, "Save the Last Dance," *New York Press*, 24 January 2001, 57.

34. *Zebrahead*, dir. Anthony Drazan, Ixltan Productions, 1992.

35. Interestingly, this marks a shift from the rhetoric of slavery, in which blackness was passed on through the maternal line. In this it suggests a difference between *legal* conceptions about what marks one as black and *imagined* or *social* conceptions of it.

36. hooks, *Black Looks*, 64.

4. CONTAGIOUS BEATS

1. Eric Nisenson, *Blue: The Murder of Jazz* (New York: Da Capo, 2000), 53; Neil Leonard, *Jazz and the White Americans* (Chicago: University of Chicago Press, 1962), 38, 33.

2. Leonard, *Jazz and the White Americans*, 38; Ann Douglas, *Terrible Honesty: Mongrel Manhattan in the 1920s* (New York: Noonday, 1995), 377; Ronald Radano, "Hot Fantasies: American Modernism and the Idea of Black Rhythm," in *Music and the Racial Imagination*, ed. Ronald Radano and Philip V. Bohlman (Chicago: University of Chicago Press, 2000), 463.

3. Ibid., 474. For more on criticisms of jazz along these lines, see Lawrence Levine, "Jazz and American Culture," in *The Jazz Cadence of American Culture*, ed. Robert O'Meally (New York: Columbia University Press, 1998), 431–47. Connections between musical crossover and racial contagion have been made in a variety of contexts. Jocelyne Guilbault, for instance, suggests that in Trinidad, "concern about music crossover could be read . . . as a deployment of the fear of racial/ethnic assimilation and acculturation," Jocelyne Guilbault, "Racial Projects and Musical Discourses in Trinidad, West Indies," in Radano and Bohlman, *Music and the Racial Imagination*, 443.

4. Nathan Huggins, *The Harlem Renaissance* (New York: Oxford University Press, 1971), 92–93.

5. Les Back and Vron Ware, *Out of Whiteness* (Chicago: University of Chicago Press, 2002), 260.

6. Barbara Browning, *Infectious Rhythm: Metaphors of Contagion and the Spread of African Culture* (New York: Routledge, 1998), 6.

7. W. T. Lhamon, *Deliberate Speed: The Origins of a Cultural Style in the American 1950s* (Washington, D.C.: Smithsonian Institution Press, 1990), 39.

8. Paul Gilroy, *Small Acts* (New York: Serpent's Tail, 1993), 7. See also Tricia Rose, *Black Noise: Rap Music and Black Music in Contemporary Culture* (Hanover, N.H.: Wesleyan University Press, 1994), 5. K. Anthony Appiah is similarly critical of the notion that "jazz or hip hop belongs to an African-American, whether she likes it or knows anything about it, because it is culturally marked as black." K. Anthony Appiah and Amy Guttman, *Color Conscious* (Princeton: Princeton University Press, 1996), 90.

9. For much of this biographical material, I am indebted to George Lipsitz's introduction to Johnny Otis, *Upside Your Head! Rhythm and Blues on Central Avenue* (Hanover, N.H.: Wesleyan University Press, 1993).

10. For more on the history of black music on the West Coast, see Ted Gioia, *West Coast Jazz* (New York: Oxford University Press, 1992).

11. Otis, *Upside Your Head*, 101; hereafter cited by page number in the text.

12. Adam Gopnik, "John Brown's Body," *New Yorker*, 25 April 2005, http://www.newyorker.com/archive/2005/04/25/050425crbo_books (accessed 22 December

2007); Stephen Talty, *Mulatto America: At the Crossroads of Black and White Culture: A Social History* (New York: HarperCollins, 2003), 59; Jean-Charles Houzeau, *My Passage at the New Orleans Tribune*, ed. David C. Rankin, trans. Gerard F. Denault (Baton Rouge: Louisiana State University Press, 2001), 84.

13. Gena Dagel Caponi cites this Otis quote on the first page of "The Case for an African-American Aesthetic," her introduction to *Signifyin(g), Sanctifyin', and Slam Dunking: A Reader in African American Expressive Culture* (Amherst: University of Massachusetts Press, 1999), 1. The volume attempts to define, as Caponi puts is, the "black" in "black culture."

14. Mike Hennessey, "Mezz Mezzrow: Alive and Well in Paris," *Down Beat*, 30 May 1968, 24.

15. Mezz Mezzrow with Bernard Wolfe, *Really the Blues* (1946; reprint, New York: Citadel, 2001), 18; hereafter cited by page number in the text.

16. At this time, writes Gayle Wald, the notion that music could turn white to black sparked anxiety in some but fantasy in others, because "shifts in social and cultural relations made it conceivable that by the 1920s, when Mezzrow was first performing, not only would whites find jazz worthy of overt admiration and emulation, but 'marginality' itself would become an object of 'mainstream' cultural desire." Gayle Wald, *Crossing the Line: Racial Passing in Twentieth-Century American Literature and Culture* (Durham: Duke University Press, 2000), 59.

17. For more on the role of whites in jazz, see Burton W. Peretti, *The Creation of Jazz* (Urbana: University of Illinois Press, 1992); Neil Leonard, *Jazz and the White Americans* (Chicago: University of Chicago Press, 1962); and William Howland Kenney, *Chicago Jazz: A Cultural History, 1904–1930* (New York: Oxford University Press, 1993). On the role of jazz in American popular culture more generally, see Burton Peretti, *Jazz in American Culture* (Chicago: Ivan R. Dee, 1997), and Gary Giddins, *Riding on a Blue Note: Jazz and American Pop* (New York: Oxford University Press, 1981).

18. Peretti, *The Creation of Jazz*, 97; Kenney, *Chicago Jazz*, 91.

19. This tension is in line with Wald's reading of Mezzrow; she describes *Really the Blues* as "a set of narrative variations on a single, but never exhausted, theme: Mezzrow's life-long pursuit of a standard of cultural or racial 'realness,' which, because it derives from his own idealized constructs of 'black' authenticity, he can never really achieve." Wald, *Crossing the Line*, 63. She calls the text "a passing narrative about the impossibility of passing," a work in which "there is a constant tension . . . between performing and 'being,' a veering between merely imitating 'otherness' and actually *becoming* 'other' " (71).

20. Ironically, one of the girls wears a star of David around her neck and passes as Jewish.

21. "Case History of an Ex–White Man," *Ebony*, December 1946, 11–14.

22. "Mezzrow Talks about the Old Jim Crow," *Melody Maker and Rhythm*, 17 November 1951, 9.

23. Wald, *Crossing the Line*, 72. Similarly, Jeffrey Melnick notes that Jewish white Negroes in general "relied in large part on language fluency to ratify their authenticity." Jeffrey Melnick, *A Right to Sing the Blues: African Americans, Jews, and American Popular Song* (Cambridge, Mass.: Harvard University Press, 1999), 121.

24. James Weldon Johnson, "The Poor White Musician" (1915), in *Black on White: Black Writers on What It Means to Be White*, ed. David Roediger (New York: Schocken, 1998), 171; Condon and Bechet cited in Peretti, *The Creation of Jazz*, 190, 192; Andrew Ross, *No Respect: Intellectuals and Popular Culture* (New York: Routledge, 1989), 74.

25. Henry Louis Gates, "The Passing of Anatole Broyard," in *Thirteen Ways of Looking at a Black Man* (New York: Random House, 1997), 207.

26. LeRoi Jones, *Blues People* (1963; reprint, New York: William Morrow, 1999), 204.

27. For more on the tension between pop and authenticity, the debate over commercial/mainstream versus artistic and independent, see Andrew Ross's chapter on the "hip" in *No Respect*, 65–101.

28. Bernard Wolfe, introduction to *Really the Blues*, viii.

29. For a philosophical examination of the notion of authenticity in the realm of music, see Peter Kivy, *Authenticities: Philosophical Reflections on Musical Performance* (Ithaca: Cornell University Press, 1995). Kivy explores the way in which "authentic" has become "a synonym for 'good,'" while seeming to confer upon a performance some magical property that it did not have before" (1). Of the four types of musical authenticity he considers, Mezzrow's fixation falls under the category of "personal authenticity," which can be defined in terms of "sincerity." See also Kevin J. H. Dettmar and William Richey, eds., *Reading Rock and Roll: Authenticity, Appropriation, Aesthetics* (New York: Columbia University Press, 1999).

30. Ken Palmer, "Mezz Mezzrow at Sixty-five," *Jazz Monthly* 10.9 (1964): 4.

31. Christopher A. Waterman, "Race Music: Bo Chatman, 'Corrine, Corrina,' and the Excluded Middle," in Radano and Bohlman, *Music and the Racial Imagination*, 195.

32. Eric Lott, David Roediger, and Michael Rogin have explored the relationship between performances of blackness—often in the form of blackface, though in Mezzrow's and Otis's cases also in the context of passing and identification—and immigrant assimilation into mainstream America. Rogin, for instance, considers "the conjunction between blackface and Americanization" and argues that, ironically, performing in the face of the Other was a way for Jewish performers to adopt whiteness. Michael Rogin, *Blackface, White Noise: Jewish Immigrants in the Hollywood Melting Pot* (Berkeley: University of California Press, 1996), 13. On

blackface and the not-quite-white Irish, see Eric Lott, *Love and Theft: Blackface Minstrelsy and the American Working Class* (New York: Oxford University Press, 1995), and David Roediger, *The Wages of Whiteness* (London: Verso, 1991); for an emphasis on blackface and Jews, see Rogin, *Blackface, White Noise*.

33. Maria Damon, "Jazz-Jews, Jive, and Gender: The Ethnic Politics of Jazz Argot," in *Jews and Other Differences*, ed. Jonathan Boyarin and Daniel Boyarin (Minneapolis: University of Minnesota Press, 1997), 158. For Mezzrow, Damon argues, "blackness becomes a way to be 'more Jewish' by providing a New World context for social critique, community, and an understanding of suffering and the 'human condition'" (157). George Lipsitz suggests that for men like Otis, black music offered "a powerful critique of mainstream middle-class Anglo-Saxon America as well as . . . an elaborate vocabulary for airing feelings of marginality and contestation." Lipsitz, *Dangerous Crossroads*, 55. Damon also suggests that the jazz world "offered a model of masculinity for Jewish men . . . that enabled difference without weakness" (168).

34. Here my reading of *The Jazz Singer* (dir. Alan Crosland, Warner Bros., 1927) differs from that of Rogin, who sees blackface in the film as a whitening agent, one that Americanizes Jack. I suggest that Jack's blackface is just as representative of his Otherness as of his whiteness. In the famous scene in which he applies blackface, for instance, Jack speaks of the "cry of my race"; the film also goes out of its way to link jazz and prayer, as when Mary describes Jack as "a jazz singer, singing to his God." Blackface seems a sliding signifier in the film, at one moment representing Jack's Otherness and at another signifying his assimilation.

35. Melnick, *A Right to Sing the Blues: African Americans, Jews, and American Popular Song* (Cambridge: Harvard University Press, 2001), 43, 109. Melnick's work explores the ways in which Jews in the music business "drew connections between themselves and African Americans in order to create a narrative about the ethnic origins of the music which then became operational as a national mythology" (25).

36. Ibid., 50, 212, 260. Melnick's *A Right to Sing the Blues* is a superb study of black-Jewish relations in the context of the post–World War I music scene. For a case study in black-Jewish influence, see Charles Hamm, *Irving Berlin: Songs from the Melting Pot: The Formative Years, 1907–1914* (New York: Oxford University Press, 1997). Walter Benn Michaels, *Our America* (Durham: Duke University Press, 1995), is also helpful on the subject of black-ethnic relations during the 1920s. In their memoir of the 1950s music scene, Jerry Wexler and David Ritz mention Otis, Mezzrow, and others. Wexler writes: "The hip of my generation, who were teenagers in the thirties, had always been drawn to black culture. In fact, I had known white Negroes, not pretenders or voyeurs but guys who had opted to leave the white world, married black women, and made Harlem or Watts their habitat." Jerry Wexler and David Ritz, *Rhythm and the Blues* (New York:

Alfred A. Knopf, 1993), 90–91. See also Mark Lisheron, "Rhythm and Jews: The Story of the Blacks and Jews Who Worked Together to Create the Magic of R&B," *Common Quest* 3 (Summer 1997): 20–33.

37. Melnick, *A Right to Sing the Blues*, 119.

38. Ibid., 76; Douglas, *Terrible Honesty*, 360.

39. Artie Shaw, *The Trouble with Cinderella* (Santa Barbara, Calif.: Fithian Press, 1992), 92. This quotation is also significant in light of my discussion, in chapter 2, of the relationship between skin color and Jewish surnames. Shaw's words echo those of Philip Green in *Gentleman's Agreement* when he decides to change his name and pass as a Jew.

40. Melnick, *A Right to Sing the Blues*, 122.

41. Locke cited in Melnick, *A Right to Sing the Blues*, 30; Bud Freeman and Robert Wolf, *Crazeology* (Urbana: University of Illinois Press, 1989), 76; emphasis added.

42. William Raspberry, "Does Rap Music Need a Warning Label?" *Washington Post*, 24 June 1994, A27.

43. "Rappers' Violent Link Stretches into Society," *USA Today*, 11 March 1997, A10.

44. Betty Houchin Winfield, "'Let Me Count the Ways': Censoring Rock and Rap Music," in *Bleep! Censoring Rock and Rap Music*, ed. Betty Houchin Winfield and Sandra Davidson (Westport, Conn.: Greenwood Press, 1999), 13.

45. Richard Greener, letter to the editor, *New York Times*, 17 September 1993, A28.

46. Crispin Sartwell, *Act Like You Know: African-American Autobiography and White Identity* (Chicago: University of Chicago Press, 1998), 186–87.

47. Brent Staples, "How Long Can Rap Survive?" *New York Times*, 22 September 1996, sec. 4, 12.

48. Steven Daly, "Send Porn Stars, Funk and Money: The Limp Bizkit Story," *Rolling Stone*, 5 August 1999, 32; Riggs Morales, "American Psycho," *The Source*, July 2000, 186; Rob Kenner, "Thirteen Ways of Looking at a Whiteboy," *Vibe*, May 1999, 118.

49. "Rappers' emphasis on posses and neighborhoods has brought the ghetto back into the public consciousness. It satisfies poor young black people's profound need to have their territories acknowledged, recognized, and celebrated," writes Tricia Rose (*Black Noise*, 11). Interestingly, though jazz emerged from both urban and rural milieus, men like Mezzrow idealized its country origins, asserting that "true" jazz came from deep in the bayou.

50. Kenner, "Thirteen Ways of Looking at a Whiteboy," 120; Alex Ogg with David Upshal, *The Hip Hop Years: A History of Rap* (London: Macmillan, 1999), 129.

51. Cited in Mark Anthony Neal, *Songs in the Key of Black Life: A Rhythm and Blues Nation* (New York: Routledge, 2003), 79.

52. N'Gai Croal, "Long Live Rock and Rap," *Newsweek*, 19 July 1999, 62; Semini Sengupta, "A Multicultural Chameleon," *New York Times*, 9 October 1999, B1; Elaine Dutka, "He'd Like to See You Squirm," *Los Angeles Times*, 16 November 1997, 51.

5. IS PASSING PASSÉ IN A "POST-RACE" WORLD?

1. For two studies of classic and nonclassic passing narratives, see Gayle Wald, *Crossing the Line: Racial Passing in Twentieth-Century American Literature and Culture* (Durham: Duke University Press, 2000), and Samira Kawash, *Dislocating the Color Line: Identity, Hybridity, and Singularity in African-American Literature* (Stanford: Stanford University Press, 1997), as well as Philip Brian Harper's chapter on passing in *Are We Not Men? Masculine Anxiety and the Problem of African-American Identity* (New York: Oxford University Press, 1996). For work on early passing novels, see Maria Giulia Fabi, *Passing and the Rise of the African-American Novel* (Urbana: University of Illinois Press, 2001). Elaine Ginsberg's essay collection *Passing and the Fictions of Identity* (Durham: Duke University Press, 1996) includes a reading of Olaudah Equiano's slave narrative, and Maria Sanchez and Linda Schlossberg's anthology *Passing: Identity and Interpretation in Sexuality, Race, and Religion* (New York: New York University Press, 2001) further expands on the subject. Recent years have seen the "passing" genre grow to include a broad range of identity swapping, including gender passing, gay-to-straight passing, religious passing, and passing for Native American.

2. Baldwin cited in Susan Gubar, *Racechanges: White Skin, Black Face in American Culture* (New York: Oxford University Press, 1997), 135.

3. Ishmael Reed, *Writin' Is Fightin'* (New York: Atheneum, 1988), 7. Kobena Mercer asks flatly: "If imitation implies identification . . . then what is it about whiteness that makes the white subject want to be black?" Kobena Mercer, *Welcome to the Jungle: New Positions in Black Cultural Studies* (New York: Routledge, 1994), 216.

4. Baz Dreisinger, "The Whitest Black Girl on TV," *New York Times*, 28 September 2003, 24.

5. Work on mixed-race identity abounds. A good anthology is Timothy Powell, ed., *Beyond the Binary: Reconstructing Cultural Identity in a Multicultural Context* (New Brunswick, N.J.: Rutgers University Press, 1999). Naomi Zack's work on mixed race is helpful, especially *Race and Mixed Race* (Philadelphia: Temple University Press, 1993). Two nonacademic books that tackle the subject are Farai Chideya, *The Color of Our Future* (New York: Quill, 1999), and Lisa Funderburg, *Black, White, Other* (New York: William Morrow, 1999). A good collection of pieces by mixed-race authors is Claudine Chiawei O'Harn, ed., *Half and Half* (New York: Pantheon, 1998).

6. Madison Gray, "A Founding Father and His Family Ties; DNA Test Extends Jefferson Legacy," *New York Times*, 3 March 2001, C1; Steven A. Holmes,

"The Confusion Over Who We Are," *New York Times*, 3 June 2001, sec. 4, 1; Larry Rohter, "Multiracial Brazil Planning Quotas for Blacks," *New York Times*, 2 October 2001, A3.

7. Edward Ball, *Slaves in the Family* (New York: Farrar, Straus and Giroux, 1998); Rebecca Walker, *Black, White, and Jewish* (New York: Riverhead, 2001); Judy Scales-Trent, *Notes of a White Black Woman* (University Park: Pennsylvania State University Press, 1995); Dalton Conley, *Honky* (Berkeley: University of California Press, 2000).

8. Barbara Browning, *Infectious Rhythm: Metaphors of Contagion and the Spread of African Culture* (New York: Routledge, 1998), 6.

9. Margo Jefferson, "Seeing Race as a Costume That Everyone Wears," *New York Times*, 4 May 1998, E2.

10. Walter White, *A Man Called White: The Autobiography of Walter White* (1948; reprint, Athens: University of Georgia Press, 1995), 4.

11. Gregory Rodriguez, "Dining at the Ethnicity Cafeteria," *Los Angeles Times*, 18 May 2003, M3; George Will, "Crude Remedy for A Disappearing Problem," *Washington Post*, 24 June 2003, A21.

12. Paul Gilroy, *Against Race: Imagining Political Culture beyond the Color Line* (Cambridge: Harvard University Press, 2000).

13. Kobena Mercer, "Black Hair/Style Politics," in *Welcome to the Jungle*, 125.

14. Kawash, *Dislocating the Color Line*, 147.

15. *The Jerk*, dir. Carl Reiner, MCA Pictures, 1979.

16. *White Man's Burden*, dir. Desmond Nakano, Home Box Office, Inc., 1995.

17. *Bulworth*, dir. Warren Beatty, 20th Century Fox, 1998.

18. James McBride, *The Color of Water* (New York: Riverhead Books, 1996), 171, 239, 218, 246, 30, 31; hereafter cited by page number in the text.

19. Philip Brian Harper argues that Ruth "simply never lays claim to any racial identity whatever" in "Passing for What? Racial Masquerade and the Demands of Upward Mobility," *Calaloo* 21.2 (1998): 385.

20. Ibid.

21. Noel Ignatiev, "The New Abolitionists," *Transition* 73 (1997): 200; Ignatiev, editorial, in *Race Traitor*, ed. Noel Ignatiev and John Garvey (New York: Routledge, 1996), 10–11, 200, 82. Ignatiev's work is part of critical white studies, which is flourishing in fields ranging from cultural studies to law. David Roediger is best known for his pioneering work in white studies; see his books *The Wages of Whiteness* (London: Verso, 1991); *Towards the Abolition of Whiteness* (London: Verso, 1994); and the anthology he edited, *Black on White: Black Writers on What It Means to Be White* (New York; Schocken, 1998). For a good overview of the field, see Les Back and Vron Ware's introduction to *Out of Whiteness* (Chicago: University of Chicago Press, 2001), 1–14; and Ruth Frankenberg's introduction to her anthology *Displacing Whiteness* (Durham: Duke University Press, 1997),

1–34. Other anthologies include Chris J. Cuomo and Kim Q. Hall, eds., *Whiteness: Feminist Philosophical Reflections* (Lanham, Md.: Rowman and Littlefield, 1999); Christine Clark and James O'Donnell, eds., *Becoming and Unbecoming White* (Westport, Conn.: Bergin and Garvey, 1999); Thomas K. Nakayama and Judith Martin, eds., *Whiteness: The Communication of Social Identity* (Thousand Oaks, Calif.: Sage, 1999); Michelle Fine, ed., *Off White* (New York: Routledge, 1997); Mike Hall, ed., *Whiteness* (New York: New York University Press, 1997); Joe Kicheloe et al., eds., *White Reign* (New York: St. Martin's 1998); Richard Delgado and Jean Stefancic, eds., *Critical White Studies* (Philadelphia: Temple University Press, 1997). Foundational studies in whiteness include Toni Morrison, *Playing in the Dark: Whiteness and the Literary Imagination* (Cambridge: Harvard University Press, 1992), and Richard Dyer, *White* (London: Routledge, 1997). In the field of law, crucial texts in white studies include Ian F. Haney Lopez, *White by Law* (New York: New York University Press, 1995); Barbara J. Flagg, *Was Blind, But Now I See: White Race Consciousness and the Law* (New York: New York University Press, 1998); and George Lipsitz, *The Possessive Investment in Whiteness: How White People Profit from Identity Politics* (Philadelphia: Temple University Press, 1998). In film studies, see two anthologies edited by Daniel Bernardi: *Classic Hollywood, Classic Whiteness* (Minneapolis: University of Minnesota Press, 2001), and *The Birth of Whiteness: Race and the Emergence of U.S. Cinema* (New Brunswick, N.J.: Rutgers University Press, 1996). On case studies of the construction of white identities, see Noel Ignatiev, *How the Irish Became White* (New York: Routledge, 1995); Karen Brodkin Sacks, *How the Jews Became White Folks and What That Says about Race in America* (New Brunswick, N.J.: Rutgers University Press, 1999); Matthew Frye Jacobson, *Whiteness of a Different Color: European Immigrants and the Alchemy of Race* (Cambridge: Harvard University Press, 1998). Ignatiev elaborates on New Abolitionism in "How to Be a Race Traitor: Six Ways to Fight Being White," *Utne Reader*, November–December 1994, 85.

22. Rob Kenner, "Thirteen Ways of Looking at a Whiteboy," *Vibe*, May 1999, 118.

23. Crispin Sartwell, *Act Like You Know: African-American Autobiography and White Identity* (Chicago: University of Chicago Press, 1998), 171.

24. Wikipedia, "Nerdcore Hip-Hop," http://en.wikipedia.org/wiki/Nerdcore_hip_hop (accessed 2 February 2007).

25. For more on the complex relationship between Jews and blackface, including debates about whether blackface represents an expression of Otherness or an assertion of Americanization, see Michael Rogin, *Blackface, White Noise: Jewish Immigrants in the Hollywood Melting Pot* (Berkeley: University of California Press, 1996); Maria Damon, "Jazz-Jews, Jive, and Gender: The Ethnic Politics of Jazz Argot," in *Jews and Other Differences*, ed. Jonathan Boyarin and Daniel Boyarin (Minneapolis: University of Minnesota Press, 1997), 150–75; and Michael

Alexander, *Jazz Age Jews* (Princeton: Princeton University Press, 2001). In "Passing for What?" Harper argues that Ruth's black identity both resists and produces assimilation.

26. Gregory Howard Williams, *Life on the Color Line: The True Story of a White Boy Who Discovered He Was Black* (New York: Dutton, 1995), 1, 2, 3–4, 9; hereafter cited by page number in the text.

27. Danzy Senna, *Caucasia* (New York: Penguin Putnam, 1998), 408.

28. Kawash, *Dislocating the Color Line*, 20.

29. Ralph Ellison, *Juneteenth*, ed. John Callahan (New York: Random House, 1999), 254. For more on *Juneteenth*, see Philip Martin, *The Artificial Southerner: Equivocations and Love Songs* (Fayetteville: University of Arkansas Press, 2001); Horace A. Porter, *Jazz Country: Ralph Ellison in America* (Iowa City: University of Iowa Press, 2001); Christopher De Santis, "'Some Cord of Kinship Stronger and Deeper Than Blood': An Interiew with John F. Callahan, Editor of Ralph Ellison's *Juneteenth*," *African American Review* 34.4 (Winter 2000): 601–20; and essays in Robert Butler, ed., *The Critical Response to Ralph Ellison* (Westport, Conn.: Greenwood Press, 2000).

30. Langston Hughes, "Who's Passing for Who?" (1952), in *Langston Hughes: Short Stories*, ed. Akiba Sullivan Harper (New York: Hill and Wang, 1996), 170–74.

EPILOGUE

1. Susan Diesenhouse, "Boston Case Raises Questions on Misuse of Affirmative Action," *New York Times*, 9 October 1988, 54.

2. Carole Rafferty, "Issue in Ouster Vote on Coast Is Whether Official Is Black," *New York Times*, 8 May 1984, 14. Randall Kennedy, *Interracial Intimacies: Sex, Marriage, Identity, and Adoption* (New York: Pantheon, 2003), reports that Stebbins had been married three times; his first wife was white, but the two others, one of whom he met at an NAACP meeting, were black.

3. Kennedy, *Interracial Intimacies*, 337.

4. Kobena Mercer, *Welcome to the Jungle: New Positions in Black Cultural Studies* (New York: Routledge, 1994), 217; Seymour Krim, "Anti-Jazz: Unless the Implications are Faced," in *Views of a Nearsighted Cannoneer* (New York: Excelsior, 1961), 73.

5. On DNA testing for college applications, see Amy Harmon, "Seeking Ancestry in DNA Ties Uncovered by Tests," *New York Times*, 12 April 2006, A1.

6. Leslie Fiedler, *Waiting for the End* (New York: Stein and Day, 1964), 134.

7. Joe Wood, "The Yellow Negro," *Transition* 73 (1997): 40–66; Hilton Als, "Young Japanese in Blackface Invade Downtown," *New Yorker*, 21–28 February 2000, 32. I myself visited Club Harlem: a sea of styled dreads and tanned faces, of T-shirts—worn by women with crimped hair and cornrows—that read "Born

Black" and "Black Women Are the Original Mothers of the Earth." I wrote about the phenomenon for *Vibe* magazine in an article titled "Tokyo After Dark" (August 2002, 30–35). "Yellow Negroes" share at least one thing in common with their American "wigger" counterparts: a taste for hip-hop fashion. Clothing is a recurrent motif of white passing narratives. In *Pudd'nhead Wilson*, Roxy enables her son to pass as white by switching his clothing, a device that returns in "The Vengeance of the Gods" and in "Mars Jeems's Nightmare." Griffin and Halsell, however, in their efforts to isolate skin color as a social factor, are quick to note that their passing did *not* involve a change of attire. Clothing and often hairstyle stand for skin, then; these are the simplest, most effective ways of putting on blackness. A young Latino today may have lighter skin than his non-Latino white counterpart, but once he sports Iceberg jeans and cornrows, he is far more likely to be identified as nonwhite. R&B singer Jon B and British comedian Ali G, both Jewish, are often taken for black or Puerto Rican on account of their hairstyles and hip-hop gear. Interestingly, because hip-hop fashion has become synonymous with youth fashion, today's "wiggers," who adorn themselves in Ecko and Phat Farm, can literally wear a black pose while retaining their white identities.

8. Gena Dagel Caponi, "Introduction: The Case for an African American Aesthetic," in *Signifyin(g), Sanctifyin', and Slam Dunking: A Reader in African American Expressive Culture* (Amherst: University of Massachusetts Press, 1999), 8, 10. Excellent critical discussions of the African American aesthetic can be found in Robert G. O'Meally, ed., *The Jazz Cadence of American Culture* (New York: Columbia University Press, 1998). Two essays—Olly Wilson, "Black Music as an Art Form," *Black Music Research Journal* 3 (1983): 1–22; and James Snead, "Repetition as a Figure of Black Culture," in *Black Literature and Literary Theory*, ed. Henry Louis Gates Jr. (New York: Methuen, 1984), 59–79—are particularly relevant.

9. George Lipsitz, *The Possessive Investment in Whiteness: How White People Profit from Identity Politics* (Philadelphia: Temple University Press, 1998), 129.

10. Robert Farris Thompson, "An Aesthetic of the Cool," in Caponi, *Signifyin(g), Sanctifyin', and Slam Dunking*, 73.

11. Joel Dinerstein, "Lester Young and the Birth of Cool," ibid., 241.

12. Cited in Kennedy, *Interracial Intimacies*, 334.

13. Rafferty, "Issue in Ouster Vote on Coast Is Whether Official Is Black," A14.

14. Sasha Frere-Jones, "Brazilian Wax," *New Yorker*, 1 August 2005, 85.

15. Gotti, "*The Source* vs. Eminem," *The Source* on-line magazine, http://www.daveyd.com/commentarysourcevseminem.html (accessed 22 December 2007).

16. "White Stars are Ripping Off Rap and R&B," *Ebony*, June 2003, 191.

17. Homi K. Bhabha, *The Location of Culture* (London: Routledge, 1994), 85.

18. Garofalo's essay appears in *Rhythm and Business*, an excellent collection laying out the ways in which black musicians have all too often been given the economic short end of the stick. Reebee Garofalo, "Crossing Over: From Black

Rhythm & Blues to White Rock & Roll," in *Rhythm and Business: The Political Economy of Black Music*, ed. Norman Kelley (New York: Akashic, 2002), 112. Michael Bertrand, *Race, Rock, and Elvis* (Urbana: University of Illinois Press, 2000), is also helpful on this subject.

19. Juliet Williams, "No Black Artists on Rock 'n' Roll Cans," 16 August 2004, http://query.nytimes.com/gst/fullpage.html?res=9F02E0DF133FF935A2575BC0 A9629C8B63 (accessed December 22, 2007).

20. Ronald Radano, *Lying Up a Nation: Race and Black Music* (Chicago: University of Chicago Press, 2003), 2.

21. George Lipsitz, *Dangerous Crossroads: Popular Music, Postmodernism, and the Poetics of Place* (London: Verso, 1994), 61, 63.

22. Cited in Peter Guralnick, "How Did Elvis Get Turned into a Racist?" *New York Times*, 11 August 2007, http://www.nytimes.com/2007/08/11/opinion/ 11guralnick.html?pagewanted=1 (accessed 22 December 2007).

23. Burton Peretti, *The Creation of Jazz: Music, Race, and Culture in Urban America* (Urbana: University of Illinois Press, 1992), 88.

24. Lipsitz, *The Possessive Investment in Whiteness*, 23.

25. Peter McLaren, "Whiteness Is . . . : The Struggle for Postcolonial Hybridity" in *White Reign: Deploying Whiteness in America*, ed. Joe Kincheloe et al. (New York: St. Martin's Griffin, 1998), 72.

26. Nelson George, "On White Negroes," in *Black on White: Black Writers on What it Means to Be White* (New York: Schocken, 1998), 227; Leroi Jones, *Blues People* (New York: Quill, 1963), 149.

27. In a superb unpublished study of Boris Vian, Celeste Day Moore argues that Vian's passing for black was indeed a progressive act, miles ahead of the sort of white Negro routines he encountered in 1950s Paris, because it reflected Vian's critical scrutiny of whiteness, blackness, and essentialism as a whole. Vian, she writes, "manages to both respect the ways in which he will never understand or be black but also undermine the constricting notion that to be black is essentially something. He believes that blackness is socially constructed but also recognizes his inability to be socially construed as black." Celeste Day Moore, "Black Like Boris: Boris Vian's Fictions of Identity in Post–World War II Paris," unpublished ms.

28. David Roediger, "*Guineas, Wiggers*, and the Dramas of Racialized Culture," *American Literary History* 7.4 (1995): 663.

INDEX

blackness, 3–6, 11–13, 18–19, 21–22, 37, 43, 47, 64, 72–73, 86, 88–91, 115, 129, 139–40, 142–43, 145, 148–49; and gender, 80–81; and Jewishness, 110–12; in passing narratives, 28; performing and posing, 24, 170n32. *See also* racial essentialism; racial passing; whiteness

Blanco, Johnny, 131

Blood of Abraham, 116

Boss, 115

Bourne, Rev. George, 1, 15, 17

Brown, John, 100, 145, 150

Brown, William Wells. See *Clotel*

Browning, Barbara, 4, 95

Bubba Sparxxx, 116, 118

Cable, George Washington, 19, 25–27. *See also* "Salome Muller, The White Slave"

Caponi, Gena Dagel, 144

Captivity narratives (Native American), 11, 32, 47

Cash, W. J., 23

Caucasia (Senna), 13, 121, 138

Chamillionaire, 116

Chesnutt, Charles, 11, 48–49. *See also* "Mars Jeems's Nightmare"

Clotel (Brown), 9, 16–20

Color of Water, The (McBride), 13, 125, 127–29, 132–34, 137, 139–40

Come By Here (Major), 121

Condon, Eddie, 106

Craft, Ellen and William, 16–19. See also *Running a Thousand Miles for Freedom*

Devil in a Blue Dress (film), 13, 121

Dinerstein, Joel, 144–45

double consciousness, 4, 149–50; and Jewish passing, 59; and *Soul Sister*, 92; and white passing, 48–49

Double Life, A (film), 57

Douglas, Ann, 9

Douglas, Mary, 24

Dr. Dre, 116

Durst, Fred, 114–16

Eazy-E, 116

Ebony, 146; featuring Mezz Mezzrow, 104–5

Ellison, Ralph, 4, 96. See also *Juneteenth*

Eminem, 13–14, 95, 114–18, 131–32, 144–45, 154n39

Everlast, 131

Fanon, Frantz, 16, 163n17, 166n30

Fauset, Jessie Redmon. See *Plum Bun*

Fiedler, Leslie, 143

50 Cent, 114, 116, 145

Fishkin, Shelley Fisher, 28

Flight (White), 5, 33

Frank, Waldo, 3, 60–62

Frere-Jones, Sasha, 146

Gaines, Jane, 41

Garies and Their Friends, The (Webb), 18–19, 44, 60, 72

Garofalo, Reebee, 147

Garrison, William Lloyd, 100

gender, 7, 11–12, 17, 48, 56–57, 72–75, 78, 86; and authenticity, 85–86; and homosocial male bonding, 56, 73, 103–4, 115–16; and music, 116–17; and passing, 73–75; and *Soul Sister*, 165n10. *See also* masculinity

Gentleman's Agreement (film), 58–60, 68

George, Nelson, 149

Proof, 115
Pudd'nhead Wilson (Twain), 3, 8–10,
   15–16, 26, 28–38, 41, 126, 158n39,
   158n36, 159n48

race, 2, 10, 13, 20, 34–35, 42, 125, 143;
   and class, 22–23, 75; associated with
   disease, 21–23; and Jews, 60; and
   "post-race" society, 139; and racism,
   60; as social construct, 5
Race Traitor (journal), 13, 129–30
racial essentialism, 3, 11, 28–30, 34, 36,
   47, 62–64, 69, 83–85, 99, 124, 144,
   150; and science, 24
racial passing, 1–14, 121–22; and
   activism, 100; and authenticity,
   12, 123–24, 132; as distinct from
   blackface, 5, 153n20; and black
   passing, 2, 6–7, 153n24; black
   passing for black, 5, 33; as detective
   fiction, 34–35; and essentialism,
   3; etymology, 4; and gender, 7;
   genres, 6; and geography, 3–4,
   8–9, 36, 53–54, 75, 100, 103, 140;
   Jews passing for white, 61–62; and
   masculinity, 7; as narrative, 28; in
   the news, 141–42; passing as Jewish,
   58–61; passing as Mexican, 79–80,
   97; passing as Native American,
   78–80; on the radio, 125–26;
   reproducing whiteness, 129; and
   sexual liberation, 75–78; skin-dye
   narratives, 67; as slave, 9, 15–16, 18;
   supernatural, 35; as transgressive, 3,
   7, 13–14, 148–49; travel narrative, 51;
   white vs. black passing, 7; "would-
   be passing," 126–27. See also racial
   passing in film; racial passing,
   white
racial passing, white: 1–14, 16, 44,
   60–61, 80, 101–5, 121–22, 125,
   148–50; as anxiety, 16–19, 24–28,
31–33, 36–40; vs. black passing, 7;
   as fantasy, 41–44, 47–50, 55, 68–69;
   white women passing, 71–73
racial passing in film. See *Black and
   White; Black Like Me; Bringing
   Down the House; Bulworth; Devil
   in a Blue Dress; Double Life, A;
   Gentleman's Agreement; Human
   Stain, The; Imitation of Life; Jazz
   Singer, The; Jerk, The; Jungle
   Fever; Love Song; Malibu's Most
   Wanted; Save the Last Dance; Silver
   Streak; Soul Man; Tales of the City;
   Watermelon Man; White Man's
   Burden; Zebrahead*
Radano, Ronald, 94, 148
Really the Blues (Mezzrow and
   Wolfe), 12, 101–10, 112
Reconstruction, 4, 10, 15, 20–23, 50,
   123, 156n12
Roediger, David, 5, 20, 143, 150
Rogin, Michael, 111–12
Ross, Andrew, 106
Roth, Philip, 13, 68, 121. See also
   Human Stain, The
*Running a Thousand Miles for
   Freedom* (Ellen and William Craft),
   9, 16–20

Sacks, Karen Brodkin, 133–34
"Salome Muller, The White Slave"
   (Cable), 9–10, 19, 25–28; compared
   to *Pudd'nhead Wilson*, 32–37
Sartwell, Crispin, 114, 131, 164n4
Save the Last Dance (film), 86, 90, 91
Schuyler, George, 1, 49–50, 58, 63,
   148
Schuyler, Josephine, 1
scientific race thinking, 10, 21, 23–24
Senna, Danzy. See *Caucasia*
Shaw, Artie, 111–12
Sheppard Lee (Bird), 42–43